how can one be offended by the truth?

a raw hummingbird

the story of
two young women
who were

never

meant to

fall

in

love

a raw hummingbird

This is a true story.

Original authors:
Jasper Faolan and Sage Taylor (aliases)

This trilogy has been compiled, edited and created by:
Jasper Faolan

SECOND EDITION

All book cover artwork, photography & design is
copyright © 2009 Cameron Gray,
Parable Visions

www.parablevisions.com

ISBN
978-0-578-01715-0
paperback

For C.a.t. & Mother

In Loving Dedication:

To everyone with a heart that bleeds, mends itself, &
bleeds again.

To the Moon.

Thank you

First Chakra.

Sacred Mother -
Miracle.
Through your guidance and constant challenge to delve
deeper, you trigger rebirth in us both,
every single day.

Daddy Bear: You amaze me with how willing you are
for me to be different to you.
You have taught me unconditional love.

Aubergine: You are beautiful. Thank you for forcing me
to assign myself a 'due date' for the completion of
this project. Without you, I may never have finished!

Extended 'family'.

To My Most Precious Editor, bella niete, thank you for
the endless *hours* of (remote!) work you put into this
project. The voice message you left after you read the
last chapter of this trilogy...left me verklempt(!) &
inspired. Thank you so, so much.

Thank you, Fatality True, for your companionship &
ideas on how to best express & promote this mission! xo.

CAMERON GRAY! Oh My Gosh.
You are such a profound artist. Can't wait to watch for
Book II's design & to continue following your career.

Rain. Rain. Rain.
You've taught me how sacred I really am and how sacred
we all are. Precious. I love you - I always will.

Ah, Unicorn. I hope that we are always homie-peas.
Love you.

Women.

Thank you, J, for teaching me that it's valuable to
know what your cervix looks like.

Thank you, B, for teaching me freedom through movement.

Thank you, Kiwi ladies, for your quirky sense of humor
and belly laughs.

Thank you, H, for bringing me flowers.

✍ FOREWORD
A RAW HUMMINGBIRD IS A TRAGEDY.

But it signifies the beginning of creating an Empowered Woman.

By confronting the shadows cast across every crevice of my mind, I come to realize the first step towards empowerment: **waking   up**.

To quote the love in my life, Rain,

"If we are serious about **transformation**, we must examine openly and honestly the present structures: social, political - all areas that affect the way we live: the layout of our neighborhoods, the food we eat, the education we're taught, the occupations that occupy us...

To bring about CHANGE, we not only need to have a deep understanding down to the foundations of our current systems, those that are generally invisible and taken for granted; we also need to overcome our own inter- and intrapersonal obstructions in order that we may   come   together   in   the power of community.

If we want to Plant New Crops, we have to dig up all the roots of the old. We can't just pretend they aren't there, or hope they'll go away on their own. These roots are within us as accepted assumptions about "the way things are".

Peering into
                                                another's   mind or living in another country's culture, we would find that quite different interpretations of experience, ways of structuring our personal interface, can and do exist. We see these are entirely human constructs and potentially

                        awaken   to   our ability   to   consciously interpret our reality, or even to lay off and allow things to be how they are without all our mental organizing, judging, editing...

Perhaps we might see more clearly, opening our minds in this way.

And   when   we   do, when we

see the way

we've been **conditioned,**

the way our lives are enslaved to deep patterns of reaction, we understand that our will is not free until we free it ourselves. No one can do this for me. (If I had to depend on someone else to do it, it wouldn't be freedom.)   Your   freedom   is   your   power.

Having investigated your depths until

you can

stand naked and **unashamed** before the world, you AFFIRM:

I am Goddess,

I am God,

& so are all of you."

- **From the Journals of** Rain, sustainable community freak, composting whore & entrepreneurial pepper spice.

"Your task is not to seek for love, but merely to seek and find all the barriers within yourself that you have built against it."

~ Rumi

TABLE OF CONTENTS

Everyone You'll Meet	1
Writing quirks & idiosyncrasies…	3
Preface. October 21st	4
Year One	11
Christina	17
The Room	21
How do you know?	28
Loft	37
How do you…Do It?	41
The Nightmare	46
Burn	55
The first of many firsts	63
Online - Our First Conversation	65
Scholastic Achievement Test	69
Sight	87
The Drive	102
Decision	131
Fear Instructs	139
Hollow objects fracture	142
Dr. Snow	148
Runes	164
Withdrawal	173
A flock, a spirit and a wolf	177
just the surface	179
At-one-ment	191
Revolution	194

Ladies Night - A Plan   199

1:21 AM   212

The Woods   218

A Phatic Conversation   229

FFFF...(friends, foes, friends, foes...) 237

wish i could run away just like that sentence.
    247

Whiskers on Kittens   253

A One Night Stand (plus a game of pool) 261

Black Copper Kettles   276

Absconder   279

Trials...   287

Fragile Formations   292

The SATs   296

Drunken Cheerleaders   304

Ache   322

Aadita   328

Relief & Oddity   340

The Appointment   342

Mother   355

🍃   368

Veracity of Falsehoods   377

Notes   405

Set in: Wellington, New Zealand

Jasper Faolan – Author – Me.
16 years old.
Spiritually 'odd'. A party girl.
I have dark hair & blue, green eyes with 'sunflowers' around my irises. Am 5'6.
Socially preoccupied heterosexual.
I have no idea who I am.

Jasper's best friends:

Melantha – best friend, gothic, brilliant, observer. hates small talk. she dropped out of school, so I don't see her as much. she makes me laugh harder than anyone else.
Nicole – blonde, athletic, tall. i used to have a crush on her, but I've never admitted it.
she's "good at everything". nicknamed 'lil miss goody-two-shoes'.
Evette – model, incredible actress and still innocent. we all used to be.

Other good friends:

Rayla – beautiful, creamy barbie doll, disgruntled about gaining weight...throws TONS of great parties.
Amy – super lovely girl, has five sisters, is half Maori, half Pakeha & crazy bright & creative because her parents rarely let the TV out.
Morgan – short, plump, boy cut brown hair, electrifying blue eyes. gossip queen.

Jasper's friends from the past:

Christiana, Julie, Aadita, & Sarah

The Jasper boys:

Steve – the ever-present charming, sociopathic, druggie ex
Henry – the hot senior (who skipped out on having a brain)
Daniel – the one guy friend who never tried to get in my pants

Jasper's Mother, Dad & sister:

Mother, Dad & Crystal - Crystal is 12 years my senior & lives in America.

Jasper's counselor & wife:

Dr. & Mrs. Snow

Sage Taylor – Socially aloof, discerning lesbian.
16 years old.
> **Ridiculously intelligent, but only an achiever when she wants to be.
> Dirty blonde hair, deep amber eyes, shorter than me. Spiritually dark.**

Sage's best friends – all live in America:

Bernadette – her most significant past lover/current friend.
Rose & Rosalyn – the other two most significant women in Sage's life. These three girls make up her 'family'.

Sage's New Zealand friends:

Nellie – dirty blonde, blue eyed, natural, hippie chick that ends up wanting to hook up with Sage. **Daisy** – good friend of Nellie's...crazy nerdy. **Kimberly** – started out being really close to my, Jasper's, set of friends but she's too bright for us. She eventually became friends with Sage and the rest of her crowd. Sage and Kimberly pretend to be 'married', just for fun, so they say that they are one another's 'pretend wives'.

The Sage boys:

Nicolas – Sage's primary gay guy friend, he's older than us. **Michael** – the token 'out' gay male at school that we all respect. Played Ophelia for our art installation course. Wears bright red lipstick, black dresses, is slim and over 6 ft tall...LOVE him. **'The boys'** – a group of 6 – 12 nerdy guys. they do drugs, play Magic and get to joke around in Math class (unlike us) because they've already finished all the exercises.

Sage's Mom, Dad & sister:

Beth, Luis & Edith – Edith is a few years younger than Sage

✍ WRITING QUIRKS & IDIOSYNCRASIES... CONFOUNDING, INTRIGUING, IRRITATING

SAGE'S QUIRKS:

Sage quite often misspells 'doesn't' as 'dosen't'. She does this SO many times i didn't have the heart to erase them.

'Damnit' or 'dammnit' obviously means 'dammit'.

'Aight' is a cute ass way of saying 'alright'. (Yo, wha?)

'Probly' means 'probably'.

'Biotch' means 'bitch', intended lightheartedly, most certainly!

'musak!' = music, music!

MY (JASPER'S) QUIRKS:

I misspell 'weird' as 'wierd' as if it's a religious right to do so.

I'm not a fan of spaces on either side of dashes or parentheses. Neither is Sage. Case in point: "i'm not trying to make you feel guilty-i'm just spilling some thoughts out that might be of interest to you(if they're not, sorry-and let me know)."

Abbreviations: j/k' means 'joking', 'lol' of course means 'lots of laughs' and 'lmao' means 'laugh my ass off'.

Ok, so the cApitAlS. Why are some sentences capitalized correctly and others unconventionally (infuriatingly?) led with lower case letters?

As far as addressing this quirk in our emails, I have no answer. I think it primarily had to do with ease of typing.

In *a raw hummingbird*, the lower case letters that lead sentences in the <u>prose sections</u> *are* intentional. These sections of writing without any capitalization indicate timidity, shyness or a sense of fear.

DISASSOCIATION.

Cold breathing down my neck.
I drift back and feel my skirt tear. Clawing my hips, the moon
slips in and fingers the stone brick nearest my aching eyes.
He is behind me.
I'm hurting. *Please.* I try to turn around.
With a *crack* he splits my cheekbone against the dripping walls.
I hear him moan his pleasure as his
cock thrusts
into me,
away from me.
My drunken hysteria swirls into slippery pools of misery and
confusion.
Why is he doing this to me?
Tears spill and fracture the slip of moonlight, my only friend.
Disassociate. Flung, consciousness becomes imagination.
Eyes close. Blood spills down her leg.
Her wrists seer in pain as he grips them to prevent her
from...*escape.* The stench is overwhelming. Scarlet ribbons of
painted bruises,
no voice, a dysfunctional slave.
Love   *and*   sex?   What   a   novel   idea.
Maybe Sage *could* teach her something;
perhaps the gentleness of Sage's cheek would heal her;
take the ribbons and tie them in bows at the end of her two long,
messy ponytails.
Perhaps. Or perhaps Sage would be another perpetrator
in the young girl's life, her love a mere guise for
eventual abuse.

`process it. again.`

`DISASSOCIATION.`

Cold   neck.

back   moon

fingers   eyes

Please.

cheekbone

into me.

Why

Tears spill and fracture

grips   *...escape.*

ribbons

dysfunctional slave

messy

ponytails

young girl's life

* * *

Anger

Year Three

Fuck you. No, really. Fuck you.

Deceit, mental dis-ease, sexual innuendos. Sex, rape, love, deception, disrespect. 'Bisexuality'. Fuck you. Shut up, my mouth isn't dirty.

I can't control this. I can't control the images in my sick, culvert of a mind. I like it this way, don't I? Fine. I'm sick; going to hell. Whatever.

She fills me.

You do not. You do not fill me. Not you or your bigotry. You suck me dry.

Fuck you.

If I'd only screamed these words nine years ago.

Shhh.

What are you saying? It sounds like you are whining...

* * *

Today

Reflection

But I want to write honestly to you. The story in your hands is as true as my memory is, and it is truer at times, as the emails, instant messages and letters in this book include bits and pieces that my mind has let go of.

Every life has a moment that needs no further dramatization. This is mine.

Thank you for reading.

Jasper

the canvas before the storm

☒ Year One

> There are two mistakes one can make along the road to truth... not going all the way, and not starting.
>
> Hindu Prince Gautama Siddhartha, the founder of Buddhism, 563-483 B.C.

September 8th

"Why did we have to sit in such a *visible spot*?" hisses Nicole. We try to make ourselves inconspicuous to the eyes of the oncoming pair of classmates.

Because you wanted to check out *boys!*" I tease.

Welcome to oh-so-tralala superficiality.

Evette laughs. It's evening. The three of us are downtown in a casual restaurant in New Zealand. We have an amazing view. Funky shop doors and people flow around us. Sitting next to the huge glass windows at the front of the restaurant, we can't hide. I'm wearing my typical all black outfit with smudged gray makeup and a violet ribbon tight around my neck. My skin glows white; I stopped sunbathing years ago. Nicole is my aesthetic opposite; she's dressed in strawberry colors that complement her radiant olive complexion, blonde hair and athletic body. Evette is our hourglass bombshell. She's confidently accentuating her figure with tight dark blue jeans, a cream top with lace ruffles and a designer jacket. The outfit was a gift from a modeling agency with which she's had a contract since she was six years old.

We're an odd threesome – no doubt about it - but for high school girls going to the arty school we are, best friends typically transcend fashion boundaries.

Nicole has finally turned 16 years old like the rest of us. We're celebrating it with an early dinner, as we have for the last three years. Though the youngest of the group, she appears to be the most put together—a model offspring on course to become her parents' "little success story". But Nicole's surface doesn't run deep enough to satisfy Melantha, one of my soul mates, who picks up on Nicole's insecurities more than the rest of us. Melantha is absent from our party-planning dinner precisely for this reason. Her intolerance warrants her fewer public appearances than most; she just can't bear the weak, or the shallow-minded. I'm more forgiving, sometimes to a fault.

Nicole begins fretting over *another* boy. I burst out laughing, "Oh right, Nicole, it's *sooooo* awful that you have to deal with all of this attention! Shush, you know you love it!" I press a teasing finger into her shoulder. She throws her eyes wide, the comical expression adorning her pretty face.

"What? I don't get *that* much attention...do I?"

I roll my eyes. "We all get plenty. I keep failing my damn foreign language classes because there's always a cute boy that ends up flirting with me. Oh, the *drama*!" I toss a lazy hand across my forehead.

Evette says, "Ha! I know what you mean! You needs school when you can play?"

Nicole looks more reflective. She's always competing with me. "Who's flirting with you this semester?"

I sit back up. "Oh, no one important."

Evette's voice drops to an incredulous whisper, "Wow. They're actually coming in here. What are they doing together?"

"What? Who?" I turn to look.

Sage. Brittany. "...*oh*."

Sage is in her typical outfit: low slung jeans, massive T-shirt, and a backpack full of books and oddities that we've never heard of. A backwards baseball cap tops off her androgyny. In blaringly stark contrast, Brittany sashays in wearing a taut white tank top, disturbingly intimate pants and painful looking heels.

Sage has never given us the time of day, so we certainly aren't about to go out of our way to say hey (why would we?). And then Brittany is one of those sad cases of neglect; she's an emotional sponge that sleeps with all the boys in a vain attempt to fill the holes leaking inside of her. It's because of *her* that we're pretty sure these two will talk to us – she's been trying to infiltrate our clique for weeks.

"For *impressions-sake,* let's make this quick." insists Nicole.

"Yea, totally. Agreed."

As predicted, they spot us and then meander over to our table. Brittany bounces through her nervousness. *What an odd thing for someone to need such approval from a group of chicks one doesn't even know.*

A superficial conversation ensues.

E..b...b and f—l---o-w of <u>bull</u>shit.   Wait.

A new social dynamic emerges. Bewildered, I watch. Sage, not Brittany, is eagerly accepting the bits of conversation flicked at her from the ends of Nicole's disinterested fingertips.

> "*Weird,*" I whisper. Sage has never been interested in us before.

Odd...

Sighing, a jolt of exhaustion ricochets through my body; the offending pinball depletes all of my remaining energy. I sink into my favorite pocket of mere observation.

It's not until she speaks to me that I come back to seek this space.

"Hey, Jasper?"

what*?*

"Can...can I stay at your place tonight?"

Huh?

a cheese grater along my backbone

I balk. *Search...search...*for the face coupled with the voice...*Sage?*

Amber eyes.

Yes, it was *she* that asked.

Interesting...the energy within her...it's dark but light at the same time.
I fall in, just   to   peek.

She's watching you.

Snapping, I seek an answer.

Well, I say! What a total social retard.
Who on *earth* just asks outright if they can STAY THE NIGHT with someone
they barely know?
What are we, six years old?!
Disbelief reigning from my glazed, tired eyes, I silently demand an explanation.
Her sudden request makes absolutely *no* sense -
our interactions over the last several months
haven't been particularly pleasant.

Three months ago.

I caught Sage alone after school one day. Her American accent drew me to her, even though she was really different to the girls I usually befriended: her IQ equals all of our intellects combined, and she has a particular taste for *totally* corny jokes (ones that often involve unnecessarily huge words). But we're both expatriates – I moved to New Zealand four years ago when I was 12, and she, at the age of 16, had just arrived – and her accent triggered 'home' for me even though we're from different parts of the country. I thought it would be neat to talk to her because of our common, American roots. Wrong.

I initiated small talk...but instead of responding in kind, I was transported into an Ayn Randian encounter:

"He stood looking at her.
She knew that he did not see her. No, she thought, it was not that exactly.
He always looked straight at people and his damnable eyes never missed a thing,
it was only that
he made people feel as if they did not exist.
He just stood looking.
He would not answer."

Distant, Sage made emotionless, monosyllabic responses to my sad attempts to connect.   Eventually she left.   My hands fluttered a dejected little dance of nerves and shock.   *Perhaps she doesn't like me because of how into being 'popular' I am.... Perhaps her nerdy friends have turned her against me.*

Sliding back into the present,

Her request suddenly intrigues me.

But she's a *lesbian*...and that word has a dark shadow that trails its every utterance.
It makes me nervous. *She* makes me nervous. She's the *only* openly lesbian girl at school...

I'm ignoring everyone. Sage mutters something to me. *She's embarrassed by my lack of response.*   My conscience claps loudly, in my face: Surely I shouldn't discriminate based on sexuality? *Pause.* ...Right? I'm always advocating for people to respect Michael, our only openly gay student.   *If I like Michael so much, how can I discriminate against Sage?   And since when have you ever even had an opportunity to TALK to a lesbian?*

Ok, answer her question.

"Yea...ok, Sage.   Sure."

Nicole whirls to face me.   Evette drops her lip balm, bends to pick it up – and keeps her eyes on me the whole time. "Really?" they ask in unison.

I cough. "Yea, sure. Sage can come over and stay the night – even though it *is* a random request." I direct my voice to Sage, "We really don't know each other at all, do we...but yea, it could be fun."

Sage's shoulders relax.

Nicole hastily grabs my arm and begins to escort me towards the bathroom. "Jasper! Are you crazy?! What are you *doing*?"

I shrug her off. "Hmm, yea, I dunno. I'm a risk taker, I guess. It'll be interesting to see what comes of it, eh?" I turn back to face the group. "Hey, so I really should be getting home – tons of sleep to catch up on y'know. Evette, Nicole, can we keep planning tomorrow? "

Stupified nods.

"Ok. Are you ready to go now, Sage?"

A reply,

"Ready."

♂ CHRISTINA
I was six years old

I remember his face. It was pale and almost albino, just like Christina's. He was Christina's brother, and his name was Louis. One morning his ghostly complexion invaded the make-shift tent that Christina and I had constructed in the middle of her bedroom floor. You know, lots of little kids build tents. We just also liked to pretend we were making love (or at least we thought we were), as a married couple of course. Christina was six as well. Our game began when we both 'fell in love' with the same boy in our first grade class, Adam. We wanted to act out what it would be like to marry him. Oh, he was just *so dreamy*. I ended up only dreaming about her, though. The way her body wriggled under my fingers and became drenched in droplets of innocence as we coached one another on how we thought you 'did it right'. We would take turns being Adam. Sometimes we would fight about who would have her sweet little body stroked more, although we mostly got on well because I always preferred to be Adam, the initiator, the one in control. It suited me.

My desire to dominate desperately retreated into remission as a direct result of those three long moments when Louis's piercing blue eyes shredded my psyche. He spit my identity back in my face, and my once happy, amorous self was disfigured.

Before he

split   me   in

TWO,

`(one, two)`

Christina and I had been tangled and giggling. Our saccharine smells seeped through her yellow, teddy bear sheets. The bears danced on the pattern above us, in rhythm with our movements. Louis didn't expect to see his little sister that way, I guess. His whole body shook. He was outraged, disgusted. At the age of 15, he held dominion over us. He threw the sheet in our faces and left. I went rigid. Somehow I knew this was 'wrong' but I didn't think we'd ever get caught. It was our private, secret life. Numbness settled in. I hid my body.

Mortification.

Our breath shallow, "What do we *do*?" I finally whispered. Wild and uncertain, Christina scrambled to put her clothes on, her tiny fingers tripping over the buttons of her pink pajamas, and fell out of the tent. I waited and then followed. I didn't want her to have to go it alone.

Louis had taken to destroying a brand new wall clock on the back porch – the sliding door was open. When I walked in he sneered at me, looked at his Mother, and with a second look at me he lifted a massive sledge hammer high into the air and...*crash.* Blow upon blow he inflicted violence on the plastic, metal and wiring. Pieces flew in all directions, showering the back porch and lawn with invisible bits of shrapnel. *They'll cut Christina's feet as she runs to play outside on their jungle gym.* It was on that jungle gym that I told Christina that Mother and I had a pact: We would always tell each other everything. And I had. I even told her about Christina. Mother was kind. She said it was normal for little girls and boys to explore one another but that I would grow out of it. I thought about what she had said for a long time. It made me happy that she didn't yell at me, but it also made me feel like what I was doing was childish. I didn't tell her about Louis finding us. Christina didn't approve of me talking to my Mother. She believed secrets were safer.

The last time I went to see Christina was at her birthday the next month. She was cruel to me then. She pushed me out of her bedroom door and slammed it on me, as everyone else from the party piercingly laughed with her. I tried knocking a few times, thinking that she was just being silly and playing a game. We were best friends, after all. She would open it, throw out her shrill, manic laugh and declare that I was unfit to play with them. She would next pretend to be joking, have me come halfway in, and then they would all proceed to push me out again. The last time she did this I felt my hand sear with pain as I wrenched it free from the slammed door. I held it, wincing with eyes shut as blood throbbed through my temples in defense. I breathed against the dark wood inches from my face, numb. The momentary calm was my only solace – I imagined it all disappearing...into the knots of the wood before me...and me along with it.

I turned around and went to study her cake. It was one of those dessert cakes from the grocery store, complete with a theme. Hers was Cinderella. I liked the mice.

Eventually her mother noticed me. Like Christina, she too had bright blonde hair. Unlike Christina, whose hair was naturally the purest white, Christina's mother *dyed* her hair to be white. Roots of black seeped from her scalp. Even though I was the only child outside of Christina's room, she didn't ask me why. She was preoccupying herself with her adult friends as they swallowed the contents of small, cloudy brown bottles. I thought about going outside, but then one of her male friends kindly asked me if I needed anything. Christina's mother appeared publicly supportive of this question, but when they weren't looking, she ignored me. Meekly I slipped off the chair towards him and asked to call my Mom. Obviously pleased by the question, she handed me the phone. Cowering, I dialed.

My Mother has this habit of decimating anyone who 'dares to hurt her child'. It's the only time she isn't overtly accommodating. When my kindergarten teacher was replaced by a strict, cruel woman who usually taught people twice our age, Mother 'had to' send my Dad to complain in her place for fear she might be charged with assault. While perhaps not the best for the adults involved, it has always made me feel safe. She is the reason I am even able to write to you today. More on that - later.

"Momma?"

19

"Momma,   she's   being   mean   to   me..."
On cue, livid protectiveness crashes forth. "Jasper! Christina doesn't know what she's doing. It's her Mother's fault for not being there for you all. I am coming over right now. I love you – you are a precious treasure. I'll be there in five minutes."   Upon arrival, her voice raked across the room to shame Christina's mother for not mediating between us girls fairly. Christina's mother told us to leave. As Mother snapped the door behind us, I was able to find, and hold, my Mother's hand.

I wanted to go home. Numb, I was already there. I like feeling detached, safely tucked away from offending emotions. I would fantasize about the first horse I would be able to buy and care for. It would be a black horse, and it would carry me
quickly   *away*   *from*   *dark*   *places.*
I would name the new 30 foot tree I had learned to climb, and I would crawl through the obscuring branches, fumbling for the sunlight at the top of its canopy, and there I would read for hours on end.

Mom and I only saw Christina's family one more time. We were in our cars going in opposite directions at an intersection near our school. Mother muttered something along the lines of "There's that bitch again," and then, noticing that I was watching her with wide eyes, she continued, "But of course we must always strive to forgive...."

∂ THE ROOM

Her **aloof** **concentration** on each image:
a unique offering for such a secret, virginal set of
memories,   untouched
 by someone
so attentive.

Sage gravitates towards the left side of my room, as all newcomers do. It's where my enormous corkboard wall stands: eight by five feet high. Photos and trinkets deck its surface. My Dad installed it when he renovated my room (Lord, do I love him). Sage appears reflective; she hasn't said a single word since stepping out of our taxi.

I know that she can probably tell that I am looking at her since females have nearly 180 degree peripheral vision, but I don't care. It doesn't seem to matter – we're in the same room yet quietly experiencing completely different pools.

My fingers begin to release my hair from the many bobby pins restricting it. It feels silken as fingertips glide up and down of black and red strands. But against my will, anxiety floods every edge in my body.

I don't know what to do with her.

I follow her gaze. It's odd watching someone take in my history so intently. The photos spin the invisible, connective threads of my life. A sixteen year old's tapestry.

```
Trinkets from all over Welling speak to
one another:


a run-over beer can, bewildered by its
new state of being (wouldn't you be?),


pictures of parties, parties, parties...

T     he Moon

a   wooden   rosary   given   to   me   by   a
Catholic nun,

(an empty spot eventually to be filled
by a Mandela bracelet from a Buddhist
nun),

...& a picture of my ass, windblown, as I
moon another car.
```

```
then. drawings. those. drawings.
```

```
        Black ink strokes TUCK away aberrant,
                   sickly thoughts and ideas,
                                    secretly
                     underneath one another,
                                      hidden
                  under less offensive material.
                     They seem to shimmer
                                  slightly,
          as her eyes brush their hidden edges.

        No one ever notices them.  But she...her
                   energy reaches out to them...

        This is horrifying.  How can she know?

        Insanity; she can't see them, they are
        covered by photographs of parties, dances,
        gatherings...distract yourself, let it be
                      like the times you steal.
              Don't let the store owner
                   know your thoughts.
```

I do **not** know what to do with her.

A knock.

Mother!

A flood of warmth rushes my clammy face. I run away, thankfully leaving Sage in my room.

"Mom! Dad! Phew. How are you guys? Something smells amazing."

Daddy smiles kindly at me. His expressions are precious; he's the introvert of the family.   The corners of his eyes crinkle as he murmurs, "Hi, baby bear." I walk over and give him a hug.

In the tenderness of our kitchen, re-aware of my exhaustion, I sit atop one of Dad's beautifully hand-made, rimu bar stools. Dad is patiently stirring his white sauce, *back and forth, back and forth,* for their chicken pot pie. My head flicks over to the counter to make sure that there is a separate dish for my vegetarian one. There's no real need for me to check – both Mom and Dad always make me a veggie version of whatever they are having – I'm just concerned about the chicken flesh that will fill their pie.... *Step by step. Maybe they'll eventually eat less meat. I mean, Mom already has, to a degree...*

Mom begins teasing me about my exhaustive social life. I squish up my nose and stick my tongue out at her, :P. She laughs and flaps her hand at me in mock defense and then gestures towards my bedroom.

```
           "So, how did you
                 hook
                  up
             with Sage?

  I thought you tried to be friends with her a while ago
                and she wasn't into it...?"
```

I mutter,

```
                                   "Oh. Um, well..."
```

Mother continues, "I know her mother, you know. I actually met Sage at a meeting we had at their house."

"Really? Oh, oh."

"Yep. Her Mom was a part of our book club for a while. She seemed depressed. (One of my Mom's college degrees is in psychiatric nursing.) Unlike us, the move to New Zealand wasn't her decision. Her husband's career swept her away from everything she loved – her friends, job, church – her identity. She's embraced a victim role here. She dropped out more and more as life got too much for her..."

"Wow."

"Yes, hmm. I should call her sometime. So...is Sage going to sleep in the loft with you?" Mom asks.

By the tone in her voice I *know* she's aware of Sage's orientation.

"What difference does it make? Yea, probably. I'd feel weird sleeping in my cozy loft and leaving her to sleep on the floor now wouldn't I?" Expecting Mom to at least semi-agree I slip off the barstool to leave.

Instead, she timidly responds, "Ok, then."

My eyes flash at her. She knows how I hate timidity – I lectured her about her needing to toughen up and deal with life after her illness. So now? She should confront me if she wants to say something! I curtly walk out. I've already had dinner anyway.

I open the door to my room. My lion cat *shoots* under my legs, against the rules. The adorable dork hides underneath the pool table sitting in the middle of my room. "Platypus! You know you're not allowed in here! You *Know* I have Asthma...ah!" Catching him, I rub his head and toss him out.

Sage is peering up into my loft on the far right side of my room, obviously curious. She glances at me. Her eyes are brighter here, in this light.

"Oh, you're welcome to go up to the loft. Dad built it for me. He's amazing. The old kitchen and dining room used to be in here before he renovated. The loft has my bed in it, and because it is soooooooooo cool," I giggle, "I call it 'My Nest'. Feel free to peek. It's super fun." A small, reserved smile transforms her face. She climbs up three of the five wide, wooden ladder rungs.

Wait.

You now have a lesbian in your room,
on your loft ladder,
looking at your bed.

As her eyes disappear above the loft entrance, I close my own and drift into horrible thoughts...

'She wouldn't even find the idea of kissing another girl disgusting. She finds it attractive, sensual, sexual, and even allowed'.

25

My body sways and churns, sways and churns, *back and forth*, at these thoughts...I force myself to squelch back into reality the moment the bottom rung moans with her descent. "So, uhhh...." I start, but my thoughts are making butter.

"Hmm?"

I clear my throat. "So, uhhmm...if you don't mind me asking, why did you want to stay here tonight?" Albeit rude, it was the first question that bubbled up on my tongue. She doesn't seem to mind. Her energy is more open now.

"My family moves all over the world for my Dad's research. We house sit for people, who are often traveling themselves. It's normally fine, whatever; you have to deal with it. But there is something messed up about the house we are currently staying in. I don't like its energy..." She peers at me, "...I don't expect you to necessarily understand what I mean by bad 'energy'..."

ENERGY.

Spirituality. Forces-known and unknown, accessible and inaccessible, physical and spiritual, often though not always, conceived as "fields" that surround the bodies of all living things: the earth, you, me, them...the energy takes the form of 'rays' or vibrations. Yes, I think I understand.
Vibrations.

"...but yea, anyway, I need a break. So I've made sure to stay out of the house over the last two days. I'll have to go back tomorrow, though."

"So that's why you stayed with Brittany last night."

"Yes, but that's not the only reason. Even though Brittany is obviously, uhh...consuming, ahem, I thought she could be a neat friend. I shouldn't have bothered though." Sage rolled her eyes. "When Brittany started hitting on me it freaked me out. I didn't know she was bi, did you?"

"'Bi'?"

"Bisexual."

"Uhh…no." I clumsily answer, not quite grasping what she means.

Sage smirks. "Right, well, I could be wrong, but it certainly seems like she was..open to me."

 "Wow, weird. Uhm, so yea - what should we do, uhh, now?" I ask.

"Well that's easy." She replies.

Talk.

✍ HOW DO YOU KNOW?

"How do you *know* you are heterosexual?" she demands.

Clearly, Sage is not into small talk.

"Well, how do you know you are a *lesbian?!*" I shoot back.

It's a stupid retort.

She rolls her eyes. "Jasper, heterosexuality is something that society engrains into us...." "*...on unsuspecting victims,*'" I think I hear her grumble.

Society engrains in us...what? Why is society doing this exactly?

"Heterosexuality – men and women loving each other - is the expected and accepted orientation of the day. People don't question sexuality like they should – just like people don't question what they *eat* like they should, hmm?" She peers at me, knowing that this statement will get a rise out of me. Vegetarianism is my way of life.

Well, that's different, it's crucial for people to care about what they eat – for their health, the animals, the environment...being heterosexual doesn't hurt or destroy anyone, right?

She carries on, "People need to question the meat, egg and dairy industries just like they need to question why on earth all women need to be married to men in white dresses. Wait, not men in dresses..."

I begin to giggle.

"Ok, no! You know what I mean, although I do love me a good trannie in drag."

"Trannie?"

"...Transvestite?" I look blank. "Oh Lord, Jasper – you've got a lot to learn.

Anyway, getting back to the IMPORTANCE of questioning sexuality...It's the same as questioning DIET and society's involvement in these. By becoming

vegetarian you've questioned a SYSTEM, acknowledged the so-called abuses of animals
in
our modern factory farms[1],

and so you change your life to have a positive effect on the world.

Every meal you're able to make an impact   - as you like to say.

Even though I think eating meat is just fine."

"What?! Ok. Don't get me started on why eating meat is so fucked up."

"Haha, ok, ok. We'll talk about that another time. My point is: why don't you challenge your own sexuality and figure out why you believe what you believe? If you don't, you're just a walking zombie and doing what society expects of you. I thought you liked to rebel...I hear stories about your driving, missy. Seems you like adrenaline."

"What stories? But ahhh, I don't know. Dating guys is normal, and so it's just...oh, I don't know!"

"It's also 'normal' to eat meat – normal is defined by the majority."

---

[1] www.peta2.com

She decides on her next tactic. Walking over to my computer, she wakes it up and sits down. Typing in a web address she says, "Ok, let's do an online test to see just how hetero and/or homosexual you are."

I stare at her. "What?"

"C'mon. It's good for people to have insight about themselves."

She's serious. `"Ohmygosh. No way. I don't want to do` `that!" I squeal.`

She laughs and waves off my stricken expression. "Haha, nope. You've got to do it. It's just a quiz."

> *Hey, don't be so quick to say no. It could be fun taking a sexuality quiz...*

> I just don't want to do it in front of her.

> *Or anyone else!*

> But she's a lesbian! If anyone is going to let you be who you are, it'd be her, right?

> Huh? No? She's coming across as pretty judgmental, so what am I basing this on?

> And what the hell, 'be who I am'?

I sit.

"Ok, here. Start with this quiz – `'Lesbian or Bisexual, Which One are` `You?'`. There are 25 questions. Ready?"

God. I didn't think we'd discuss this so soon, if ever.

Numbly acquiescing, I obey.

Where did they get these questions from?!

> `'Do you find yourself daydreaming` `about what a girl would feel like?'`

30

Of course I do.

Doesn't everyone?

Merciless challenges. They swim through my head and sever my identity. Reality? Dismembered.

I am, secretly, shamefully, curious about girls...

Don't you dare tell *anyone*.

* * *

Skin

I am a little girl with raisin skin.

I spin in deep water –   jelly, dirt.

The light will touch me and sink stitches of confusion
into my skirts..they will wrap their thick bodies
around my legs.

The stitches begin...*Ouch!*

"God, she's hot."

Shut up.

                                        What am I?

        *I'm just curious about how women can love one
another...that's all. It's not bad to be curious about
                                        love, is it?*

        It's when the love will send you to hell.

        *Right. Ok. So you are just appreciating 'beauty'.
                        Nothing more. nothing more.*

                        nothing more...

I glance sideways at Sage. She's watching me. My nerves stitch.

Maybe I just like girls because of the abuse.

Beauty.

My thoughts are just a normal, dammit, normal appreciation of beauty.

nothing more....

My hands shake. I press the final button for the computer to tally my score.

my body is numb..the stitching is wrapping me,
tight, in a 'coon i never asked for.

You can't be gay. You can't be bisexual. This has to end <u>here</u>.

Now.

I sit up straight.

I can bolt, leave this place...

Sage gets up to dim the room's light. "I like softer light in general; it's so bright in here."

I am solitary, for these few moments. Tick, tick...

I feel my shoulder blades hit the back of my chair, and my eyes wince.

The change in illumination bends to black the beads of light across the threashold of my eyes.

Dimmer light means dimmer inhibitions. I have to take care not to say too much.

Help me.

My eyes ache into slits. I see the quiz's blurry results. I hear her step over some of my clothes littering the floor. I whip around to look at her. Before she can sit back down, I attack the computer screen's 'off' button and flick it to gray.

She nonchalantly joins me again.

"So...your results?"

I respond with nothing but an apprehensive shrug and a casual laugh. "Oh yea, well, we don't have to focus on that. Why don't we do something else??"

Like, you know, play hopscotch or something.

Cascading into stillness, her profile...shimmers.

Her energy is far clearer than I first realized. It's the color of a plum sky. Wow, I can really see her; her aura is far more palpable than other's I've been around.

What does this mean?

```
                                     It is wrong
                          to think that love comes from
                  long companionship & persevering courtship.

        Love is the offspring of spiritual affinity & unless
                        that affinity is created in a moment,
              it will not be created for years or even generations.

                                      - Khalil Gibran
```

34

She leans forward, her arms tucked in around her stomach. The clearness of her skin slips underneath...

... she's beautiful. I can even see the outlines of her eyelashes...

Stop.

"This ex of mine...I found out a few days ago, is pregnant." She begins. Apparently we're going to talk more before we turn the computer screen back on. I relax, slightly, but –

I don't move. As she talks, her leg brushes my hand. I close my eyes against the onslaught of hatred and love and curiosity and hell and family and self. I let my head tip back, a vain attempt to remove myself from her presence long enough to breathe. Time stretches, and we talk for some time about teen pregnancy, parenthood, sexuality, identity, social networks and psychology. At some point I realize that I've never had a friend - or boyfriend (ha – that'd be really strange) - teach me like this.

```
            It makes me happy
                   listening
                 & talking

                    to her

            -

            in that order.
```

I distance myself another three inches. I need to sleep, but she doesn't notice. Words drain over me.

Then she leans in to turn the computer back on.

Congratulations, Jasper!

You are 70% into **males** and 30% into **females**.

You are bisexual!

Ice. Self preservation.

"Ok this is totally fucked because like I've been *saying* all *night* – I AM NOT BISEXUAL." I'm more spastic than I mean to be.

She looks at me, her disbelief evident.

"Anyway, enough. I need to sleep. Are you ready to go to bed?"

She considers me. Perhaps noticing the paleness of my cheeks, she nods.

We both go to stand up. By accident, we press against one another. Pausing, my psyche splits and hovers, suspended, waiting for the next moment to dawn.

She's 5'3, I'm 5'6. She looks up at me. My body begins to tremble. I clasp my hands behind my back.

Her eyes...they hold so much of my future within them...I can see us...in three months, in nine...

"Whoa..."

"Pardon?"

My eyes widen. "Oh, sorry, nothing. Just mumbling about how that quiz has got to be wrong. You know." I extract myself.

Breathing deeply, I head purposefully over to the other side of the room, pick out my night gown and turn to see whether or not I can turn off the light. She says 'yes', and I flick the switch.

Shadows. Peace. Anonymity.

God. Fucking thank you.

I'm finally safe, here, in the darkness – I can't see her face, she can't see mine, I can pretend we're totally separate, autonomous beings again without a voice shuttling threads between us; two girls without a connection.

You can still see her aura.

The moon offers a gray candy cane design through the cracks of my curtains. It compliments her glow. She stands very still.

"Can I turn the light on, again?"

"Sure."

Pupils - assaulted.

I squint at her. Apparently she isn't going to change out of her clothes. Contrary to the assumption I had made, she hadn't planned to stay out twice in a row.

She spontaneously decided to come be with me.

Why?

Creaking up the ladder, I slide under the covers, telling myself that she's just like any other friend. She flops down next to me, the casualness so opposed to my tension that I laugh.

♉ "How do you...do it?"

The darkness and laughter over the next hour (we are <u>never</u> going to go to sleep!) put me into the dangerous position of being totally relaxed. Ha.

She's hilarious, and I suddenly get curious about something I've never been able to ask anyone before. I'm also So Sleep Deprived and that silly, giddy feeling is clouding my mind.

So, crazily, I burst out boldly and say, "Hey Sage, before we go to sleep, can I ask you a personal question?" My fingers gather my comforter tightly around me. The inevitable caress of a deep blush rises from my tummy to my cheeks.

"Yea, alright. If you want to." Her voice seems to show her tiredness too, now.

Well you have to ask her now, you've already started.

Lame excuse!

I breathe in.

Am I really going to say this?

"Errm, this is going to sound rather naive and dorky."

She says nothing, her breathing now the only indication that she's even next to me.

"Ok, well...*ehem*, right then. Ok. So, *Sex*. As a topic..."

Her breathing becomes slightly shallower. "Hmm..?"

I pull my hands out and fretfully smooth the covers. "Well, uhh...how do, uhmm..well," BLAH, "how do lesbians uhhm, do it?"

Pause. "Seriously?"

"Yea, I sound retarded – thanks for noticing. Yes, *seriously*, dork. I've been having sex with guys since the age of 14, so I know a thing or two about how a girl and guy 'go together'. I just can't figure out how **girls** have sex. It all just seems so...*bizarre*."

imagine having to wait for an answer to this question.

Sage,

after an

INDETERMINABLE

amount

of

TIME

finally responds by saying, "Sex isn't about anatomy, Jasper."

She doesn't go on.

> *Of course it's about anatomy! Sex is about fucking isn't it?*
> *And fucking involves bodies...aka our anatomy...*

"Huh? Can you explain a bit more? You're not giving me much to work with here." The sarcasm flies out without considering just how difficult it might be to answer.

Awkward.

"You'll just have to wait to understand."

> *Uh! Annoying. Wait for what? I'll never experience sex with a woman. Why*
> *won't she at least describe a little bit of the process...*

Dodging any more questions of mine, she starts to grill me again.

Apparently she likes to see me squirm.

Challenges rain down as jokes scurry off and instead she begins to throw topics in my face: religion, theology, spirituality (yes, she argues, there are differences), the importance of my friends, the meaning - or lack thereof - of *my life.*

She actually cares what I think. She wants to know *me.*

My head bobs. My eyes hurt. It's 3:36 am. With the most embarrassing of my own questions out of the way, and without any indication from Sage that she'll be finished talking any time soon, I let my mind wander to thinking about what I will fire back at her.

I want to tell her about my nightmares.

That's a bit of a leap. How can you trust her? Do you trust her?

I better be able to. With her incessant interrogation, she now knows more about me than most of my friends do, maybe even more than Melantha.

But she doesn't give much in return.

Maybe she'll open up later. If you're going to be awake, you might as well take advantage of her obsession for analyzing situations. Maybe she can give you feedback on whether or not your abuse fucked you up sexually.

It's strange how connected I feel to her already.
What do you see in her?

She's a wishing well. I toss pennies into her mouth, hoping for magic that will make me whole...

You shouldn't look outside of yourself for ways of being whole.

I know, I know.

She agrees to listen.

☾ THE NIGHTMARE

It's a **shame** to wake up from a nightmare...

>   ...only to walk
>   straight
>   into another.

* * *

seven and a half years old

i'm trembling.

it was just a dream! A dream dream DREAM –

i lift away from the pillow that pools in the horror of my nightmare. i peer up at Julie's top bunk.

she is dead to the world; an unconscious rag doll; a reminder that i too, will die. i shut my eyes tight and fall back into my blankets.

i should be happy she appears lifeless – she tortures me.
>   - just differently from how her mother soon will.

>   she forces me to carry her on my shoulders; i
>   bruise. she screams at me if i try to put her down.

i think my pain...thrills her?

>   *i can't decide if it thrills me, too.*

carrot, horse; feather, cat; approval, child; excitement, dog.

she does scare me during those times...but i don't know how to stop being friends with her. we're just playing, right?

i need to find the light switch…

oh that's right. it's broken. julie had that flashlight…

i press my hands along the cold, dirty carpet. the flashlight is gone.

eek!

i ache with anxiety.

is it in her bed with her?

find the door, open it. the living room lamp might still be on. her mother always forgets to turn it off.

i crawl and reach up to turn the doorknob. lifting onto my knees, a crack of light bathes my stricken face.

surely her mother is awake. GO. find her.

potential safety almost makes me throw up. as i tip toe down the hall, the carpet shifts beneath me, – No! – i pause and self soothe, *'shh…it's ok Jasper, you're almost there…'* two more steps…i shrink into Heidi's doorframe. i look up. her huge door overwhelms me. should I knock?

please don't be nervous, jasper. hurry, go in.

i tap lightly. i wait anxiously as images of monsters taunt my mind. *'Stop it, STOP it..'* i tap again. no answer. i put my tiny hand on the door knob and with a deep inhalation, i turn it. now holding my breath, i hear the lock *click*. the door starts to fall open -

Her room looks like my bad dream.

> Thick, dark red curtains. A single dying lamp feebly retreats with each passing moment. Snakes and ladders of discarded panty hose litter the carpet, the couch, the bedpost.

> *The posts i will be tied to.*

Panties. Magazines. Dirty, dirty magazines. Senses overwhelmed. Colors: sinister and rebellious. Crushed beer cans. Red, broken high heeled shoe. julie and i tried it on weekends ago. Its mate remains trapped to the foot of her mother, Lady Macbeth.

i back into the doorframe.

> fleeting relief: i am distracted by my back pressing hard into its corner, i almost forget where i am.

> a vertical bruise.

>> *delicious.*

run. run.

> *...Momma?*

On her left side, a black silky nightgown is pulled tightly against her tiny, 105 pound, 5'2" body. Her breasts are exposed.

i don't understand. My Momma never looks like this.

Snap. Her neck cracks.

Awake.

Coiling to rise upon her elbow, her eyes are fused shut with stitches of mascara. Scraping the filth from her face, she notices me.

Her eyes are bleeding.

Spidery veins hiss the presence of popped vessels. The red digits of her clock mirror the trapped blood. It blinks to 11:53 p.m.

> i have never, ever forgotten that clock.

Her boney back reflects in the mirrors behind her one thousand times. She leers at me as she throws her arm towards a vulnerable beer can. it squeaks.

> *it squeaks just like the red cartoon shoe in* Roger Rabbit, *just before the mean destroyer of animation dips it into a cavernous vat of deadly eraser fluid.*

48

The beer evaporates.

"What the fuck are you doing in here, you stupid brat? Did you want to see me, like this? ...Do you want to see *more* of me, pervert? Tell me what you want, *little girl.*"

```
innocence.

                        that      once      dripped.

        from my legs.

                is

                        destroyed.
```

i shrink down the wall...

Shrinking

    Shrinking

Shrinking

          down

  the

                Wall

Shrieking

                wet stains of **shock** cut down my
ankles

Take me. Take me away.

Momma?

    Daddy?

Make me better, make it better, make her disappear.

i'll wait for you. . . .h e   r   e.

                                                                    i

promise.

F a i n ting...

all is still.

"I'm going to counseling for it now." I take a deep breath. "Hmm. I *love* my counselor – he rocks. He has this reputation of being crazy awesome as far as his work with teenagers. He has one of the highest success rates…"

There it is. She's about to respond.

Shards of glass. At first I don't feel it, but after a few stings their tinkling presence makes my skin bleed. The ear closest to Sage, my right ear, is most affected.

She begins to laugh. *Laugh.*

Yes, laugh.

At me.

>At my abuse.

>At my counselor.

At my ridiculous idea that she would *give a damn*.

She laughs so hard that she appears to stop gulping air.

>*Fuck you, Sage.*

>*Go on, do it. Asphyxiate.*

Moments draw watermarks along the shame filling my ears. Her lungs irritatingly attempt to inhale.

>I smile…a twisted smile. It spreads along my lips as I imagine…

>*…licking blood.*
>*Her blood,*
>*in retaliation for her violating me here, in my own bed.*

I CAN NOT ALLOW PEOPLE TO VIOLATE ME, NOT ANYMORE.

55

Not true. You let people violate you all the time, and what for? Popularity?

Fuck off. You know nothing.

Perhaps you could just push her out of your loft...

My chest restricts appreciatively.

She gasps.

She's alive.

Unfortunate.

In the midst of her disjointed, fiercely persistent mirth, she splutters,

"Well hey, that doesn't sound **too, too bad**, I mean, it could have been *much,* MUCH worse – ahaha – you know, you, ^{you} could have been abused by an older *GUY*."

`Bitch.`

`RAGE.`

I'd experienced an opposite reaction from others - a shocked look, sympathy, or a supportive murmur, a shred of insight. But her!

Horrid.

I can't get out of the loft. She is lying on the side of the bed that is nearest the trap door...
I would have to climb over her to get out.

I'm fucking trapped.

Don't cry. DON'T CRY!

Weak. Always so weak.

Sarcastically she oozes, "Ha! Hmm...Sorry if I upset you. You'll *soon realize*," each syllable dramatic and infuriatingly comic as her hands waffle midair, "*why I do NOT maintain friendships with anyone other than my three best friends in the States, aka 'mis chicas'. I am a master of my own demise.*"

What is she, like, totally unredeemable or some such shit?
Like fucking Doctor Faustus or something?
Drama queen.

"You'll no doubt learn to hate me, just like the rest of them."

Three moments pass. I turn to look at her – the sun is rising. I can see her face now. Her expression hints at a depth of thought not expressed by her tone of voice.

I am not in the frame of mind to give a shit.

"I'm 'just like the rest of them', huh? Oh. You think I'm 'just like the rest of them'?" Shivers of fury charge through my wrecked, shredded body.

How dare you insinuate that you know anything about me.

"Well, we'll see about that," I snarl.

Her eyes observe me and click through an old black and white slide show:

First. She shines with surprise.

Click

Next. She becomes entertained.

Click

Finally. She settles on unmistakable detachment.

*To hell with you, Sage. I'll destroy
you.*

*No one should be as cynical as you are... Fine, you're deranged because you can't
maintain even the most casual of friendships.
But I know you need friends and fucking LOVE. D'uh. Stupid bitch.*

You need fixing, and I'm going to be the one to fix you.

A vicious twist bends my face.

*Then, as your savior, I will be able to tear down the image of you
laughing...laughing at the little girl that timidly sways inside me.*

If only I hadn't gone in...

I must try and curb this manipulation.

*But she hurt me.
I need her to become dependent on me,
rather than my emotions
depending
on her.*

'Tis true. I will teach her to wipe that cruel grin off her face.

I will own her.

* * *

5:30am.

Eyes close.

An array of dreams.

* * *

Five hours later.

Mute consciousness.

I stare at the bars that line the side of my loft... dark, light, dark, light, dark, light....my mind scans them. My back is to her.

45 minutes pass.

With each thought, I blink...

...light, dark, light, dark, light, dark, light...

My eyelashes flutter two thousand, two hundred and twelve times....

"Jasper? Are you awake?"

I make no sound.

Learned helplessness.

You mean nothing to this girl.

"Jasper? Look. I'm sorry about laughing last night. It was probably…ok it *was* insensitive. You threw me off – I didn't expect for you to tell me what you did. I'm sorry about the stupid jibe, too. It won't happen again."

really?

Intuitively she replies, "Truly. I'm sorry."

Ridiculous tears embarrass my pillow.

Talk to her, you know you need to. It's the healthy thing to do.

"Yea, well." I surreptitiously fling off the tears. "I want to believe you, Sage…but you were so mean last night. I hate being hurt."

"Me too."

"I don't know. I don't even know you, and I opened up to you far more than I ever should have. I'm sorry for letting you in."

She's quiet.

I feel a familiar ache dawn in me. Fear, in a way.

What if we don't properly make up this morning? What if we never talk again? What if we go back into a space where I have no one, absolutely no one, to talk to about my life and all of my psychotic questions about identity? What IF?

You might never meet another lesbian – you've already lived 16 years, and you've only ever met her. You might never be able to ask another honest question; you might never discover your truth – whatever it is.

Bursting, I cry, "Oh fuck it! I'm lying! I love talking to you. I just don't understand why you *laughed*!"

"I know. I'm sorry…"

"Ok, whatever. Stop saying you're sorry – it's over. Just know that I have limits – I'll eventually have to let you go if you hurt me too much."

You have limits? Since when? You're always maintaining friendships with people you shouldn't give the time of day.

I turn over slightly and see her smile. "Ok, Jasper, it's a deal. We'll try our best to not hurt one another."

Oh.

Happiness tugs at the edges of my mouth. I let my right shoulder fall so that I'm now lying on my back, staring at my loft ceiling.

Dammit. So predictable.

"Thank you…"

She turns over onto her left side and looks at me. Her energy - an affectionate rainfall on my chest - its drops tip, & pour…

We move gently into other conversations. She crinkles up her nose and sticks her tongue out every time she spouts off a philosophical or psychological theory that she knows goes WAY over my head. Her humor is sharp and uninhibited.

She's teasing me.

Wonders.

Wow, I forgave her so quickly…

Giggles escape from my lips more contented than I've seen them in a long, long while.

In the spirit of release, I turn to face her.

Proximity…the raindrops pour anew, shocking my senses into a space of poised apprehension.

Her eyes, her nose, her eyelashes, her lips, her hair…her messy, bed slept hair…

I tense up, but I needn't have worried. Closing her eyes, she takes a deep breath, sits up and swings her feet down the opening of my loft. She descends and falls out of sight, safely away from me in my nightgown.

"Jasper? Thanks for letting me stay. I need to go now, so I'll see you later."

Perhaps predictably, I missed her.

✑ THE FIRST OF MANY FIRSTS

A man who publishes his letters becomes a nudist—

nothing shields him from the world's
gaze except his bare skin.

A writer, writing away, can always fix himself up to
make himself more presentable,

but a [wo]man who has written a letter is stuck with it
for all time.

- Elwyn Brooks White

****

Subject: Saturday night

To: Jasper
From: Sage
Date: September 9th

hey.

your mind. how is it?

-sage

****

****

```
I am so much more casual
than                  she.


        At   least   in   the
beginning, hmm?
```

Subject: Re: Saturday night

To: Sage
From: Jasper
Date: September 12th

Yay! Our first email exchange! Exciting!

Thank you so much for Saturday. I've thought about it a lot. It was insanely awesome. I can't believe we talked for...what like, eight hours or something crazy?! Yay!

About my mind...hmm. Well, let's talk on online ok? I'm going to start instant messaging you on ICQ now...my alias is Lovers_End – it's reminiscent of the time when I considered double suicide with my ex-boyfriend, Steve...AH! it's all so difficult isn't it. :P

jasper!

****

✍ Online - Our First Conversation

September 12th

NorthDaughter 5:18 PM

hi, Jasper.

AH! so many e-mails!! ::looks like a child in a candy shop::

Lovers_End 5:26 PM

hi Sage! yea, I know what you mean! emails rock.

Oh AH! Dammit! I *know* I shouldn't care about Steve because he is my ex...& he's also a sociopath, *sighs melodramatically*... but he's definitely going away! ☹ he's been accepted into this drug detox program in Palmerston North. AH! He is my sex toy(!) & Auckland is so far away. HUMF.

NorthDaughter 5:28 PM

poor you. i guess you'll just have to find a surrogate sex toy..::smirk:: ahem...::laughs:: actually forget that last remark..other people have been rubbing off on me

Lovers_End 5:31 PM

haha no it's ok (even though it's really not my style!). i don't mind...ew just don't lick my ear without me knowing!!

NorthDaughter 5:33 PM

i don't lick ears...well...not without permission....who said i lick ears!!! i never licked anyone's! ok well..maybe once or twice..dah! sooo::change of pace:: does this mean i can do anything BUT lick them?

Lovers_End 5:35 PM

hehehehheeee, sooo silly. nope nope, not what i meant. i was referring to the time when a guy on the bus thought that i was hot and so when he was sitting behind me on our way home he ACTUALLY STUCK HIS TONGE OUT AND DAMN WELL LICKED ME, humf--he was really perverted, but he was a ½ friend and so i didn't mind too much, but licking me? uhhhh....i hardly knew the guy. lol.

NorthDaughter 5:36 PM

so you are comparing me to a hot guy...is this a good sign or a bad one?

Lovers_End 5:37 PM

so silly. you=chick. me=heterosexual...so hmmm. yes. lol

NorthDaughter 5:38 PM

hehehehe foiled again! ::stretches:: it's ok though i am sick of relationships anyway

Lovers_End 5:38 PM

foiled??

NorthDaughter 5:39 PM

yes....? you know..'my plan has been foiled again'? c'mon! VOCAB WOMAN!!

Lovers_End 5:39 PM

AHAHAA, ok...looking "foiled" up......shush i'm allowed to be retarded...it's a valid state of being :P hehe.

Lovers_End 5:40 PM

so yes. relationships have lost their novelty. no doubt they will be appealing again sometime...but for the moment fuck buddies are good, hehehe *aaaaahhhhhh* and mine's gone!!! ☹ ☹ (you're gonna be hearing about this quite a bit i am sorry to inform you ;) lol)

NorthDaughter 5:41 PM

maybe not novelty per se...i see it as more of a..'i will never find love again' type of thing...yeah except fuck buddy type relationships can get soo screwed up later on, you try and say 'no feelings' or anything yet they are still there...oi ve it's confusing, i just wanna go to a bar and find me a one night stand or something

Lovers_End 5:52 PM

....sorry about taking forever to respond i had to set the table and talk to   my   mother. you'll 'never find love again'? of course you will miss!! you're awesome i say. do you still talk to that chick who would have been you're your fiancée?

NorthDaughter 5:53 PM

uhm well yeah Bernadette [the ex-fiancée] has been avoiding me..no e-mails; no icq messages..i don't blame her but damnit we've been friends for seven years..i mean you'd expect her to care a little...ach! sorry didn't mean to babble..

Lovers_End 5:55 PM

why do you think she's doing that?

NorthDaughter 5:55 PM

i don't know..perhaps i'll find out sometime. anyway.

Lovers_End 5:55 PM

ok.

so i was wondering you know how we just kinda spilled our guts out on Sat. night, do you do that often? like tell lots to people? i'm indifferent on whether or not you do, just wondering cuz i don't know how you usually move through life (either really open or not really or somewhere in between...etc) and i wanted to let you know that a) it was soooo good telling you stuff, even better after you apologized about the laughing attack...lol ;) and b) i don't go around telling everyone all the things that I told you, so shhh shh about it all plz ok?

NorthDaughter 5:56 PM

> i basically dont tell people stuff..my nickname used to be 'THE CLAM' except on those rare occasions i get no sleep or am influenced by substances

Lovers_End 5:58 PM

> hmm...right ho.

> well...i promise not to tell anyone (hehe pinkie promise! lol ;) cuz i don't tell people personal stuff. ☺ i think if it turns out that we can tell each other things, and everything we say be totally confidential, that'd rock.

NorthDaughter 6:01 PM

> as long as you don't hurt my feelings..::sniff::

Lovers_End 6:02 PM

> ☺ nah, i won't hurt your feelings. ah! must go – dinner time!

NorthDaughter 6:02 PM

> i try to be a good listener..just sometimes I laugh at the oddest places..i guess eventually you'll realize how screwed up i am anyway

Lovers_End 6:03 PM

> that's cool, makes our conversations interesting cuz you totally throw me off sometimes, lol

NorthDaughter 6:03 PM

> good!

NorthDaughter 6:08 PM

> ...night hun

☒ SCHOLASTIC ASSESSMENT TEST (SATS)

****

Subject: Excited! You are so amazing!

To: Sage
From: Jasper
Date: September 15th

Miss Sage!

It's so neat that you suggested we study for the SATs together! What a great idea. I had no idea I could still take it as an American citizen living in another country...neato cheeto! :D hehe.

& so it begins! aahahhaaa im a dork...yay!

eeeeee! hehe. I'm sorry to sound like such a sop but I really love spending time with you. It's so...odd. Like, we're totally different but wow. It's just...yea, maybe it's because we're both American in this crazy Kiwi country, what with their tall poppy syndrome (its so ick how they put down on people achieving here – so different to the american outlook) ;) hehe. I'm not sure. But thank you!

Jasper

****

```
*****************************************************************
```

Subject: Re: ←prefix for 'again'

To: Jasper
From: Sage
Date: September 15th

i have decided through
careful observation
and limitless stipulation,
that
you are insane.

thank you yourself missy
-the sage
(p.s. btw-now all my boyz are calling me prissy thanks to you!)

```
*****************************************************************
```

Subject: 'pps'

To: Jasper
From: Sage
Date: September 15th

ok and i also must rant about the complete and utter self-centeredness of my best friends, obviously i was either blind, or we have grown so far apart that there is nothing left to us except superficial remarks on the 'weather' of our lives!

::breathes::

::bows::

that is all

stop

```
*****************************************************************
```

```
************************************************************
```

Subject: Friends…hmm.

To: Sage
From: Jasper
Date: September 15th

Hey chick,

I'm so sorry about your friends! Sometimes people can be so wrapped up in their own lives and forget to contact the old best friend that's moved away. I found the same thing with my friends when I moved here four years ago -- sadly, 12 year olds don't make for great letter writers. It's really quite sad. Hmm…I hope you hear from them soon.

On another wave…what makes you *tick*? I've been trying to figure you out.

Jasper.

```
************************************************************
```

Subject: Re:*()*….koala

To: Jasper
From: Sage
Date: September 16th

fortunately for me, the ones who stopped emailing within a few months i don't actually care about that much, but these are mis chicas you know? rose, rosalyn and bernadette (the ex). my three best friends. we were inseparable and now it's like I am forced to say 'my ex is avoiding me' and i HATE the word 'ex'. it's soo cliche.

but anyway despite being self absorbed myself, i also love to argue philosophy and sociology so do send comments and we can discuss. i'm big on figuring people out, it's fun to be disillusioned

later babe

-sage

```
************************************************************
```

September 17th

NorthDaughter 10:01 AM

   mlaaaa

Lovers_End 10:09 AM

   how are ya prissy? neat neat studying last night

NorthDaughter 10:09 AM

   DAH! i am not prissy! ::said in a very prissy fashion::

Lovers_End 10:17 AM

   ahahahahahahahahahaha sooooo cute! lmao (lmao = laugh my ass off...)

NorthDaughter 10:17 AM

   cute? CUTE??!!! I AM NOT CUTE!!!

Lovers_End 10:17 AM

   YES YA ARE!!!!! YOU KNOW IT!! AHAHA :P

Lovers_End 10:17 AM

   ooo! so i've done lotsa studying today yay!

   :P *sticks her tongue out at YOU miss smarty pants*, haha im not gonna be as dumb anymore :P

NorthDaughter 10:17 AM

   we'll see about that

Lovers_End 10:18 AM

   ahhhhhhh, pthhhhh :P

Lovers_End 10:30 AM

...ok question! (speaking of mis chicas – *my* chicas are going through some definite drama)→ would you go out with your best friend's best guy friend of whom she has been in love with for three years?

NorthDaughter 10:31 AM

i would consider it, but i wouldn't do it aye

Lovers_End 10:31 AM

yea neither. humf! Nicole apparently doesn't see it that way. She bloody well went ahead and hooked up with Sam, Evette's best guy friend that she's secretly been in love with for three years! Who *does* that? Man she sucks!? ok so she is a wonderful person......but I think she's one of those people that is so gorgeous that it means she's highly sought after, and she hasn't learned how and why to say NO THANK YOU to these guys who are "hot" or "popular". It's strange – it's like she needs to have people crushing on her to feel good about herself...

Maybe it has something to do with her dad being too demanding and making her feel like she's not good enough all the time but aaaaahhhhhhhhh!!! She has no loyalties when it comes to a friend's crush or love object! She just has to learn to say no! grr...

NorthDaughter 10:32 AM

Nicole? she has a friend? that she isn't shagging? and it's male? huh?

Lovers_End 10:32 AM

if you're gonna get all technical about it

Lovers_End 10:37

oh it's all so sad! my poor home girl Evette!

NorthDaughter 10:39 AM

your home girl? what the....can't you talk correctly? and i find this amusing i mean either Nicole is vicious or she is dumb..i prefer dumb...it endears her more..

Lovers_End 10:40 AM

yea dumb is much betta i reacon. anyway sorry for bitching, i try and keep it to a minimum, but ugh --sorry, im being most childish

Lovers_End 10:40 AM

all these silly people! lol, how are your mates? have they written yet?

NorthDaughter 10:41 AM

you can bitch... By the way can you believe i actually left the house yesterday without any gel in my ahir? whoa talk about mind fuck....well one friend wrote me, but it was superficial bullshit...

Lovers_End 10:43 AM

'ahir' is not a word dear. try and keep the spelling up to an appropriate standard now won't you? mustn't have fun whilst on the internet (ahaha) and superficial bullshit eh? nice.

NorthDaughter 10:44 AM

DAH!!!! ::levitates-head spinning:: i am never wrong! if ahir wasn't in the stupid dictionary (who knows how mentally retarded the people who wrote that are) then i'll put it in!!!

Lovers_End 10:45 AM

ahaha...ehem. that's nice dear.

Lovers_End 10:44 AM

what exactly qualifies as superficial? i ask because it seems to be
becoming a theme of ours...and because superficial has a wide range

---

Which answer is correct?

SUPERFICIAL is to **PENETRATING** as:

a.	Shallow	is to	Deep	(spatial)
b.	Facade	is to	Structure	(architectural)
c.	Cursory	is to	Analytical	(philosophical)
d.	Insignificant	to	Profound	(intellectual)
e.	Surface	is to	Authentic	(arguments)
f.	Minor	is to	Severe	(medical)
g.	Trivial	is to	Substantial	(editorial)
h.	Trivial	is to	Significant	(substantial)
i.	Careless	is to	Thorough	(intentional)
j.	Frivolous	is to	Serious	(attitudinal)
k.	Apparent	to	Actual	(visual)

NorthDaughter 10:45 AM

yeah yeah i know.. "superficial" applies to things that have no meaning
aight? For example, 'hello, school is nice, my boytoy is nice, everything
is blah blah blah, and well i have to go now cause i have a life..' no nooo
i'm not bitter never....

Lovers_End 10:46 AM

who's boytoy? thought this was an ex of yours?

NorthDaughter 10:46 AM

NO I'm talking about mis chicas my ::breathes:: ex(i HATE that word) has not talked to me since

NorthDaughter 10:46 AM

mis chicas are three people rose, rosalyn and bernadette – i've only dated bernadette

Lovers_End 10:47 AM

ok.

she was probably hella hurt i'd say. maybe that's why she's not talking?

NorthDaughter 10:47 AM

SHE was hurt? oh MY ASS!

Lovers_End 10:47 AM

why don't you think she would be?

NorthDaughter 10:49 AM

hahaha if she was hurt then why do it?...::ok enough bitterness please...must be joyful::

Lovers_End 10:50 AM

ok so you're not making TOTAL sense, but I'm here if you need to talk? but you probably don't.(as has been the habitual response from you, you moo)

Lovers_End 10:51 AM

guess what? all that shit that i was gonna write to you has just kinda done a disappearing act from my conscious mind eh

NorthDaughter 10:51 AM

i know how that works..::smirk:: comes with the blondeness..

Lovers_End 10:51 AM

I AM **NOT** BLONDE!!!!!!!!!!!!!! fuck that.

NorthDaughter 10:52 AM

i understand that you are not physically blonde...just act like it

Lovers_End 10:52 AM

ah!! pthhh *pthhhhhhhhh* not true! I just chose to focus on a social life rather than my brain for a few years. *smiles*

NorthDaughter 10:52 AM

indeed. well you have fun dear

Lovers_End 10:52 AM

yup. i have had fun...but you, yes *YOU* :P, have inspired me to think about the future and begin planning for it (shock horror).

NorthDaughter 10:52 AM

nice try miss but i don't inspire people

Lovers_End 10:52 AM

force?

NorthDaughter 10:52 AM

nope. you'd know it if i did. everything is a choice. ::nods sagely::

Lovers_End 10:54 AM

nah, you did inspire me eh. Mom's been trying to get me to study this whole year. but just a few times of being around you studying was just...ok, no other word for it other than INSPIRATIONAL :D. i love how you have a big vocab—makes communication soooooo much more interesting, it's cue man cue (cue = cool!!!)

NorthDaughter 10:55 AM

::sighs:: the 'cue' again...do you know that 'cues' are used in billiards?

Lovers_End 10:57 AM

yup yup, most certainly did. but 'cue' is my word for cool.

hey yes, and i also know that psychologically you might not be able to appreciate my complements, so I'm sorry if that's the case

NorthDaughter 10:57 AM

are you saying i am screwed up?:: torn between laughing and screeching::

Lovers_End 10:57 AM

no

NorthDaughter 10:58 AM

::rolls her eyes:: no one ever comes up with a more interesting comment than 'no' you'd think they'd expound or something...

Lovers_End 10:58 AM

i'm telling you from what i know of your background that you aren't all that keen on letting someone get close enough to actually give you a complement without you rejecting it. am i wrong?

NorthDaughter 10:59 AM

ok so you figured out one thing...but that's the nearly most obvious trait..EVERYONE gets that eventually..

Lovers_End 11:00 AM

    uh-huh...rite ho. EVERYONE gets what eventually?

NorthDaughter 11:01 AM

    the compliment bit

Lovers_End 11:03 AM

    ok then. well then you must pardon my attempt at being intellegently perceptive--it was obviously a stupid observation huh? ahaha, ;) :P

NorthDaughter 11:04 AM

    intellegently? huh? ::sighs:: sooo uhm right moving on?

Lovers_End 11:04 AM

    i'd say. yep, lets move on.

NorthDaughter 11:05 AM

    you see..i have so many ideas running around in my head i don't have time or the typing skill to explain them all

Lovers_End 11:06 AM

    yea...noticed, lol

NorthDaughter 11:06 AM

    mmmffff

Lovers_End 11:06 AM

    hehehe

Lovers_End 11:13 AM

    silence eh?

NorthDaughter 11:14 AM

    should i be talking?

Lovers_End 11:15 AM

> i don't know. probably not

NorthDaughter 11:16 AM

> that's good then. commence with the silence.

NorthDaughter 11:17 AM

> later babe madre home

Lovers_End 12:06 PM

> rite ho, later

> Among those whom I like or admire, I can find
> no common denominator, but among those whom I
> love, I can: all of them make me laugh.
> - W. H. Auden

September 18th

Lovers_End 7:27 PM

   hey chickie ☺ hehe, mmmffft

NorthDaughter 7:31 PM

   mmmffffness! stop stealing my phrases missy

Lovers_End 7:32 PM

   what other phrases have i stolen missy? i doooo believe that "prissy"
   etc is MAH word! as is MAH...:P lol...riiiight

NorthDaughter 7:32 PM

   mah? MAH? where da hell are yooo from missy?

Lovers_End 7:33 PM

   TEXAS BABY! ahahaha

NorthDaughter 7:33 PM

   GOD KILL ME!! NOT BILLY RAY!!!

Lovers_End 7:34 PM

   ahaha, see look at THAT started doin' MAH sized letters...ie:
   capital....ahaha

   OK, YES SO HOW ARE YA PRISS?

NorthDaughter 7:35 PM

> i am NOT prissy! and you don't OWN capital letters missy, MAH ASS!
> i'm ok.

Lovers_End 7:35 PM

> ..that's nice dear *pat pat*

NorthDaughter 7:35 PM

> mmmfff!!!

Lovers_End 7:35 PM

> *evil grin*

NorthDaughter 7:36 PM

> ::turning purple:: DAHHH!!! that's nice honey bunches

Lovers_End 7:36 PM

> aahaha, honey bunches eh? bunches of honey? lmfao

NorthDaughter 7:37 PM

> bunches of missy type honey flavored Texan....::looks vaguely red::

NorthDaughter 7:37 PM

> nix that last bit ::smirk::

Lovers_End 7:37 PM

> nix that last bit? hmm?

NorthDaughter 7:38 PM

> hmm? what did i miss something? i have no recollection of the events
> described

NorthDaughter 7:38 PM

    sorry being an evil twin means i act strange sometimes

Lovers_End 7:39 PM

    lol, silly eh? ahaha ya wee punk ass...

NorthDaughter 7:52 PM

    'ya wee'....what da hell? good god woman what da hell happened to your head? why, i do declare it must be shrinking! must be all that 'not-so-smart-as-sage' leaking out all over.. ::smirk::

Lovers_End 7:52 PM

    BIAAAAAATCH!!

NorthDaughter 7:53 PM

    ::laughs::

Lovers_End 7:53 PM

    nooooooooooooooooo laughin' at me girl! dammit woman, you are infuriating!

NorthDaughter 8:00 PM

    thank you missy

Lovers_End 8:05 PM

    no welcomes...not a complement! :P lol

NorthDaughter 8:05 PM

    silly girly ok fine if you want to be a meanie then go ahead

Lovers_End 8:06 PM

    yups.

NorthDaughter 8:07 PM

>::sighs:: eh you cliquey's are all the same

Lovers_End 8:07 PM

>cliquey's?? missssss we weren't snobby at all today!! we welcomed you with open arms miss :P

NorthDaughter 8:08 PM

>yeah thanks for straining yourselves to accept me

Lovers_End 8:09 PM

>what the hell? ok...so you're suffering from low self esteem today huh? you're awesome mate, it was a cool change to see ya round more. ☺

NorthDaughter 8:10 PM

>agggg! go away.

Lovers_End 8:11 PM

>see? there you go again...not being able to accept complements...would you rather i say: "Ya wee munter, why the hell did you come and say hello? i mean it was just soooo rude to penetrate our cliquish bubble!"

NorthDaughter 8:12 PM

>yes that would be funny then i could mock you and not feel guilty. can't we have one conversation without mentioning me?

Lovers_End 8:12 PM

>hmm...ok so you wanna talk about something else? me? or issues? issues eh? ok then

NorthDaughter 8:13 PM

>so talk woman

Lovers_End 8:15 PM

>hmm..yes right. *thinks*.....*strains herself*...ahh

NorthDaughter 8:15 PM

>no hernias dear

Lovers_End 8:15 PM

>i'd say. that that would be something you couldn't wiggle your way out of

NorthDaughter 8:16 PM

>uhm wiggle? me? i never wiggle

Lovers_End 8:17 PM

>ahahahahaha, hmm dear that would be a figure of SPEECH

NorthDaughter 8:17 PM

>my ass! (which does NOT wiggle)

Lovers_End 8:18 PM

>hmm...wouldn't know i say..but i'll take your word for it, lol!!

NorthDaughter 8:18 PM

>::rolls her eyes:: ok fine then you gonna tell me an anecdote or do i have to start?

Lovers_End 8:19 PM

>I'd say you should start cuz whatever i say will be retarded :P but oh yea, one of the things i was gonna say to you in one of the spillage emails was that I like spending time with you more studying (ie: without hyper assed peeps...lol) not that i am requesting anything, just that was one of the things that you are really fun/cue when i get you on my own.

NorthDaughter 8:26 PM

eh? indeed. well watch out i have a split personality and bad things happen to little girls who try to be my friend..::attempts to smile::

Lovers_End 8:27 PM

there isn't any "trying to be your friend" about it. I'm simply your friend. :P

NorthDaughter 8:28 PM

::blinks:: you are insane

⚡ SIGHT

****

insanity, eh?

    hmm.

        ...why do i see the things i see?

am i damned?

am i blessed?

what do these words mean?

what do you mean?

what do...they...mean?

        they

                they

they

      why do i not remember everything i see?

he said i wasn't insane.

i try to believe him.

          focus on the light of this place...

...and i do, focus, sometimes. i'm just still so young –
i don't know how to control things, yet –

The First Time I Talked About It

I'm three years old. My bed is populated with soft toys – I love animals – I've named every single one. My Mother is kisses me goodnight...but I leap out of bed the moment my head is s'posed to hit the pillow.

"Momma! I want to pull the new light switch string! I wanna turn it off! Watch me!"

I grab onto the string and wait. Hooray! Once she's on her way out,
I'll turn off the light, then boOOOoound back into bed.

She comes over and leans down to kiss my forehead. Crying out, I exclaim, "Hey, Momma!

Look! Look! Who's that lady sitting over there?"

My head tips to the side. Exuberance hushes.

Now it is time for quiet observation.

Mother turns and scans my pink and purple room, searching for a lady. The only two people in the room, insofar as she can tell, are herself and her daughter. "Hmm. Jasper, honey? Are you looking at a picture or at one of your book covers?

"...What do you see?"

"A lady of light. She's so neat. Her colors are *beauty-ful*..." I trail off and begin murmuring to myself, seemingly in conversation with her. Dipping in and out of the conversation...

The lady is transparent but easy to see.

> She's sitting
> on my bed in
> the place i
> just left -the
> place still
> warm from my
> little body.

Her smile
is soft and kind.

> She
> makes me
> feel
> SAFE...

I am precious.

Mother considers her response. Rising to her fundamental values - openness, belief in every possibility, unconditional love and absolute support – she instantly

affirms

my

world.

Thank you...

> "She looks like Jesus's Mommy in my Christmas books...ohhh! Her light just got brighter!"

* * *

Mother has spent much of her life studying world religions and mysticism, an interest that sprang from a unique summer when she was 12 years old.

Just after Mom's 11th birthday, her father had a major stroke and was bedridden, paralyzed and unable to speak well. Mom's mother had a nervous

89

breakdown caring for him, so for three months one summer Mom stayed with her maternal aunts.

Every week, she would switch houses, moving from one aunt's home to another.

Each aunt had a special gift.

The Aunts

One aunt was a Sufi priestess. Sufism is the mystical branch of Islam. She was also a talented astrologer, and decades later she notes on Jasper's birth chart that she would be a mystic with psychic abilities.

The youngest aunt was a house wife with marital problems (paranoid schizophrenia can get in the way of intimacy). She was responsible for introducing Mother to dirty jokes. Her life also provided color to family stories: "It was never the same between her and her husband after she flushed his dentures down the toilet."

Her great aunt, who was 69 at the time, was a retired store clerk. As a strict Baptist, discussing astrology, marital problems, world religions and telling dirty jokes were strictly taboo. Cooking, cleaning, domino games and gin rummy occupied Mother during the weeks with her.

The fourth aunt had lost her hearing at age five. She saw the world. ghosts, spirits, angels. premonitions. ESP. dreams. She bequeathed her sight to Jasper when she passed and thus supplemented Jasper's gifts with her own. Jasper was eight when she did.

* * *

Before my Mother went to bed that night, she transcribed my first vision of the lady of light. She saved and filed it away on her computer in a folder labeled, 'Jasper'.

While supportive of me, a year later, and after many more visions, she called my pediatrician and family friend, Dr. B. She would leave a message on his answering machine saying that we needed to arrange a psychiatric exam for me; her daughter might be schizophrenic, like one of her aunts.

My mother has multiple university degrees, two of which are in psychology and nursing. My pediatrician sincerely trusted my Mom's judgment, so he took the situation seriously.

He agreed to perform a psychiatric exam on me.

It took a whole hour. When I came out, Mother was fully prepared to love me through any diagnosis.

The doctor came out pale faced. 'Well, she's not hallucinating. She did, however, give me some personal advice based on certain details she never should have known. I can't explain it, but she isn't mentally ill...' Then he then muttered, 'As a four year old, she shouldn't know how to give such advice....' I danced around my Mother's legs and asked if we were able to go home yet. I had a new puppy, and I wanted to go home to play with him.

From this point on, Mother never doubts my gifts. No matter where I was, or am, she listens to my spiritual whisperings – and more – helping me translate my spiritual world into concepts others can understand. The computer folder labeled 'Jasper' has grown and grown...thank goodness. Reading through her records helps me remember.

why can't i *remember* EVERYTHING i see?

why see the things i see?

...what does it mean to be damned?

what does it mean to be blessed?...

* * *

Lovers_End 8:34 PM

> ...umm 'little girls'??? hello dear i am OLDER than you!

NorthDaughter 8:35 PM

> i may have been a fetus when you were 'born' but mentally i am older..::smirk::

Lovers_End 8:36 PM

> ...my soul is older so ha! :-P

NorthDaughter 8:37 PM

> oh NO she did not..are you telling me we have the same religion too? ::knowing smile:: the plot thickens..did i ever tell you my wiccan story?

Lovers_End 8:38 PM

> nope. go for it.

NorthDaughter 8:39 PM

> eh nevermind erase last message

Lovers_End 8:39 PM

> no no no! you've stepped in it now, fess up

NorthDaughter 8:40 PM

> about what? i don't know what you are talking about...besides i was messed up then even more so...ahh how the past haunts us

Lovers_End 8:41 PM

> and how other people's pasts entertain us...(if you will kindly remember my sexual abuse story, and remember you're mirth as a result of it...)

NorthDaughter 8:41 PM

   i was sleep deprived! ::looks guilty:: but yes, i have no desire to speak

Lovers_End 8:49 PM

   hmm...DAMMIT WOMAN! BY THE TIME I AM THROUGH WITH YOU,
   YOU ARE GONNA REALISE THAT YOU ARE AN AWESOME,
   INTELLEGENT, DAMN WELL FUN PERSON-and therefore don't have to
   put down on anyone else, and you can be quite content in life. ok? ok.

NorthDaughter 8:51 PM

   ::shakes her head::
   you   know   i'm
   getting sick of
   telling people to
   stop trying to fix
   me..can't we just
   take it for granted
   and get over it?

> If you treat a person as she
> appears to be,
> you make her worse than she is.
> But if you treat a person as if
> she already were what
> she potentially could be,
> you make her what
> she should be.
> - **Goethe**

Lovers_End 8:56 PM

   ? oh.

   i am sorry. my bad...

NorthDaughter 8:57 PM

   hehehe.

NorthDaughter 8:58 PM

   so tell me about your life..

Lovers_End 8:59 PM

   Ok, #1: i have an awesome family. I would be totally fucked and lost if
   they were any different.

NorthDaughter 8:59 PM

   always a good thing? my family – mis chicas – is in new mexico. right.

well, what do you think about?

I think about sex mainly (being honest) and relationships, and why we are here...and why I see the things i see

NorthDaughter 9:00 PM

what do you see?

Lovers_End 9:00 PM

...things.

NorthDaughter 9:01 PM

do you see yourself?

Lovers_End 9:01 PM

no *(whoa, that was a weirdly fast response.)*

NorthDaughter 9:01 PM

yeah. i thought so

Lovers_End 9:01 PM

that's why you are so scary, you force people to see things about themselves that they'd rather ignore.

NorthDaughter 9:02 PM

unfortunately i see who i am and i know when to be afraid.

me = scary? never!

NorthDaughter 9:05 PM

hmmm complete serious silence....not a good sign?

NorthDaughter 9:05 PM

must make joke..::grins:: so there was this chicken right? and well she wanted to cross the road (as they do). soo-oo....wait...ok i think i ruined the punch line sorry...lemme start over

NorthDaughter 9:09 PM

this blue monkey met a chicken by the side of a road, and he asked her why she wasn't on her nest preparing for easter...unfortunately for the joke, the hen was a christian thus ruining all of our fun ::stretches:: ok then...well i'll just be hiding now......

NorthDaughter 9:10 PM

whoa how weird

Lovers_End 9:10 PM

hello

NorthDaughter 9:11 PM

::grimaces:: tell me this isn't a ruse to get me to babble incessantly so that you can make a judge...ment...oh nevermind

Lovers_End 9:11 PM

perhaps.

NorthDaughter 9:11 PM

::rolls eyes:: i always fall for it damnit

NorthDaughter 9:12 PM

you'd think i'd see it comin ya know? it's hard when you are not in person but then in person bad stuff happens just as much...like..'oh nevermind' etc....damn must stop babbling ::yawns and plays the strong silent type::

Lovers_End 9:13 PM

okies. ☺ actually i got a call so i couldn't very well respond

NorthDaughter 9:14 PM

uh huh ok then just paranoia settin in heh heh.....nix all of those messages

Lovers_End 9:14 PM

nix?

NorthDaughter 9:14 PM

nix = 'delete'

Lovers_End 9:14 PM

ok, figured as much

Lovers_End 9:14 PM

loved your joke mate

NorthDaughter 9:14 PM

why? it was lame

Lovers_End 9:14 PM

that's why i liked it

NorthDaughter 9:15 PM

::rolls eyes:: ahh no sense of humor always a good thing

NorthDaughter 9:19 PM

ok so: my fav song on this cd [I Don't Wanna Die Anymore by New Radicals]..will be long quote sorry but i am torturing you

two months of fun   add it up

two years of pain   and get a life of rain

97

i need to scream but too ashamed

it's gonna rain, it's gonna
rain

you wanna go you wanna
stay

you really blew my world

i wanna live and there's
only one way

I don't wanna die anymore

i want to live it up

I don't want this high
anymore

but I can't give it up

I won't live a lie anymore

I need to give you up

won't you save me?

NorthDaughter 9:27 PM

   ::grins:: give me attention damnit hmm...

NorthDaughter 9:30 PM

   ::whistles instead::

Lovers_End 9:34 PM

   ahaha, hey i really gotta cruise cuz i've still got my english speech due...

NorthDaughter 9:37 PM

   ok then run away..::smiles:: have fun

Lovers_End 9:38 PM

   lmao. cya

NorthDaughter 9:38 PM

   later babe

are you ready for this?

Lovers_End 7:27 PM

>hey dorwk. ☺

NorthDaughter 7:28 PM

>woman, what da hell? get your ass over here missy, we must continue to study for the SATs TODAY or else we shall perish! hehee. i am feeling so good right now man

Lovers_End 7:30 PM

>i just got back from the gym, and i am just having tea [dinner]. relax. and uhh....YAY for feeling good! (i guess?)

NorthDaughter 7:37 PM

>i love it...my mood right now crazy happy brilliant. be afraid be very afraid...happy is when i am the most.....well....uninhibited...oh and hit me if i bore you to death with my babblement

Lovers_End 7:39 PM

>okie doke. ;) all good i say...oooo me=leaving in a sec so i'll see you soon then ok? ok.

NorthDaughter 7:39 PM

>ok babe

```
*********************************************************************
```

Question asked of Ken Wilber

Q: "How do you know these [spiritual] phenomena actually exist?

A: "As the observing self begins to transcend...deeper or higher dimensions of consciousness come into focus. All of the items on that list are objects that can be directly perceived in that worldspace. Those items are as real in [that] worldspace as rocks are in the sensorimotor worldspace and concepts are in the mental worldspace. If cognition awakens or develops to this level, you simply perceive these new objects as simply as you would perceive rocks in the sensory world or images in the mental world. They are simply given to awareness, they simply present themselves, and you don't have to spend a lot of time trying to figure out if they're real or not.

Of course, if you haven't awakened to [this] cognition, then you will see none of this, just as a rock cannot see mental images. And you will probably have unpleasant things to say about people who do see them"[2].

```
*********************************************************************
```

---

[2] Wilber, K. (2000). *A Brief History of Everything.*

****

Gregory Smith's *Caledonian Antisyzygy.*

There's no use screaming.

****

I have to feel fear; I have to let go; be vulnerable. Are you ready for this? I'm really not.

American Heritage Dictionary

vul · ner · a · ble   (vŭl'nər-ə-bəl)

adj.

    1. Susceptible to physical or emotional injury.

    2. Susceptible to attack.

    3. Open to censure or criticism; assailable.

    4. Liable to succumb, as to persuasion or temptation.

There's never been a more difficult piece for me to write than the section you are about to read. Honestly.

I've tried to avoid it; not to write it...to let it wash away.

Years of avoidance.

But you have to understand.

****

Are you a good girl?

Sometimes.

****

Sage is suckling on my petticoats, an infant, wailing promises of a time when I will be lost to her. Thankfully. She is a social aberration, my only assurance that this life isn't as fake and transitory as I first feared: a damning maelstrom, she's insisting I notice her for who – and what – she really is, an **oxymoron** *capable of demanding me to feel as chaotic and centered as she does in*

one

single

moment.

~ she is note just 'another girl' ~

****

Don't go tonight.

The last bite of dinner slides down my throat.

I can't shake this... sick craving to know more, to experience her in between my hands the way she spins cobwebs in my mind, to feel the way she places cotton candy in my mouth and morphs my thoughts into something we both under-stand.

I want her. To hate her.

You mustn't go.

I pace the carpet of my room, not seeing the foamy blue paints that drown my walls.

****

****

She's waiting for me.

What will I say when I call her?

"*Hi, Sage, I'm sorry. I know we were going to study for the SATs tonight, but I just have this feeling that I shouldn't go out. I'll just see you tomorrow at school, ok?*"

Bizarre.

Dammit, we simply intend to study. That is it. I can go. I'm just edgy because it's going to be the first time I visit her house.

Yea, the first time to visit the same house that she was running away from the night of our sleepover.

Shh. Don't worry about that now. It not your intuition; you're just being crazy.

****

****

Twist

Key ignites engine. The motion sends shards of distress through my nerves. I place my hands on the steering wheel.

Trepidation – punctures holes.

Warning lays painful connections in my skin. We will be alone; her parents will be gone.

I begin to quietly gasp.

Breathe

Think of something light

Itsy, bitsy spider, climbed up the water spout. . .

Explosion of music. *The offensiveness of its bite calms me – there's something about the honesty, rawness, and lack of boundaries in violent expression....*

Breathe. Directions. Look at the directions.

> - Head down the hill, turn left at the traffic light.
> - Go through two stop lights and turn left.

Ready, girl?

Stretching behind me I place my left hand on the passenger seat and guide my parent's silver Nissan Primera backwards onto the street.

****

****

She looked so good today in her school uniform. She always wears the gray pants and maroon sweater – she doesn't own a kilt. I do. I wear my pants and kilt equally, but almost always with a sweater, too. The extra layer comforts me.

She's beautiful. I can hardly wait to see her – even for these few moments of driving.

I can't wait to see her?

I've never known androgyny to be so striking.

You have a split personality, it seems.

****

Ok, there was a third direction...

> - Head down the hill, turn left at the traffic light.
> - Go through two stoplights and turn left.
> - **Follow the road for about two miles and turn right, just past the Dairy**

Shit! Turn here!

Electric nerves crush into reaction. I swerve so forcefully that the tires of my parent's car collide spectacularly into a curb. **Energy compresses.** Winded, I blink with fingers tight, legs braced. *Saved.* Blood throbs. Shakily, I look down at my lap.

The street is a dead end – only 10 or so houses.

> - Go through two stop lights and turn left.
> - Follow the road for about two miles and turn right, just past the Dairy
> - It's the last house on the left.

The lighting. It's different here...

absent.

Hmm.

Fingers tighten.

home, home, home...

Feeling obligated to others...it gets the better of me.

Music out of place; jarring, driving beat too overt for the secrecy required to survive this place. Off. The street lamps flicker gasping, sickly breaths. The road is a tunnel, with my headlights disappearing, *falling*, over its slick, aphotic edges.

movement exhales the health of a Tibetan singing bowl only to inhale the birth of one recently possessed.

Harmony, lost.

Fingers lift thickly. Focus slips from here   to

there.

It begins to suck energy out of me – I feel it insert itself into my fingertips and begin to pull them inside out, forming invisible threads...*it wishes to take my essence and replace it with its own.*

I recoil – hands to my chest.   *Protect me, protect me*

How...?

Horror stretches and forms perfect cylinder beads of sweat on each vertebra, their order an alarming mockery of the chaos in my head.

```
You're  going  insane,  again.   Stop  feeling  so  much.
You're                  fucking                       fine.
Conform, freak.
```

Pressured toes - the car moves forward.

The entire underside of my parent's car is violated by her driveway. *Shit!* Rolling my eyes, I turn off the engine, grab my backpack and swing out.

...was...?

I don't know. Did you see something?

Well...no, but there was definitely something there.

I know...

Ignore it.

down, down, down. . .come the rain and washed the spider out. . .

Seven foot high wooden fence. A gate handle. I am not allowed in; the rust shouts, NO.

Suspension

Please let me in, I'm suffocating.   3, 2, 1...CLICK.   I
step.

My vision fades to permit the world behind my eyes to take center stage; societal expectations ("There's no such thing as Energy.") slide down my cheeks and fall away, absorbed by nature, humming below. I scan her garden.

Vertical stones - artificial barrier. Shrunken plants and weeds desperately trying to claim their worth between the cobblestones at my feet.

This courtyard is pregnant with Rosemary's baby.

I could learn a thing or two from such a baby.

What?

If I explore it, it'll become less scary...

Sage opens her front door and stands at the top of her five entrance steps.

"Hey, Jasper. You coming in?"

My mind is unraveling to a place little girls surely should not go.

I look up into her face. I can hardly see her; my eyes water. I want to explore this scene, the hallways and heartbeats of the ones who live here...I want the syringe's plunger to press deep in me...to have their essence injected into my arm...I want to truly know what's real...

She stares at me, with full understanding.

I walk towards her.

She's felt this too.

The door closes behind us.

****

We make our way into the dining room. SAT books and blank notepads lie neatly, soon to be defaced.

"Mom finished photocopying all of the study books and put the 2,000 pages into these two folders." She indicates the two white monsters with a nonchalant wave of her hand.

My eyes slide into focus. "What? We have to learn everything in these two binders? You're kidding, right?" *Wow - it's nice to have something else to center on.*

She surveys me, bemused. "Nope, not kidding. All of it. Well, that's if you want to do well."

My chest tightens. "But we only have a month or two to study!" *And I don't even know HOW to study.*

Flipping through the introduction she shows me the sections of the exam: vocab, verbal and math.

"Ok, yea thanks for the overview but it's just retarded that so many words exist! And please! What weird relationships between words…"

She raises her eyebrow at me.

"What?! It's true…"

"Hmm. I prefer to absorb knowledge instead of discredit it."

Doctor Faustus said that too and look where it got him.

"Yea, well…I suppose that's a decent view…."

She circles the table and sits. I follow her, slip into the seat at the end of the table and end up catty corner to her with her on my left side.

****

She's teasing me, as she loves to do (during her hyper moods...). I love it...although this vocab list is kicking my ass.

"Are you studying a hard word, Jasper? Your face is contorting. Don't strain too much. Let me know if you need my help..."

> "Help?! Oh pleaaaaaase! Whatever, dorkface. I am a *total* master of the words 'abate', 'abdicate' and 'aberration'! You're a goofball if you think I need you."

"OOooOoo...a 'goofball', huh? Ouch!" She leans over and tickles my side.

"Ah! Ah! Aaaaaaaah! Not allowed!" I squeal as my index finger shoots out an accusation. "NO touching allowed!"

She seems a bit miffed by this, so retreats and folds her arms. "Oh well. We better study so that you can come up with a more momentous allegation than 'goofball'..." She reviews the sentences I'm writing to help myself learn the new vocabulary. Her eyes pause over,

> '*The aberration seemed to be expressing a psychic inclination.*'

Breaking her moment, I mutter, "Goose."

Looking back at me, she cocks her head to the left, forms a kissy face and *honks*. Yep. She honks.

Honk!

I gape at her and burst out laughing. I don't come up for air for quite some time. The release and permission to find happiness in this thick space spins nervous merriment through my body - mini bubbles of saliva stream down my face making me self-conscious, so I laugh more...and she keeps giggling at me, pretending to be more mature than I, and the crinkles at the edges of her eyes do nothing other than convince me that she's having JUST as much of a ball as I am...*gasp!* Ahahahahaa! Oh, air! Yes, pleeeeease....

I grab a tissue out of my discarded backpack and mop up the rivers of mascara twisting down my cheeks. "We have to *study*!" I squeak and burst into laughter again as she mocks me with a face forever held precious in my mind. I sit back and gulp, air, air, air...she grins – *gorgeous* - and begins to write notes on my study page. Now the air caught between my lips has nothing to do with this delightful laugh attack. *She is just so gorgeous.*

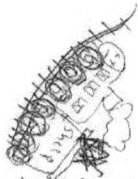

- abate: When the speech was abated, the crowd became ~~uncomfortable~~.
~~After the winds~~ The wind shall abate.

- abdicate: By wearing trashy cloths to ——— she abdicated her position in society.

Abdicating the prince was very sad.

- aberration: She blurted out aberrations which startled & amused the crowd.

The aberration seemed to be expressing a psychic inclination.

abet: To abet a criminal is illegal. The bully attempted to abet to his
The bully abetted the child to breaking point. breaking point

abeyance: ~~Until~~ The plan ~~is postponed~~ will be held in abeyance till further notice.

abhor: I abhor drugs and what it does to people's minds,
ahaha- esp 5?aha.

~~No hablo el englais.~~

~~abscond:~~
abscond: to run off in secret.   absconded

absolve: to free of guilt or blame: to exonerate, exculpate

abstemious: I was abstemious when I drink water in between glasses of vodka.

abstract: a written summary
abstruse: extremely difficult to understand.

114

We go back to studying. All is well until I notice that she's gone through three times as many vocab words as I have.

Yikes.

Each question accentuates my lack of intelligence; insecurities. I fall back into my secret, private space.

****

"Are you
making it
up

out of
nothing? is
she

really not
there at
all?

I don't
even know
how

to respond.
:) Smile
you're

being
watched.

I am so exhausted because there is a human body that I haven't ever trained with the "big boys". Confusion. Ignorance. and doubts image - yet exist as a human. When the stars open up + let the dark juice seep out... is even the power of stars are released.

To not remember all of what you see ⟹ why

You're making ME FLY AGAIN - HIGHER + HIGHER ... again the path. The question → why? If I get to that I might fall.

Are we making life out of nothing? Are we already dead? What is dead?

Are you making it up out of nothing? she really not there at all? I don't even know how to respond. :) Smile you're being watched.

****

"So   what do you believe?"

her energy echoes, faintly, inside me.

"What do I...be**lie**ve...?" I consider poking fun at her and telling her that she's just being a distraction again, but her serious expression establishes the importance of going another route.

"...do you mean spiritually?"

She nods.

It's so rare for anyone to ask about this sort of thing. "Well, that would be a fairly long conversation, actually. I'd love to have it now but only if we have time?" *I'm already asking her permission to do things...odd.*

She leans back in her chair and arches, ever upwards - arms high towards the ceiling – and stretches. Her short hair falls back onto her shoulders, and she tips her head to the right, eyes closed.

God.

Sweat reweaves a delicate pattern on my neck.

Heat.

Moments later, I too stretch.

Am I on automatic pilot? Am I subconsciously mimicking her or...?

> *People subconsciously mirror those that they find captivating; if the object of your affection lifts their hand to their face, your own hand will reach the surface of your cheeks. Visa versa. Mirror neurons.*

She stops stretching and watches me. I let my arms fall.

"Well, we've been studying for a while now so yes, I want to know what you believe. Mom, Dad and Edith should be gone for another couple of hours, so we should have plenty of time to discuss this – after the movie, they were getting dinner."

"Edith?"

"My younger sister."

117

"Oh, right – I remember you mentioning her. Ok, so they're gone for a while more, huh?" I act casual.

"Yep."

Why am I suddenly so nervous...?

Without studying as an activity, we might get into something we later regret. I'll end up bowing to THAT...energy...

I look into the lounge. I've been ignoring the energy all this time. It's easy to do when you preoccupy yourself with material things. Moments trickle by - it comes back into sight. I watch it for a few moments. "One sec. I need to think about something." I begin to write. My thoughts need sorting.

She leaves me and goes into the kitchen to get juice.

I look back into its current center. The walls, television, paintings, couches all look ordinary, but it, this, is not normal. I sit quietly. *It's waiting for us - to take us away.* The energy swoops and hovers in front of me.

```
                              Offering  a  single
                              crippling
                              fingertip  to   my
                              lips, it Dares,
```

```
     'Taste me.'
```

I've always loved the thrill of stepping over the edge.

I lick.

Sage comes back into the room holding two glasses, "I assume you want some?" Artificial blue liquid swirls as she gestures with it.

"Oh, sure."

Abandoning our study table, we make our way into the lounge. We sit on the smaller of the two living room couches.
We   land   mere   inches   from   one   another.

This is the closest we've ever been without a chaperone.

My breath catches.

Here's your first choice.

The left side of her mouth turns into a small smile.

Again, she knows your thoughts...

She looks beautiful, here, in this moment. In every moment. She glows. The carpet is cream, the couches a shade darker. Her amber eyes deepen as she waits for me to fully absorb everything. *She's so intuitive with me. Sometimes at school I doubt her social graces, but spiritually....*

I choose to rest the left side of my face against her couch's cushion. My eyes close. The shaded respite is a moist grove – comforting, reassuring.

I'm not ready to talk. "So this belief question. How about we start with *you*, oh-so-mysterious Sage? I really don't like talking about myself." I get up and move to the other couch. I can't stand being this close to her.

space.

In reply to her eyes, I offer, "Oh. I just want to sit over here because...well...then you'll have more room to yourself and whatever, you know, this way you won't be *squashed* by me..." I attempt a smile.

Brushing off this explanation she says, "I don't like talking about myself either."

"Umm, right."

Stalemate.

"Well, I guess we'll just sit here quietly then."

"Sage! You can't just sit there and not talk."

"I didn't say I would never talk, you just have to go first. Start with your sense of spirituality and how it relates to your beliefs."

"I don't think you want to know all of that. It's a little...off the beaten path."

She looks at me intently, "No, I do. Tell me."

"No really, it's probably not a good place to start tonight's 'chit-chat'. It's not something I discuss with a lot of people."

The silence ingests us. I force myself to be ok with it. *Just relax; don't be impulsively react to how awkward this is.*

Out came the sun, and dried up all the rain...

****

I suppose I could win favor by making small concessions...even if I hate being told what to do.

"Well, fuck it. Do you promise, promise tell me what <u>you</u> believe after I tell you my story?"

Subtly triumphant, she agrees.

"Ok, so my sense of spirituality is kinda different to other people's, at least as far as I can tell." I inhale. *Appear cool, calm and collected.*

> *Right.*

> *There.*

You've got it now.

"Ok, so I'll just run through it all, from start to finish.

"I sense things. When I was four, Mother had me take a psychiatric test..."

Her expression hasn't changed much...I can't tell if she is interested or not.

"Hey, Sage, am I boring you? I mean...if I am...I don't have to continue."

"What? No, you're not boring me. You have confidence issues."

I stick my pierced tongue out at her. "Right. So I went in for my psych exam, and..." The story finally ends.

She leans forward and begins to interrogate,

```
"Ok, Jasper. What do they look like?

        Can you interact with them?

            How often do you see them?

                What's their purpose?


                        Your          . . .
                        purpose?"
```

"Wow, right-o, then..."

She turns her head away. Her energy folds – she hibernates.

"Umm...Sage?" Her aura deepens in its violet intensity. *Is she angry?* "Hey - I'll just rattle off general answers to your questions, ok?"

Sage, you're safe with me.

"Ok. Your first question was

```
        'What do they look like?' so:
```

"Angels are more beautiful than one can ever imagine – it's like standing in the rain and reveling in its exquisiteness with every part of you rejoicing. Viewing or interacting with them is an entire body experience – no sense is left out. I feel a lot of love and compassion when they reveal themselves.

"Super crazy importantly: their beauty doesn't waver during the moments with them. This is in contrast to daemons who can either appear as disgusting as their name projects, or they can appear angelic for the purpose of tricking you. Don't let them.

"Now,

        'Can you/I interact with them?'

"I never try and 'conjure' spirits, angels or visions. I feel weird about doing that – who am I to dictate what they should be doing? Ridiculous. So I work on their terms – if at all. So if they wish for me to help someone here on earth that's having a hard time listening to...listening to...hmm. What do you call it? Let's see...the language of...yea, yea – the language of our world's interconnected energy, as through signs, coincidences, etc., (there are so many ways that the world tries to speak to us to break us out of our patterns) they can use me and other mediums to give guidance of some kind. It's really weird, I normally have *no* idea why I'm saying a certain thing – it's all so cryptic to me since I don't usually know the people, actually it helps to not know the person because then a personal connection doesn't get in the way.

(KIWI BIRDS)

"Like one time an older man ghost started wandering around our house. He hung around for several days, so I finally told Mom about it, saying I hadn't talked to him but he was around. In her notoriously supportive (and forever curious) way, she retrieved 50 of her old funeral bulletins to see if we could identify him. She loves mysteries.

"After a couple of minutes,

        yes –

        a man's photograph 'leapt' out at me. 'Yes….' I looked back and forth between the man and his funeral service. 'It's him.' It was an older, dark crème bulletin and his photograph was cropped to fit inside of a vertical oval. It was uncanny to find the resemblance between this photo and the transparent man standing next to me. Oddly, no matter how many times this happens, I can never quite get used to my visions somehow being validated in 'reality'.

"So she was just about to go off to an appointment, but before she left she asked me to ask him what he needed, what he wanted. It's strange – whenever she asks me to do something, I slip deeply into the freedom behind my eyes, where all makes sense...on such different terms...such different waves. My vision falls out of focus...and he's there, with us in the brightly sunlit kitchen, me standing at the bar. I asked, 'Hi, so what is it that you want or need? Can I help you?' His face softened, and he said, 'Yes. Please. It's my wife – she's in pain. I can't go on until I know that she knows I am safe, happy and ok. Please tell her I'm ok.'

"I relay this to my Mother, who quickly turns a lighter shade of white, but she's still with me. 'Ok, Jasper, I know his wife, I was the minister for this service – I've been working with his wife all this time. Ask him if I can relay this message to her, and if so - how I can prove to her that this is real –'

"My stomach swirls. I ask him. He replies, 'Kiwi birds. Just mention kiwi birds.'

"I cock my head and ask him again, 'No, really – what should Mom say to her to make sure she believes us?'

"'Kiwi birds.'

"Several minutes pass as I consider actually saying this out loud. Sounded pretty outrageous. How on earth would a mention of 'kiwi birds' have any impact on making sure my Mom didn't sound insane?

"'Mom? This is weird. I don't know if I should tell you...it's so far out,' I say to her.

"'Jasper, since when have I bowed out because of weirdness?' She smiled at me.

"'Yea...true. Ok, kiwi birds is apparently the message that should go along with whatever else you write to her.'

"She stares at me and then cracks into a grin. 'Really? Wow, that is strange. Kiwi birds, huh?'

"'Yep.'

"'Ok, well I'll have to think about how I'm going to do this. Maybe an anonymous letter would work better.'

"She leaves to go to her appointment and later that evening she has a letter all written up.

```
Dear Mrs. X,

I come to you with a strange, but kind, message.  I hope that
it is more comforting than disconcerting. Blessings.

Please read it all.

A person, who has contact with the departed, has told me that
your husband wants you to know that he is OK. He loves you and
the children.  He wishes he could do more than let you know
this, especially at this difficult time.

So that you can know this is a real message from him, he told
the person to say to you, "Kiwi Birds".

If you wish to discuss the contents of this letter with
anyone, I suggest you talk to a minister or counselor of your
choice.

Sincerely,

Anonymous
```

"Holding it, she says, 'I am going to send this anonymously. It'll just be better for my career for people to not know of your gift. I do sneakily mention in the letter that she can contact a minister so maybe she'll actually come to me! That way I can be a support for her without being the messenger.'

"'Ha! Fun.'

"Two weeks (and several heart attacks wondering whether or not she'd figure out it was me, the minister's daughter, and send a witch hunt after me...bah! *shivers* crazy) later, Mother received a phone call. It was her.

"She made arrangements to meet the man's wife and all of her children that afternoon (she always wants the complete the story immediately – she can't even read a Harlequin Mills & Boon without reading the end sometimes). When she arrived, the entire family met Mother at the door. They went into their living room.

"Held neatly in the woman's hand was a now well worn piece of paper, folded two times – just like Mother's letter to her.

"After small chat came the big admission. 'Reverend, we had something very unusual happen to us about two weeks ago. We're not sure what to think of it – we can't decide if it's good or...

"The story eventually slipped out, timidly. The woman waited to hear Mother's interpretation of the message from her deceased husband.

"Of course Mom was totally supportive. It was wild. Once the woman realized that she wasn't going to be chastised for considering (hoping?) that this letter might be true, she opened up. The family told Mom that there was one reason they considered believing this message was from her husband, their Dad. It was the inclusion of 'kiwi birds'.

"Apparently the man was obsessed with them – he had a kiwi birds on everything. Kiwi bird clocks, kiwi bird soft toys out the wazoo, kiwi bird boxers...all things only his family knew of – it was a family joke of sorts since as a tough bloke, he didn't want anyone else to know. When all of her adult children swore that they didn't send her the note, she couldn't help but start to believe. Neat, huh?

"By the end of the visit, she was definitely calm.

A familiar kick angers me.

"So, so, sooooooo. This next point is **CRUCIAL**, Lady, crucial. I kid you not. Right:

"All of this, every single experience, is God's. I do NOT have any personal 'conjuring powers', except to ask for protection. NOTHING, fucking *nothing*, COMES FROM ME. I can't stress this enough. I am not some saint, some angel, some this, this or that or whateverthefuck. I am just a chick with a peculiar sense of the world. Period.

"So. I can't look at someone and tell them what they need to do to save their life or something just because they ask. My involvement has to be initiated by a request from an angel, vision or a truly deep sense that God is requesting my presence in some way – and even then Mom and I have all kinds of psychological checks and balances to make sure I'm not just going 'crazy'."

I note how harsh my tone is.

"Sorry. It really does piss me off how people try to use me for their own gain." I feel porcupine quills expose their tips through my ribs. "GRRR...Ok, next - what was your next question? Something about...

'How often do I see them?'

"Yea, I see mostly all the time, although it's definitely way harder to be open when I am mentally or emotionally exhausted. One only has so much energy..."

The Law of
Conservation
of Energy

"...Although blah, blah, blah - it does get *really* confusing, because sometimes I'm able to see way more when I'm totally exhausted and trashed and in an alley somewhere...hmm. So like, being intoxicated can heighten my senses, which kinda sucks. I wish I was able to be open without needing it...but hell, what can you do?

"So, yea, I do have 'down' times where I can't see anything but I'm not totally sure why they occur. Overall God has blessed me with a consistent flow of people to help. I do kinda wish I had someone else to explore things with – it is hard not having a spiritual mentor of any kind.

126

"DAH! I am talking SO MUCH! This sucks. I hate hearing my own voice for too long. How are you?"

"Keep going."

I sigh.

"Right, so uhh…last questions…what were they?"

She reminds me.

"Ah, got it.

        "What's their purpose?

                     "'Your   ..
                     purpose?'

"Mom says the meaning of life is to serve God…wow, yea – I still remember when she said this. She's so cool. Hmm. So perhaps this 'truth', if it is one, applies to ghosts, angels, etc. too. I dunno – it's a nice thought, but it kinda messes with my sense of wanting to be independent – like, I go back and forth between accepting God's presence and just wanting to live my life, you know? So I'm not sure about it all. Otherwise it seems fairly clear that the purpose of ghosts (people who are voluntarily or involuntarily stuck between different consciousness layers) is to communicate to their loved ones things they wish they could have said, work through memories they have, or sometimes something else. It's really about healing, learning and accepting a new space."

"So your Mom is a minister, hence the God comments. What is God to you?"

"Oh! Oh! Oh! Uhh, good point. While I do use the term 'God' a lot, I'm not really referring to to the Christian concept of God. I mean, I go to church every Sunday and whatever, but I do love all world religions, one of Mom's degrees is in world religions so she teaches me a lot about all of them, and so I don't get into saying 'they're all wrong' or whatever, whatever…"

Joseph Chilton Pearce says,
"...Spiritual transcendence and
religion have little in common.
In fact, if we look closely, we
can see that these two have been
the fundamental antagonists in
our history, splitting our mind
into warring camps. Neither our
violence nor our transcendence
is a moral or ethical matter of
religion, but rather an issue of
biology. We actually contain a
built-in ability to rise above
restriction, incapacity, or
limitation and, as a result of
this ability, possess a vital
adaptive spirit that we have not
yet fully accessed."

"Church is full of barriers and rules, even though I do love it – it's just this really strange part of my life that...well, what I mean to say -- Mom has always asked me to keep my stories to myself when we're there, because she doesn't want to freak anyone out or get in trouble with the managing body or anything – people can be so nice when they first meet you and so scared & violent once they *truly* know you...hum. So I've been taught all my life that what I have is special, but it's also to remain hidden."

"You see ghosts, auras, and...daemons?"

DAEMONS .

Why would she focus on daemons?

"And angels." Moments bend like water droplets along the ground. Our faces reflect in them, distorted.

"So we're similar," she whispers.

128

"Pardon?"

Her aura inserts itself into my skin.

SAGE, You Have to Ask PERMISSION

I glare at her.   "What the fuck was that?"

"What?"

"You know. Don't play games with me."

She stands.

The energy cradles her; she's one in the same. *She's sold herself to this energy...and now it, not just she, knows me.*

I said too much.

Who is this, this girl?

****

My nerves fraying, "So this Wiccan story of yours. You mentioned it when we were talking on the Internet the other night, but you didn't give me any details. Tell me about it now, hmm?"

She doesn't answer me.

She never would.

She walks swiftly back and forth, back and forth.

Her socially acceptable set of expressions have `vanished`.

She looks at me hungrily, from the corners of her eyes.

`Malevolence.`

She begins to scare me.

`"You. Drive."`

****

We are walking out of the door, down the steps of the courtyard that both captivates and repels me. I'm becoming an oxymoron – a moron deprived of air.

She's leading you to your death.

I know.

```
*****************************************************************
```

✍ DECISION

Decision has the same root as incision or excision = "cis". The base of the word is "cut". The prefix "de" means "from, down or away".

So de-cis-ion means an act that cuts off/away options.

The gate swings open. I touch the cold exterior of my car. I look over the top of the car's roof. A creature.

Her eyes escape color. The moon attempts to find her, but it is blind– she has slipped into the other world, the world that consumes an eager, self-mutilating crowd that would like nothing more than to drink their own blood, just to feel the heat surge through their body

one   -
more   -
time

before they

finely   let   go.

Her face

        screams.

Fear shocks its delicious fingers through my skirt and clutches my hips.

I don't understand this world.

slave...

131

I unlock the car doors.

Merge...

****

"Jasper, you believe in angels do you?"

I used to.

"Daemons are more satisfying. Drive."

The angels are frozen.

I don't look at her. I turn the car on. Pulling out, we face the beginning of her dead end street.

```
"You   are   nothing.   Neither   am   I.   We   are
meaningless.   You  and  your  little  story  mean
nothing.  There  is  no  God.  We  are  pathetic
nightmares.

We are their fucking amusement."
```

****

rope stitches endearing inadequacy through my lips and forces my mouth to shut. i listen to her. i can't escape; i never want to escape. trapped in an empty chasm of nightmares, i tell these stories to the children within me. they are all dying, slowly, as they rotate and take turns gasping for breath as i stand underneath their nooses and collapsing trachea...soon they will cease to be. all of them.

****

I feel my body dive, in slow motion, straight into the belly of salty foam. I gulp greedily, not sure of the transformation that is about to take place – but desperate to seek it.

*No one has ever allowed me to explore this side of me. But she...*she's set to release me.

Let go

Her words are impure salt, an aberration, an irretrievable recipe for a state of mind that will decay my form and create another...*then they will find me locked inside a room, dead on the laboratory floor.*

Mephistopheles...

****

I accelerate. The windows are closed, but I still feel the wind. The curves in the road fall far more quickly on the front of my car than will ever be legal.

Will you let me murder you, Sage?

I feel her energy quiver.

Yes.

The turn is laced with solid metal poles – each pole another ridiculous reason for destroying our earth, another satellite, another television, another whateverthefuck. *Everything is so fucking cliché.* My knuckles turn white as I don't let up on the gas – her words...

She begins to laugh. High, cold, delicious.

She's ready to die.

Leave these frivolous demands, which strike a terror to my fainting soul...

My body disobeys my mind – fingers screech the car dangerously away from death and into the sickness of life.

WEAK !

Her laughter ceases.

You've angered her.

"Why did you stop, Jasper? What are you afraid of? We're not going to feel anything. I promise."

See? She promises.

"Sage? I'll make it up to you."

****

Is she still talking?

I run a red light. Three more. *8:09 p.m. Too early for this type of driving to be 'safe'. Good. Safety is worthless – it's all so worthless.*

The road arches into a deeply carved blind turn – I change lanes to drive into oncoming traffic.

Perhaps this will be our final moment, hmm?

120 kilometers per hour.

Fiery heat pulsates sweetly through my veins. This adrenaline, this high. This is why I wish to live and die. This is what makes life real.

I glance at her. She is breathing rapidly. *Beautiful.* I sit back and close my eyes.

She is a mix of blood and strawberry juice on my lips. My tongue slips and caresses my mouth – yes this is the truest beauty I will ever digest.

Necromancy drains from her flesh and into my mouth. Hungrily, I lap up the disgusting fluid that flows from the knowledge of knowing you are mortal.

Pearls of truth dissolved in a cup of wine:
the aphrodisiacal effect will surely slit our throats and fill my clit with blood.

It's thrilling thinking about how I will kill her. Yes, I will die too – that's mandatory. I can't kill her and then survive.

I rip the hair tie from my ponytail and shake my head free from restriction. Black and red twists release and frame my ashen face, silken strands between my fingers. Vision after vision glorifies sight. I press harder, harder, harder...

I feel like I'm raping death, and by God I am enjoying it.

The curve ends without a challenge from another car. My heart still beats.

Never mind, Death will sink you soon. Oh, so, deliciously, soon.

I look up to the sky and smile detachedly as our blood pours out upon the pavement and whips up to deform the clouds. I relax my neck. The droplets attempt to congeal as she pulses in her soliloquy, and my breath caresses the platelets for a moment too long...

Her teeth break open our wound and refresh the current of heat pooling in our laps. Salvation cannot reach us here.

****

Her words reach me in ways   she, I, we   never knew possible.

```
It's because we're one and the same.  We're connected.
Even in death.
```

Slipping in and out of arbitrary stripes of paint, I seek the freedom of our high school's grounds. Tucked quietly away from all other distractions, it's deeply embedded in a forested, sunken valley.

```
We will be alone there.
```

"We should die tonight, Jasper. There's no point in us living any longer."

"I know."

"Drive off the end of the wharf, near our high school. We'll both drown. We'll never feel pain again."

I nod.

The field near our school gives my eyes aching release from agregious amounts of concrete and the rows upon rows of Edwardian houses. The road opens to a vast expanse of forest and hills. We're here. The water is dark & thirsty just on the other side of this field.

I never thought I'd be a murderess.

                                        Murderess...Suicidal victim.

Am I really a victim?

                                        ...Is she making me this way?

                If I die this way, I will never see tomorrow morning.

Fear tip toes on eight little legs, on a journey around my ankle. I slow down
ever so slightly...*I'll pull into the school's roundabout first. I want to look at her
before we die – before my last, final moment.*

I see a couple walking on the side of the road. "Is their life for naught?"

"Of course. You should know that by now."

Of course...?

"Really? How can you be sure? God is supposed to love us, so surely he gives us
a purpose?" My words are odd and distant.

I pull into the roundabout and pause underneath the farthest lamplight. I stare
straight ahead.

*I'm shifting away from her. She doesn't like it – we're sewn together, I'm ripping
the threads. Not only does she disobey God, but she consciously and even eagerly
renounces obedience to him, choosing instead to swear allegiance to...*

Is God even real?

                "God isn't real."

She unravels the crucial, single thread. I collapse. The world goes dim.

It's true.

I look at her.

Protuberant eyes project the horrors of our desire to suckle the teat of damnation. Menacing and dominating, the transparent manifestation of our downfall settles just above her body – I must look through him to see her. I feel fear more tangibly than I have, and ever will, feel again.

She thinks she is in control, but she is not. We can't control this. It's hubris to think we can.

His canine snout nearly touches my forehead. His breath wraps the gauze of *new truth* around my face.

> God
>
> Isn't
>
> Real.

I begin to asphyxiate.

He hisses, "Let's do it. Let's die."

****

I put the car into first gear and let up on the brake.

Her breathing is shallow now, we're mere droplets on the pier. I'm calm, resolute, tranquil. This makes sense.

Around this corner, and the next. You've always wanted to be free.

Steve was going to kill you this way, remember? Except he wanted to drive us off a cliff, not a pier. Instead of drowning, I would have died upon impact. Drowning is nicer. I've always loved the water. Inundation in the sublime.

Hmm...had Daddy not told me about Steve's plans, I wouldn't be alive now. Dr. Snow, both my and Steve's counselor at the time, told Daddy in confidence, to save me. Protecting the patient and others overrules patient confidentiality.

Daddy told me...

Dad.

Mom.

137

My sister, Crystal.

My cat, Platypus.

Family.

I halt at the stop sign just before the end of the pier.   *This is it.*
This is your choice.

They'd hate to find my dead, bloated body pulled from their own car from the bottom of the harbor. It would be a sad day. Am I ready to torture them for all of their kindness? They've been nothing but good to me.

'Suicide is the most selfish act you can commit', Mom had said when she recounted a story of one of her psych patients. He attempted to kill himself eight times. One of his attempts – to die jumping off a three story building - was foiled by an awning above of the first floor. He just wasn't 'meant' to die. Or was he?   Were all of the 'miraculous saves' just flukes?

A snag in the fabric?

I can't say what is true or false about life. But I can say that for whatever reason, my family will cry. I won't make them cry.

"I can't do this to my family."

She resumes her soliloquy, but her words thin and fray on deaf ears. I look left down at the pier. Black water laps at its old, creaking steps. I look right, towards home. I do not consult her. My choice is made.

****

the itsy bitsy spider went up the spout again.

****

Fear Instructs.

Yes. But how was she able to manipulate me so totally and get me to do all that I did? How much was her, how much was me? Or will we always spin together...like that?

Scraping the underside of the car along her driveway, I pull up to her house, again.

```
                                              That  energy.
Where  did  it  come  from?   Was  it  from  within  us?   Was  it
                       possession?   Are  we  in  danger?
```

She prances out of the car and through the still ajar gate. Dumfounded, I think:

```
Why  the  hell  is  she  prancing?
```

I follow her inside – I'm not sure why. Maybe I'm trying to recreate normalcy in our lives, somehow make everything different – revert to over an hour ago. She turns on the living room light again (when did she turn it off?) and laughs about something unimportant. She comments that her family should be home any minute now. I'm apparently free(?) to go whenever.

Right. Thanks.

I walk catatonically over to the first couch I sat on, the little one, and cave in.

"Sage?"

"Hmm?"

"What just happened?" I look up into her face once more, instinctively flinching.

"We went for a drive, didn't we? And why did you just flinch?" Her eyes gleam. *Oh fuck.* She looks behind her, perhaps at the door. It's clear. She turns back to look at me. "It was nothing, *really*." She goes and touches the left side of her jaw with her right hand. Lingering there she turns her hand up...up. To take her face off.

She becomes a bloody disarray of veins and flesh. The white of her eyes dance.

Ohmygod.

I cry out, mouth closed.

She brings her hand back down. "What was that sound, Jasper? Are you scared? Oh, you're so silly. I'm just *playing* with you, Jasper."

Click.

The front door slides open and in walk Sage's father and sister. Her mother is still getting her purse, it seems. Sage looks back at me and coyly smiles. I return no such expression.

She frolics off to meet them.

****

I
am a good
girl.

...*are* you a good girl?

i
try to be.

****

"Hey."

"hey, Jasper."

"That was a good English class. Katherine Mansfield's work it pretty cool; lotsa layers."

"Yea, pretty interesting."

We're walking towards the huge double doors that lead to the outside. Nicole is chatting, incessantly.

Focus slips away.

      `..chit chat, chit chat`

      `the world is dissolving us in this act..`

Sage pulsates around me – her influence over space has not ceased. I feel the brush of her arm, the quietness of her replies. Her   aura.

      `We are two people after a one night stand.`

      `Except`

`instead of`

      `fucking`

            `last night`

`we`

        `nearly killed ourselves.`

The   perversion   of   what   we   almost   did...
I swoon.

Is it perverse? Is *loving* yourself enough to *kill* yourself
"perverse"?

What am I saying?

                                        I can barely hear you...
Droplets   enter   my   eyes,
they   swirl   and   tunnel   their   way   to   whittle   my
insides...she   forms   a   cave.
Comforted. In this single moment. She has seen and
accepted a **side of me** that all others would discard as
insanity.

        I drift to nervousness.

To accept me is to allow me the freedom to create.

Will   she   find   out   that   my   pregnant   hollowness   is
because   of   her?   Will   she   find   out   that   it   is   she   who
washes   away   the   dull   meaninglessness   of   life,   and   I
long   to   be   with   her?   To   watch   where   this   goes...

            to be filled and drained, filled and
            drained...

        She would have too much power.

"Hey, I need to talk to Sage for a few minutes." The whir of conversation stops.
Sheepish, I bow an apology. Stretching towards an opening in our clique's
bubble, I find my way out. Sage will follow me. She has to; we are inextricably
linked.

I burst out of the double wooden corridor doors into sunlight. The buildings'
parameters shout irrelevancy in comparison to the heated questions begging
relief from my aching mind. *metal! wire! concrete!* I aim at the most isolated
spot on campus at this time: a vast courtyard. Posts and walkways splash
upwards on all sides – we are surrounded by watchful, overbearing balconies.

I look at her.

Relief crushes me. *Her eyes. It's her. She isn't someone – or something – else.* I lean forward and place my clasped hands between my knees. I push a deep breath out.

She begins, "You look different."

I look back up at her. "So do you..."

Watching me intently she murmurs, "Hmm, yes. It's your hair. It's all pinned up and restricted today. Last night it was wild. I like it better wild."

My...HAIR?

You've got to be fucking kidding me. I did my hair like this for you, you, you, SAGE.

Steve likes it best when my hair is tightly pinned up like it is today – I only assumed that everyone else would have the same opinion.

Priestesses and witches conjure and control the spirit
world

on the wisps of their hair.
Tantric sages bind and unbind women's hair to

activate the cosmic forces of

creation and destruction.

St. Paul **feared** women's abilities

to call upon angels by letting their

hair fall loose.

Steve is like St. Paul. Sage is an...appreciative witch?

I should have known that she'd like my hair down.

I pull out two of my bobby pins. I reply, "O...k...weirdo."

"Alright, then. What do you have to say?" she snaps.

144

"Well, what the hell was last night about?" I retort, far more severely than I had intended.

"How should I know, you're the one who's supposed to be 'enlightened'."

"What the...? What do you mean 'enlightened'?"

"*You're* the one, who claims to understand the spirit world."

"Fuck you! I was just telling you about my childhood and my sense of spirituality. I don't know anything important. I just know that you scared the shit out of me last night and that *you* were the one in control..."

"*I* was in control? You were the one driving...and if you are soooooo experienced, since birth it seems, then *you* should be the one explaining last night to *me*."

"*You* were in control! *You* started it, *Sage*!"

"I...was...in? Control? That's insane."

"Is it insane?! I have no idea if it's insane! Are we both insane?! What the hell happened last night?!"

Her lashes fall, and her head tips back ever so slightly. Dark circles. *I wonder if she slept last night.* "Jasper, I have no idea what last night was about. Your guess is as good as mine."

I stare at her. Long moments pass. *If she doesn't know...if she wasn't controlling it...who was?*

"Well,
not good
enough." I
callously. I
leave. *This
ridiculous.*
just keeping
answer
me.

Slipping
into
bitterness,
taunts, "Oh,
Go and play
your *actual*
friends
before they
you too, too
much...Ah,
look!" She
a mocking
at them,

```
Which answer is correct?
```

SUPERFICIAL is to **PENETRATING** as:

a. Shallow is to Deep (spatial)
b. Facade is to Structure (architectural)
c. Cursory is to Analytical (philosophical)
d. Insignificant to Profound (intellectual)
e. Surface is to Authentic (arguments)
f. Minor is to Severe (medical)
g. Trivial is to Substantial (editorial)
h. Trivial is to Significant (substantial)
i. Careless is to Thorough (intentional)
j. Frivolous is to Serious (attitudinal)
k. Apparent to Actual (visual)

---

that's
say
go to
is
She's
the
from

back

she
right.
with

miss

points
finger
sitting

---

at our wooden lunch tables a mere 100 feet away. Grandfather trees form the backdrop of the scene; our school is nestled in one of the land's great valleys.

```
Vast, lush forest
              echoes
         the horrors
    of our episode last night.
I drove and twisted around those very hills..
```

Token admirers have congregated around my girls. I pause, midstride, and watch them as Sage continues to bite out words behind me, "We've been talking at school for a total of five minutes! Oh no! Your umbilical cord is stretching! You're SO far away from them...watch out! It might snap and then you'd be ***all alone***..."

I hate her. "Oh, whatever, Sage. You and your stupid fucked up vendetta against light hearted fun. They're my family. Leave them the fuck out of it." *And stop threatening me.*

"Light hearted fun. Harmless, is it? Let's think for a moment. Don't you think that you are all just a leeeetle bit shallow? Shallowness rots your mind. I mean, what else do you girls talk about other than parties and boys?"

"We talk about stuff!!"

"Stuff. You talk about 'STUFF'. Great. Let me know when something else equally as revolutionary takes place. I guess our little talk is adjourned then, hmm?" She turns and abandons me. My cave is silent. I stand, hands clenched, jaw tight. *Bitch.*

The bottom of her left pant leg catches on her heel over and over and *over* again.

Realization and appreciation of her challenges trickle into my consciousness, despite my best attempts to remain angry. I am paradoxically infuriated and in awe. Deep in thought, I let my hands relax.

Seems I am *tickled* to have someone so determined to

       confront,

       challenge,

       DEFY &

       break me.

It'sabout time.

⌀ DR. SNOW

Curious   because   death   makes   life   real.
(Just imagine a life where death wasn't possible.)

Curious.

14 years old. I drown in half a bottle of vodka for the first time. 22 hours pass. Pseudo-alive, the remnants of alcohol linger in my dehydration. My first 'hangover'. How novel.

I learn to love it.

Two weeks later. My Mother is taking me to Dr. Snow's office, for the first time. She's arranged it all.

She's taking me to him because of the

       spit splashing slurs I managed to splutter

at some point during my

       infantile, intoxicated inching

along on her kitchen floor.

I made wet spiral patterns out of my drool that night. I was very proud of it. I'm glad the floor was varnished so well by Daddy. If it hadn't been, my bubbles of spit would have dried right through the wood and splintered the beautiful kauri.

At one point I lay feverishly down on my back. I began by throwing out wild jokes and hilarious noises – I was thrilled to be as giddy as I was; I was *happy*. But Mother peered into my eyes, tears streaming down her face. She stayed with me the whole time, so did Daddy. She moaned, "Why, Jasper, why Jasper honey, why?" In the same moment as she knelt, she grabbed my hand and held my fingers to her flushed cheek and tortured expression. She always feels so much. She's just normally hiding it.

Looking into her, I ached to give her a solid reason for why her baby girl was acting(?) like such a delinquent...so I fabricated the syncopated delivery of a flat out lie:

"Mom?"

"Yes, honey, yes?"

"I...DRANK DRANK YES, ME, MY,

     I DRANK I THINK BECAUSE DRINK DULL PAIN,

        DULL PAIN...

        I, YES ME CONFUSED

           — THE ABUSE —

        I DON'T KNOW, MAYBE DRINK, DRANK, DRUNK —
        HAHAHA - BECAUSE OF THE SEXUAL ABUSE...

           YOU KNOW?"

A **bold faced lie** to soothe maternal worry: yes! There's a *reason* why her baby girl was drunk!

She shouldn't have paid attention to me.

I just got trashed because I'd never tried hard alcohol before. Steve and Daniel happen to get a hold of a bottle. I thought it'd be fun. It *was* fun...sort of. I remember giving Daniel what would become 'the infamous naked hug' – a drunken swirl of bodies...in the midst of chaotic displays of hysterical giggling, spotted with shadows...mixed with illumination from only one lamp...swirling...swirling...Daniel has always been nice to me; he would never take advantage of me. We're still friends.

150

Steve and I were actually dating at the time (rather than being mere fuck buddies – it was early in our relationship). He was having his way with me just down the road from my parents house, in the empty place I was house sitting. I remember being very sore in the morning.

The two boys dropped me off on my Mother and Father's doorstep a few hours later. I became too difficult to handle and too unresponsive to fuck. I don't remember it happening – I had descended into my first black out of the night. Daniel wanted to stay to make sure I was alright, but Steve dragged him away to cover his tracks.

****

Mid night, I wake up in my parent's bed, their feverish hands filled with cold wash clothes and bowls angled for my impending vomit. In the morning they tell me that I sat on the toilet for an hour threading intimate details about my life into a deranged bit of tapestry. I spoke in slurs. I bound my torso in straps of corny jokes and tearful reflections, up and down, up and down. They made sure I didn't hit my head.

I was pretty horrified – I elaborate on what I said, but euphemistically.

****

Mother makes me promise to go to at least four appointments with Dr. Snow. If, after that, I'm not convinced that seeing him will help, I never have to go again. She always keeps her promises. So I'm here, in her car, waiting for us to pull up to his office. Just one more traffic light to go.

She slows down and parallel parks. I sit and stare at the dashboard.

"Ready, honey?"

I turn and look at her gentle face, her imploring eyes. *Ok. Just four one-hour appointments. It's the least you can do.* I take a deep breath. I nod, step out and look up at his office. It's in a quaint, Victorian building, San Francisco style.

here we go...

****

"You must be Jasper!"

I mutely agree. *Nausea.*

My Mother responds more enthusiastically. Looking sideways at me, she begins, "Yes, this is my beautiful, younger daughter, Jasper. She's a great combination of spirituality, intelligence and social awareness. She's very loved by all of her peers and her family..." She wants me to feel supported and not squashed, open but not afraid.

I try to go numb.

I hug my Mother. I enter his office and sit.

I am on the left side of the room in one of his poofy, black leather chairs. There is one other chair and two couches. I wish they weren't leather. 75% of all leather sold comes from India's sacred cow population – *not* the meat industry[3].

There is a circular coffee table in the middle. Long vertical windows reach

UP!

up,

up

toward the 20 foot high ceilings. Trees burst from the middle of the courtyard just behind his office building. I would watch birds fly and nest on those branches for years to come.

A six part series of striking paintings line the walls. The series was painted by one of his patients. There are 18 more bought and sold elsewhere, but she gifted these to Dr. Snow. Each painting is dedicated to one of the psychological stages of emotional and physical abuse, then transformation and rebirth.

I settle in for my first appointment. Despite my doubts, his charisma and talent for dealing with teenagers, for dealing with *me*, replaces my defense

---

[3] google search the words: 'leather, india, sacred cows'.

mechanisms with desperate hope. The man is incredible; he becomes not only relevant but paramount. Dr. Snow's my Gandalf.

Psychoanalysis,   damning   realizations, gaping emotions...

More honesty occurred in his office than anywhere else in my life.

I tell him *everything,* and his feedback never disappoints. His training steers clear of using psychiatric drugs – instead he teaches me the power of the mind and its ability to create and experience all that I ask it to. He joins me on the journey to become the woman I so honestly wish to be.

He speaks to me with words far longer than my little finger.

He gently asks me

      to stretch up,

as if I am the little boy in Shel Silverstein*'s The Giving Tree,*

      to grasp psychological patterns of self sabotage,

      and to cry, for hours.

He demands that I look myself in the face; he doesn't let me have excuses; he doesn't let me avoid myself; I'm never allowed to be numb here. His office is the only place I have for safe exploration, away from social expectations, drama and power dynamics. In here, it's like I've escaped every plastic bag waiting to suffocate me.

He apologizes after a session of crying by saying, "Jasper? If you weren't as quick at processing and as sharp as you are, I would make sure we took things slower. But you can handle all of the challenges I throw at you. I've never known a teenager to be so in love with growing. So I push you, and I will *always* do so. Neither of us knows your potential but by damn, we're going to find the true you."

Conversion, fastidious Goddess,
loves blood
better than brick, &
feasts most subtly on
the human will.
- Virginia Woolf, "Mrs.
Dalloway"

Crying. A sign of growth and a symbol of transformation.

Then there is **trust**...hmm. Sometimes I think I can trust Dr. Snow completely, other times – like when considering whether or not I'm going to tell him about my suicidal driving escapade....

I wonder.

****

Now.

Today, I could have called myself a murderess.

"Jasper! How are you doing today? Welcome, welcome." Dr. Snow booms as I step, utterly dazed, into the reception area of his office. The huge bay window on my right side forces me into the sun again. *I always keep my curtains closed at home...my big sister, Crystal, thinks I'm crazy.* The light from his window infuses me with a stunning amount of liveliness I'm really not used to.

"Uhhh...yea, hi!" I flush. "Can I go in?" I wave at his open office door.

He glances up from his last patient's papers and smiles, ever so kindly, and nods. *I always feel like relaxing when he does that, his energy is so reassuring. Man, I never want to lose him as a friend.*

I swiftly set up a protective fortress of pillows around me, like I used to do when I was a little girl. It's not that I'm scared of him, I just know we all have limits of what we accept in others (at least we should). His defining limit; the line he draws in deciding whom he counsels, might very well exclude potential murderers...so if I tell him I fancied the idea of killing myself and another girl last night...he might report me as an "endangerment to myself and others". I feel like an endangerment. He might send me away to an insane asylum. He might refuse to continue counseling me. He might stop being my friend. I might lose him.

154

These pillows are awesome. If he does reject me, their protection will be like a hot cup of cocoa after busting your ass falling a thousand feet in an avalanche. I snuggle deeper. *I might not tell him, and then I wouldn't have to worry about all of this.*

But Mom and Dad. They are paying for this - $80 a session. How can I waste everyone's money and not talk about what is most bothering me?

True, but how on earth are you going to explain what happened..?

"SO!"

I jump.

"JASPER!...Oh, my apologies – I didn't mean to frighten you.

"Tea?"

I nod wide eyed, and he sets me up with my usual– earl grey with brown sugar and milk. I wasn't vegan yet, instead just recently vegetarian. It would take me 10 years before I learned about the connection between milk and veal calves. He squeezes lemon into his tea, stirs it and smiles at me.

"How are you doing then, Miss Jasper?"

I feel my feet fret in a dull panic. *I want to run away! I can't do this!* I lift my feet up and tuck them underneath me. I shrug. *My throat is dry, uninhabitable, taciturn. I'm never going to be able to talk like this.* Minutes assault my skin; burning the reality of my silence into raw sweat marks; I am branded as the veal calves are the day their sweet Mothers give birth to them.

Five slow minutes sear scars of fear into my neck.

"So, Jasper, how's school? Life? Your drama production? Friends?"

Ten minutes.

Next I will dehydrate – this heat is too intense.

"How is your Mother? Father?

...cat?"

My cat. Yes, fine. So is my family, my precious, precious family. They're the reason I'm still alive today, listening to you ask questions I have no voice to answer.

15 minutes. "Well, if you don't mind I'm just going to begin sharing various theories, alright? They really are quite fascinating....."

****

"I'm ready, now."

The words of the latest theory scuttle back along invisible threads to wait until they are needed again.

I wish I didn't feel like my life was so insignificant in comparison to the other things going on in the world.

I just have to know: Is she insane? Am I? Will there be another time when the opportunity presents itself, and I'll actually go through with killing?

I begin my tale slowly, careful to whisper so that I might avoid deafness. I choose every word excruciatingly, aware that with one slip up I may very well end up in the insane asylum.

EEK!
I saw one, once – a 1900s insane
asylum - it was made into a museum.
People died there. Cages lined every
wall with leashes of wrapped, dead
cow skin for patients' wrists attached
to thick hooks in ghastly cells. Tape
recordings of what the screams were
like were available to play at each
station. I listened to three. I hated
the pictures of the system - all that
power. The doctors, nurses, office
staff, all telling you how to live your
life. Horrifying.

I CANNOT be sent there.

"Dr. Snow, I'm nervous. I know I've just prattled about how I have this new friend, etc. etc., but I haven't told you *really* what's on my mind. I don't know how to talk to you about this. It seems too insane. I'm scared; I don't want you to throw me into a straitjacket. I just couldn't handle it, my f r e e d o m...!" I begin to whimper, "I just couldn't handle it, you know? Like seriously, straitjackets are my number one fear along with Great White sharks and rape..."

Words continue to tumble out, steam.

"Jasper."

My eyes dart to him, then rest on my lap, ashamed.

"Look at me, Jasper." He leans in towards the coffee table that separates us and puts his forearms on his knees. His kind blue eyes inspire relief just by being attentive. "Jasper, you are not insane. You know I'm not fibbing – I'm always honest with you. I will also never, ever violate your trust by leading you out of here in a straitjacket.

　　　You 　　 have 　　 my 　　 word."

After a few brief moments of disbelief, tears spill on my school uniform onto the pillows, and I emotionally cave in. He waits with me.

"Umm..." Snot soaks my upper lip. "Thank you."

I murmur a silly, little joke to lighten the mood but manage to keep crying throughout, "I mean, I mean, I may very well be insane you know, you can decide after what I'm about to tell you – then maybe that straitjacket won't look so bad..." I grin and splutter. He smiles reflectively, hands me a tissue and sits back again.

Thank you, thank you, thank you, thank you..

"Alright, soooooo...I have a new friend." I mop up my face.

"A new friend. How lovely."

****

her   eyes...

"Her eyes were...satanic almost." Dr. Snow knows all about my spiritual side – he too is blessed.

her   voice...

"She shrieked commands at me. I felt totally out of control, at least initially. As the minutes passed and she just kept feeding me these thoughts, I suddenly felt really powerful, like something else took over my soul. It was unbelievable."

Her   manipulation...or   mine

"We were lost, you know? And, and...we almost...I almost..."

I told him.

space   space   space

****

There's something about the moment you trust someone with your life that is as exquisite as it is terrifying.

I think it's because being honest brings us closer to our   truth,   closer   to who we are.

"Hmm.

"Jasper, this is a very interesting story. Thank you for telling me. May I give you my interpretation?"

I feel my head nod a little too quickly.

"Sage sounds fascinating. I think it's wonderful that you have someone like her to discuss such things with in addition to your Mother and me. I'm also glad that you two decided not to end your lives last night.

Hmm that was particularly nonchalant, you'd think he was congratulating us for resisting the temptation to eat a slice of cake or something.

"Now bear with me - I am now going to attempt to give you my thoughts on why these events transpired. Ready?"

I nod.

"People are fascinated by death

because

Death makes life real."

He pauses and observes me.

What...?

"Ok, so here's the thing. Teenagers often subject themselves to morbid interpretations of their own world because it assures them that their rather tumultuous lives are transient. It makes each moment you *are* alive all the more thrilling. Being obsessed with death, life's opposite and definitive qualifier, makes life more real."

"Whoa, that's crazy." Blink, blink, pause.

"But what do you make of the spiritual nature of it all? It's one thing to say we like the idea of death because it's a fascinating concept, but the daemon energy...her reasoning about God..."

160

"It sounds as though Sage is a very sensitive and spiritual person as well. Good. You guys should definitely continue exploring your spirituality with one another – sounds as though you'll catalyze one another's learning."

My heart leaps.

"Just understand why death is so intoxicating – it is the counterbalance to life. I think that when you both find that you can focus on life without being insecure, or as though you want some sort of temporary release from it, you'll then see just how thrilling it is to explore life. We can work on this."

"For real?"

"Yes."

I pause one, two, three minutes and let the   `news of my sanity` sink into my skin.

"...........AH!!!!   I'm   excited!   I'm   not   insane!   Ahahahhaaa,   ok. Thank you, Dr. Snow. Thank you." I grin at him.

His bright, smiling blue eyes fall into the edges of his white, white beard and he nods confidently.

"Indeed!"

****

September 20th

NorthDaughter 8:05 PM

    hmmmf damn computer not listening to my orders...graaa

Lovers_End 8:06 PM

    hi

NorthDaughter 8:06 PM

    ok so tell me your pain

Lovers_End 8:06 PM

    lol, pain eh? humf. no thanks

NorthDaughter 8:06 PM

    ok see this is my point exactly

Lovers_End 8:07 PM

    your point? what is that may i ask...yes i can? oh good....what's your point?

NorthDaughter 8:07 PM

    i can't judge your voice and expression online thus reducing me into acceptance of the situation which i do NOT like. damnit woman. my point is wanting to know what's going on in you're head

Lovers_End 8:08 PM

    my head? *raises eyebrow* what about it? :P

    yea, emotive voice changes come in handy

NorthDaughter 8:08 PM

gee

Lovers_End 8:08 PM

hehehehehee *giggles*

soooooo are you in a better mood this evening than this morning?

NorthDaughter 8:08 PM

thus we smile..::superficial smile::

no, im better than i was when we talked earlier today, yes. but not in a good one. are you in a good mood?

Lovers_End 8:10 PM

yea, i'd say i am. My counselor didn't disown me after me telling him our little story from last night...he didn't even try and convince me to not be your friend. (uhh...acquaintance)— i told him he wasn't allowed to say that...but anyway. yea. im in a pretty good mood.

Biology class. She's sitting to the right of me, writing furious notes. The words she scripts are indecipherable – they are in a different language, the letters are like buildings.

The class bell rings.

Casually bobbing behind (as you do), I stall. She doesn't wait for me – I'm practically invisible to the conversation going on inside of her head. She's so intense right now. Walking paces in front, she screws her notes into tight balls, and throws them away. My heart jolts. *Stall, stall!* I bend down to tie my Doc Martins. I wait until I'm the last person to file out of our classroom.

Dipping, I bow and retrieve the precious pieces of paper. Some are torn. I put every single one of them into my pocket.

   I feel giddy.

I'll repair and translate them later.

* * *

Home again, I ask Mother to tell me what she thinks of these words I've collected.

"Oh my goodness. They are runes. I haven't seen them used in this way for decades...where did you get these?"

I whisper, "Sage..."

I fold into my room to look up *'runes'*. Runes are:

> "The letters of the ancient
> Germanic alphabets, such as
> the Elder Futhark [alphabet].
> They are used in magic and
> divination. The word "rune"
> is also commonly used by
> modern Pagans to mean any
> magical alphabet or symbol,
> as well as a chanted poetic
> incantation[4]."

The alphabet as transcribed by me:

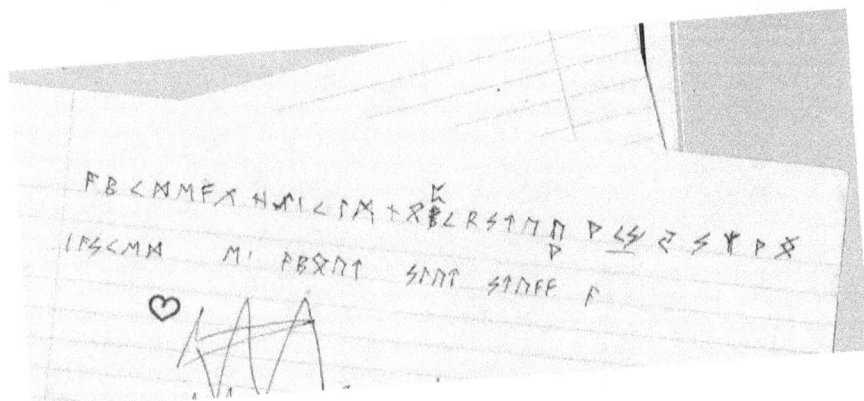

[4] www.mysticcauldron.com/dictionary2.html

F ₐ B ᵦ ⟨ 𝒸 ⋈ 𝒹 Ⲙ ₑ F 𝒻 Χ 𝓰 Ν ₕ I ᵢ 𝓈 ⱼ ⟨ ₖ Γ ₗ

Ⲙ ₘ ✝ ₙ ⦵ ₒ Ⲓ ₚ ⟨ 𝓆 Ꝛ ᵣ ⧢ ₛ ↑ ₜ Ν ᵤ Λ ᵥ Ᵽ 𝓌 ₓ

Υ 𝓎 𝓏

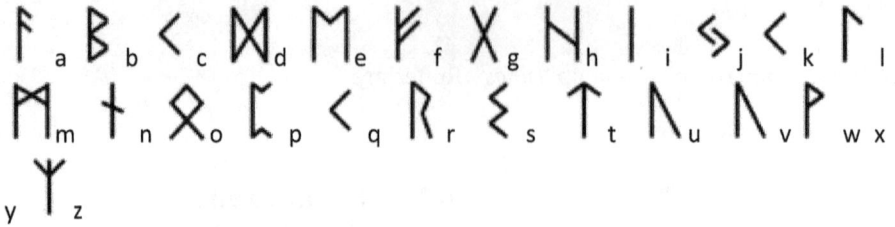

After carefully making sure that Mother doesn't want to hang out any time soon...I sit at the beautiful art table my Father made for me.

The photos to my left b l u   r...

Beauty settles into the nest of the island's harbor; hues of gold.

I scatter her pieces of paper across my art table.

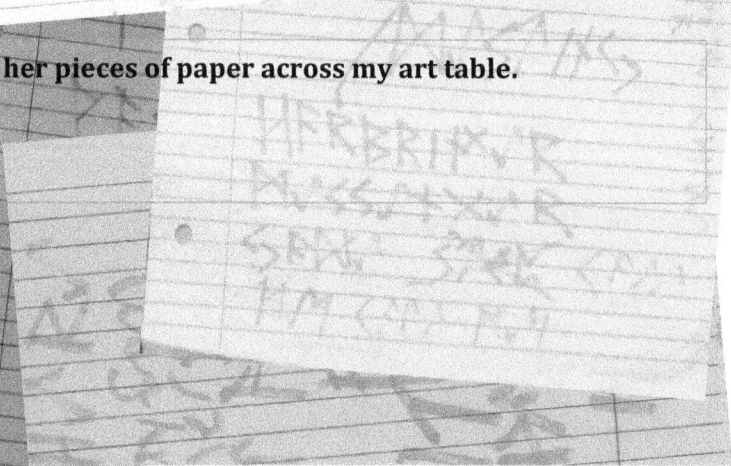

should i just let go?
it's
I have to try
IT IS SO

always?
letter is messed
up?

① I DONT want to happan again!

plesk not again
plese not again
plese not again

make it stop
plese stop it from happening

AGAIN

$\sqrt{} = i$
but

is
using it as

NOT AGAIN

I start translating all
I ME WE **of her pages.**

or is
she?

we have to do this we have to do
this plese

④

She must stay
I don't want it to

(english)

④   She must stay
       I don't want it to happen again but she must stay
damn you   why I can't look past it i _____ but
__ shes won't go away   the marks are there _____
fly _____ i can't run away   I don't want to
remember

169

(runes:)
⑤ I try to be good
I am trying

Should I just let go? (english)
it's my flow (runes)
my ___ I have to try (english)

it is so hard
always I have no choice

always i have no choice

cry for her
she
must
from
getaway
run nit away
she is lost from it
NIT Away
from it
she cannot
your
lasting
she know?
call (Messenger)
[written on right side of page:]
The blot the witch the
cry for
her
childs

Does she know?
    no
    she cannot
    it is your
    Fate/Destiny

Harbrenger
Messenger => (Messenger)
--- she is mixing i's for e's
jade stop call me call me

[written on right side of page:]
    The blot the witch the childs
        cry for her

170

cont. ⑤

Se no
hear no
touch
spek

ᛋᛗ ᛏᛟ
ᚼᛁᚨᚱ ᛏᛟ
ᛏᛟᚢᚳᚼ
ᛋᚲᛗᚲ

⑥ BECOME
no
EVIL

ᛒᛗᚲ ᛟ ᛗᛁᚢ
ᛏᛟ
ᛗᛈᛁᛚ

At some point it starts to rain outside.

The mountains begin to form the rivers of their birth – the moon. Nature drips down from Her legs. The rainforest is alive.

From my room, I can see the cusp of the ocean burst into white foam.

```
What   does   she   not   want   to  happen  again?
       Who     is        she       talking     about?

Why          doesn't          she          have          a


                        choice...?
```

✄ Withdrawl

September 22nd

NorthDaughter 7:36 PM

hey. mother called from the states – i am officially motherless

Lovers_End 7:37 PM

how is she?

NorthDaughter 7:38 PM

ehmm...ok i guess. kinda dazed sounding. a 24 hour flight will do that to you.

Yuck i just spent 5 hours studying for the SATs

Lovers_End 7:38 PM

oh wow, really? five hours! awesome!

NorthDaughter 7:38 PM

uhm. sure it was...::looks at her funny:: how was the beach?

Lovers_End 7:39 PM

yea, pretty good eh. ☺ got to catch up with mah girls Christina and Nicole. hadn't seen them in a while. lotsa cute guys....hehe and i've got to start getting ready to go out again soon...dammit! but the party that we were going to go to isn't on anymore...well it is, it's just at the guy's house, and not an event hall which means they'll charge us to get in. ugh. piece of!!!!!!!!

NorthDaughter 7:41 PM

oi ve. you just can't keep your mind on the topic can you? ::grins:: well i had a fun little spurt of writing but it went away after i took a break. ....ok well have fun then...uhm tomorrow are you going out?

Lovers_End 7:41 PM

at night? or during the day

NorthDaughter 7:41 PM

both. i found that movie we could watch and how are you doing? i'm a tad worried about you man

Lovers_End 7:47 PM

yes, I am out tomorrow night-I have my singing competition!!!! (ahhhhhhhhh *whimpers*) and then this Women's Spirituality group that Mom and her friend started...etc. anyway. Dunno about during the day, probably going to try and go to gym, and we can study. sound good?

NorthDaughter 7:48 PM

sure fine. be warned though i am not a morning person..::grins::

NorthDaughter 7:53 PM

so...uhm yeah..are you ok? did you answer? ::blinks:: sorry i'm insane ::grins:: pester pester

NorthDaughter 8:01 PM

okies well i gotta go i'm being bitched at on all sides. so have fun, goodnight, and call me later if you want. later

```
*****************************************************************
```

To: Jasper
From: Sage
Date: September 22nd

i have decided that recently i have become entirely too
dependent on you. so i am just going to do what i have to, to make
this go away. forgive me if i sounded hostile or angry or whatever, but
i really do need to use my own two feet to stand.

-sage

```
*****************************************************************
```

****

To: Sage
From: Jasper
Date: September 23rd

Well alright so that came out of the blue...I agree that everyone *should* be independent (or interdependent if you're really fancy, just ask Dr. Snow)...but I guess I didn't notice that your independence was being compromised by our friendship..well at least for the most part...does this have something to do with me being so crazy busy and therefore distant? If so, I'm sorry – I'm not trying to be unavalible, really, I just have a lot going on!! eeeek!

ehem. hehe alright. If you want to talk let me know.

Jasper.

****

Subject: meh

To: Jasper
From: Sage
Date: September 23rd

well. i wrote two messages but they died, thus you never got them..::grins:: erg to summarize my last two e-mails: i am a duck and....well, i am going to join a gym, (it's all part of my self-progression theme) but i haven't decided which one yet. i'm glad we got to talk today – im sorry for being so sensitive. i am GLAD you are busy – many fun things to do.

-sage

****

✍ A flock, a spirit and a wolf

Subject: meh

To: Jasper
From: Sage
Date: September 23rd

is it just me, or does your father seem a tad hostile to like...people outside of his flock? i know how to fix that...::dark smile, flexes fingers:: hmm so i have been lurking online for a bit. found a good shamanism site that explains things a bit...the funny part though was at the bottom, under the sub heading 'first journey' it says..'DON'T BRING ANYTHING BACK' i could not stop laughing. it's funny you see. they never explained that one to me. hmmf i was a poet and i didn't know it. but that's all past, not present. oh and i just realized that rose and rosalyn (funny how they both share the same real name) were/are in choir...how odd is that? oh and i have to discuss the concept of guardians with you. but for now i'll leave you in peace and sanctuary. -sage

Subject: Re: meh

To: Sage
From: Jasper
Date: September 23rd

Two of your messages died?!?!?! geez woman don't DO that! haha, ;) send them, send them! (I'd try and pretend to be less eager, but I'm on a sugar high so I've decided to just go with it.) I always want to hear what that mind of yours has to say.

Ok whoa, what's this about my Dad? Surely he doesn't come off as THAT severely exclusive. Although yea I can see where you're coming from. Lots of people get the wrong impression about him by thinking that he hates them

177

(which can be true of the boys I bring into the house...haha and they know it). Really he's a sweetheart - just introverted (opposite of Mom!). Some of his introversion might be because of this thing that happened to him when he was a baby...when he was just learning to talk he was crawling around and exploring, you know, doing baby stuff, and unfortunately he finds a bunch of ant poison. Then he *ate* it. ☹ When he was found there were apparently signs of poisoning, so he was rushed to hospital and had his stomach was pumped etc. He had a tube inserted in this throat to do this. THEN when he returned home he was apparently so traumatized that he stopped talking completely. THEN the stupid doctor recommended that his Mother STARVE him unless he *asked* for food. And he was only a little bitty kid during all this!! So yea – maybe he's been conditioned to not really dig talking – I mean, I'd probably be the same.

Now other than that, your line "i know how to fix that...:dark smile, flexes fingers::" was creepy. You hurt my Daddy (are you some kind of villain?) and I'll orchestrate some serious ass kicking...

Shamanism site huh? I'd be interested to look at it...but yes, shamans are beautiful, at least the genuine ones are. I love how the Cherokee Native Americans had such an incredibly peaceful approach to healing through their shamans/medicine people. There is something so amazingly spiritual about an elderly lady that can read the wind and create a story out of autumn leaves left by a man that paid her a visit during an afternoon thunderstorm. I'd like to be a shaman.

my totem animal is a black wolf...i first saw him when i was a little girl. at first he was really, *really* scary...& it wasn't until i was 12 in New Zealand that I met a healer/intuitive woman who told me that he would remain scary so long as I didn't fully embrace his power & his lessons...now he is beautiful & walks along side me.

all for now,   jasper.

✍ just the surface

****

To: Jasper
From: Sage
Date: September 23rd

mind over matter dear, or if i must be insane then i guess i just play the game.

i am seriously doubting my motives at this point. it's funny, i have watched myself slowly dissolve friendships in the last few hours. or rather i haven't prevented them from deteriorating.

don't worry, i don't fancy myself a super-villain, i'll leave that to the experts.

****

To: Sage
From: Jasper
Date: September 23rd

wow, who are you not friends with anymore?

...*blinks*...

ok so...umm, yes thank you for asking about henry today. yes, henry is *fabulous darling, fabulous.* ☺ it's so crazy that he just randomly decided to take me off and kiss me at rayla's party!!! ahhhh!! amazing. it's incredible because he's older but still baby face cute...and hot...haha, and coooolio. :P hehe...oh dammit, fuck this. *frowns* I'd talk more about my growing affection for him(!), but I'm worried about swamping you with superificial 'crap' and offending you with my oh-so-cliché

179

life...AH it's so hard, like I want to tell you things but then I don't know if you can even understand why I am the way I am/ why I am superficial a lot of the times...wow, I'm learning so much about myself, sheeesh!. AH. *slightly annoyed* anyway

OoOOoo also as a total sidenote, our study times have slipped in terms of actually studying, hmm??? I love studying with you (of course) but since we only really see each other when we study we seem to get sidetracked and absorbed in other conversations (which I love, but yes). so maybe we should brainstorm on this. Feel free to splurt out all your thoughts upon this page *holds up a blank pad for you*. HUMF. I wish we didn't have to care about this.

Yea so I'll take whatever you throw at me.

Jasper.

****

        hmm...spirituality is...

                    risky.

    yes

    escaping to the superficial is much
    safer.

****

To: Jasper
From: Sage
Date: September 23rd

no i won't be offended by you talking to me about henry, how can one be offended by the truth? i wish i could talk and jabber about superficial stuff, but i don't know how to turn on some sort of switch or whatever to make it work. you'd be surprised how much of my life is superficial though. perhaps because i have no other outlet besides you it is overwhelming (you see how wonderful selective memory is?) and i do understand believe it or not. i understood before you told me.

i have decided that soon i am either going to get completely fucked out of my brain or write a novella. it's been in my head for a while you see...my concept of god and the devil (per se) at first it started out as a play but now i realize that it just won't work given all the details i will have to convey with dialogue alone. so i babble. yup see i can (attempt to) be superficial when i try. although i generally call it babbling. in case you haven't noticed.

although on occasion i have hesitated to use the word 'friend', since we are using it now to refer to one another, i guess i have to just apologize beforehand on my sometimes intense possessiveness. please don't be alarmed it's not a sexual thing. just one of those things, you know? erg.(erg=expression of annoyance at not being able to explain things satisfactorily). thus i leap into asking you how it went with henry (although he doesn't particularly appeal to me) – i want to know you are ok. i am assuming from your comments that he is a good thing. ::small smile:: i could be wrong however.

and here i am going to babble self centeredly again. perdon senorita. so 'friends' (here in New Zealand). i have my boyz here (yes, all the ones i sit with in math class and tell 'corny' jokes with, as you like to say). and i have my drug friends...(these overlap on occasion) and i have my art/rave/overlapping into all categories friends, and then i have these new (frighteningly girly) 'acquaintances' (you, nicole, etc.) who surprisingly enough work a **balance** in my life..::small gasp from the audience as jasper's precious word is plagiarized:: just by existing. i am not particularly girly...(understatement of the millennium) but i guess everyone needs to have a feminine influence in their lives...no matter how small, or appealing (in an annoying fashion)...you see i told you i was babbling. anyway the point is, (when i get that far) that i do enjoy your company and theirs for the pure superficiality of it, as well as the amusement. you're wrong if you think my life is unsuperficial. but if im becoming too superficial i can 'back off' and just avoid them/you entirely. wow that sounds horrible doesn't it. but it's as close as i can get to explaining in a not so subtle fashion.

also i really do want to work, i don't plan for things interrupting our study time, and i'm sorry they did. if you want to study separately it's ok, i mean you might get more work done that way. i don't know. and i do enjoy spending 'quality time' with you. it's sad isn't it? we had one evening of normal(or near normal) relations, and then poof. no more normality. well i think part of that is my attitude, and my overly concernedness about things(erg), rather than me trying to make things better. ach! sorry this email is huge i really am babbling now. suffice it to say that i am agreeable to whatever changes you want to make, (unless you plan to side with the evil chihuahua in his diabolic plan to take over the world by seeming ignorance and through taco bell commercials-in which case i would have to step in and object) and well goodnight, you're probly sleeping but i won't for a while. still busy thinking. anywho. later babe...

-the sage

****

Lovers_End 2:42 PM

oh yes, by the way--i have decided that i like superficial things. lol...ok raaandom

NorthDaughter 2:42 PM

hmmm i see.

Lovers_End 2:43 PM

do you now

NorthDaughter 2:43 PM

yes i do.

well then i guess that's that – we'll stop having a deep friendship and just get to superficial, surface relations, hmm? grand.

Lovers_End 2:43 PM

struggles not to laugh because she's in the middle of another thought...oh no... ahahahhaaa

Lovers_End 2:44 PM

ok so you're weird and really things need to be half and half. I choose not to dabble in the crazy 'invisible' spiritual world too much--if i did i would loose my semi-alright hold on reality. Superficial stuff is REALLY REALLY REALLY fun, so yea. Balance.

NorthDaughter 2:45 PM

sad for me then, since i refuse superficial stuff unless i lose my mind, or am under the influence

NorthDaughter 2:45 PM

well your approach could be a reason why things are as they are

Lovers_End 2:46 PM

perhaps. there must be some reason for why they are mostly left unseen (which is a good thing, i think – im not ready for them to be everywhere ALL the time)

NorthDaughter 2:46 PM

eh.

NorthDaughter 2:46 PM

are we going to study? or are you too busy with superficial things?

Lovers_End 2:48 PM

two things about that, #1 - we need to actually study when i am over there because i don't have the book etc. and #2 - i can't study today cuz i've got a another singing competition that i will be practicing for...etc.

yes i am too busy with *'superficial'* things

NorthDaughter 2:50 PM

well one, i was going to say that anyway. And two, perhaps one of these days i'll just stop trying to figure things out and try to be normal and superficial, AND the day that happens maybe you should look at your future.

yes, i am being selfish

Lovers_End 2:51 PM

look at the future? umm

NorthDaughter 2:51 PM

or not, perhaps it's a game to you. i'm happy that you are amused

Lovers_End 2:52 PM

right. ok then, when you want me to understand, let me know and no, I'm not amused sorry.

NorthDaughter 2:52 PM

nope sorry that's the point i feel, you don't understand at all

Lovers_End 2:54 PM

perhaps i am not meant to "know" everything. Fine by me

Lovers_End 2:54 PM

ok, that was a lie--not fine by me..anyway

Lovers_End 2:54 PM

you're always saying that you're practically driven insane by the spiritual energy in your house and bedroom (which is absolutely fair enough, it's petrifying) but then when I offer to do a healing/cleansing ritual with sage (the spice, not you in this context) in your room where I ask blessings from the guardians for your home so that you can have a better time of it, you *refuse.* I can't do anything more until you decide to let me help you or you at least start learning about how to help yourself by letting me teach you about what I deal with.

NorthDaughter 2:54 PM

i don't need your help! c'mon jasper focus on the superficial man...

Lovers_End 2:55 PM

ok, let's see. Superficial! henry, kyle and evette stayed last night and henry and i are getting along really well (as mates) and he is so hot! yayay, ☺ me happy with whatever happens cuz i like having him as a mate. ☺ methinks something more might come out of it...hehe yay. :D *smiles*

NorthDaughter 2:55 PM

i feel like my hands are tied concerning you. i am sick of this. there is nothing i can do, and when i want to talk the only time is when you get over here and study, but you can't talk because of needing to study, and thus me being angry and upset.

NorthDaughter 2:56 PM

good i'm happy let me know when something else dreadfully important comes up

Lovers_End 2:56 PM

okies. if henry and i start going out-i'll let you know.

NorthDaughter 2:56 PM

that is the problem, i can't hurt you. perhaps i'm going about it the wrong way. or maybe i am sick today and therefore not thinking about this right.

Lovers_End 2:57 PM

uh....right, well i dunno how you see that one--but that's ridiculously awesome that you cant 'hurt me' (what the fuck?).

let's keep it that way and yes - perhaps i'm not weak and pathetic like all the other people who you have "destroyed".

NorthDaughter 2:58 PM

weak? you never knew them if you think that, one of them perhaps but not rose not ever. when i said i couldn't hurt you, i didn't mean that i literally don't have the power, i meant that i won't. i am unable to do anything, i want control

Lovers_End 3:02 PM

you want to control me? yes well...hmm. sorry to disappoint, but i've got complete control over myself. perhaps not the things that happen around me--but myself, sweet as.

NorthDaughter 2:59 PM

maybe i'm just going to destroy myself then, hmm? wonderful! we all learn so much when we cease to exist! and i guess part of me is lonely for at least a tiny bit of something resembling understanding from you yet it is all the superficial things that throw themselves in the way!

Lovers_End 3:02 PM

superficial things are so awesome!! mate! you've lost that...you've lost...the feeling of laughing hysterically, etc. it's like—chill *out* mate.

NorthDaughter 3:03 PM

'chill'? sure jasper, ever feel the temperature of a corpse?

Lovers_End 3:03 PM

what the hell?

Lovers_End 3:03 PM

ok. low blow

NorthDaughter 3:03 PM

gee, point made?

Lovers_End 3:05 PM

are you insinuating what i think you are?

NorthDaughter 3:05 PM

obviously it doesn't pertain to this, it's only superficial! WE ARE JUST MATTER!

Lovers_End 3:06 PM

OK   SO   THERE   ARE   BOTH   SUPERFICIAL AAAAAAAAAAAAAAAAAAAAAAAAAND DEEP THINGS!! i'm juuust saying you need a BALANCE.

Lovers_End 3:07 PM

i have to have a nap before my singing lesson. oh yes and then i am going to that women's spirituality group that i mentioned before. <--- amazing group. anyway, so I have to go...yay! seeing henry again tonight! lol, laterz.

NorthDaughter 3:07 PM

superficial things don't create a balance they don't even matter, you need a balance inside yourself so why should things on the surface count?

NorthDaughter 3:07 PM

later goodnight

Lovers_End 3:08 PM

because people exist on the surface. so of course it matters.

NorthDaughter 3:08 PM

no we don't

Lovers_End 3:08 PM

uhh...ok well i do. cya.

NorthDaughter 3:11 PM

    is love superficial one wonders?

NorthDaughter 3:32 PM

    ah. you're back. speak of the devil.

Lovers_End 3:44 PM

    or so you keep liking to do.

NorthDaughter 4:12 PM

    indeed. well, i only speak of what i know.

✍ AT - ONE - MENT

****

To: Sage
From: Jasper
Date: September 24th

Ok Sage, I'm about to go to my singing competition...but you know what? I'm sorry about our last online conversation. We probably just need to arrange some quality time for just you and me. Maybe we're getting all funked out and weird because we're not playing enough (yes, yes the word 'play' insinuates superficial but perhaps we can managed to do both serious and superficial play). What do you think?

Ok – gotta go.

jasper

****

To: Jasper
From: Sage
Date: 24th September

well, i will wish you good luck for your singing competition tonight, even though i know you are already in there. if you can't get me through the phone, it means i am online. yes – you propose a good idea. let me know when and where you want to 'play'. good luck today babe -sage

****

This is how it Happened.

Play.

Geez. She is *lying* on my lap. We were on the bigger of her two couches and she is just...*lying* on me.

> Wtf? (what the fuck)

Ha.

We are talking about something, probably about....hmm, yea. There's no way for me to remember. I just remember the **sensations** in my body.

She came and sat next to me while I was talking.

> prickling in my chest.
> Air runs away.
>
> WAit! Come Back, Air!
> i need You

Bowing, the top of her head meets my right thigh...

> she lifts and scoots her shoulder along my lower body,
>
> then her left cheek meets my left hip,
>
> > she is touching me

just for a moment, before

> she turns over - her back is on my lap;
>
> she looks up at me, but my gaze does not reach for her.
>
> Her lungs take breaths on my lap –

192

my body fractures along fault lines, each line has a name:

chaos,   fear,   turmoil, excitement
and   not knowing what is right or wrong

each fissure sickly caresses my aching —

I whisper words. Resisting her, I kept my eyes fixed straight forward.

It is, we are in, A Kissing Position – her lips are far closer than they should be.

> But I send you a cream-white rosebud with a flush on its petal tips; For the love that is purest and sweetest Has a kiss of desire on the lips
>
> -Robert Burns, A Red, Red Rose

She gazes at me, contentedly.

Her index finger makes contact with my chin.

...I throw my mind against its walls – *I need to get out.* Jerking, I look down on her, demanding that she **BEHAVE**.

"Hey, look Sage – what's going on? I'm not really comfortable, here."

```
          Don't go hiding,
      Hiding, in the shade,
          Don't go hiding,
      Hiding, in the shade,

        -  Silverchair, Shade
```

She stalls – a caught deer. Moments tick. She sighs, tenses her muscles and lifts away from me. Her feet take her to the opposite side of the room.

Relief.

****

♂ REVOLUTION[5]

September 26th

Lovers_End 6:32 PM

> hehe, twas cue having you over today-good fun i say :D and it was awesome being over at your house yesterday, too...ooo!

NorthDaughter 10:53 PM

> indeed. well have fun tonight out with the girls!

Lovers_End 11:44 PM

> I decided I wouldn't go out– for the first time in what seems like years. I *always* go out. But yea,

change...

---

[5] Italics in this section are paraphrased from: Hall, Joseph (Bishop of Norwich). "Hard Measure", London: J. Cadwel for J. Crooke,1660. Autobiographical.

Last night's study period percolated into an outrageous
but glorious
moment when I returned home.

As I step through my sliding glass door, I   **heave**

between my current and distant, potential
life.

Her vocabulary, reading list, allegories and perceptions...they spin. The threads of a cocoon slip in and out of my skin – just below the surface – then deep within my tissue.

The threads will stay within me for many months to come. Just until I'm ready to emerge, or die.

In slow motion, I slip by my snoozing Father. Feet cross the threshold into my room.

> *The door is heavy, like the entrance to a cathedral pre-Reformation. The sanctuary stretches up but more so out...the length of the building accentuated by rows and rows of triforiums deeply chiseled into stone walls.*

Masses of clothes litter my floor. The material insignificance makes my eyes water.

> *What a collection of icons decorate these otherwise plain, wise walls...statues and paintings beg allegiance from church goers – they distract through beauty and offer instant, aesthetic gratification. They offer no lasting promise. They offer no tangible assistance in*

connecting with God.

I walk over to my desk. I look down on it. Its surface is covered, cluttered. Indiscernible, unusable.

> *A communion altar. It is meant for rituals intended to feed us with substance, with peace, with love. But here...this table is covered with pieces of empty history, mere obstacles to one seeking and receiving the gift of this table.*
>
> *Idols must be banished.*

I kneel down to rest underneath my desk and discover the clutter there too...

I throw myself up.

Abruptly, my breath rapidly increasing, I begin to pace.

1643: The English Civil War. Troops and citizens are encouraged by a Parliamentary ordinance to destroy churches as a sanctioned rebellion against the superstitious and idolatrous act of worshipping mere 'things' in the place of God.

Yes.

I hurl the contents of my desk across the room.

`God must mean more than things; the divine within me, within you, must break free.`

Now.

The more delicate pieces of my shallow history are shattered.

Lord what work was here! What beating down of walls! What pulling down of seats! What wresting out of irons and brass from the windows! What defacing of arms! What demolishing of curious stonework! What tooting and piping upon organ pipes!

Pictures of childish dates are discarded, magazines scatter the floor, and I lose ridiculous notes of gossip – the thorn of every woman's side.

Rid yourself of it.

I start to see the entirety of
my desk,
a possible foundation.

Nice to meet you.

...[W]hat a
...[W]hat a
...[W]hat a

...[W]hat a
hideous triumph
in the market-place before all the country,
when all the mangled organ pipes, vestments, both copes
and surplices, together
with the leaden cross which had newly been sawn down
from the Green-yard pulpit and the service-books and
singing books that could be

carried to the fire

in the public market-place were heaped together...

To burn.

Every discarded, fluttering piece of paper finds her height of flight and descends. Private joy smiles on my face.

I find the SAT study sheets I made with Sage and place them in

in in in

a neat row upon
my desk.

☒ LADIES NIGHT — A PLAN

I have her over to my house to study, next.

Good space.

****

To: Jasper
From: Sage
Date: September 26th

alright so my mom called my dad and she bitched at him, thus he bitches at me..but really the point is she dosen't want me to study anywhere but here...and she doesn't want the SAT study books out of the house..just because she doesn't want them lost..and i realize you won't lose them but they are yelling shit at me so i guess i really need them back, uhm i'm sorry mlaa etc. and right so call me if i don't call you first alright miss? ok..talked to bernadette. slightly confused yet happy...but save that for later. have fun...be happy and so on. -sage

****

September 28th

Lovers_End 8:01 PM

  ? ugh re: your email. tell him to shut the hell up and go yell at a mirror

NorthDaughter 8:02 PM

  cannae do th' miss jasper

Lovers_End 8:03 PM

  humf. *i* will then!! dammit, ok no i won't. HUMF! i am so sorry!! ☹ I'll get the books back asap ok???

NorthDaughter 8:04 PM

  jasper, had an outburst! ::gasp:: mark your calendars everyone!!

NorthDaughter 8:03 PM

    btw me, nellie, daisy and i wanted to know if you wanted to come out with us this weekend

NorthDaughter 8:10 PM

    ::pokepokepokepokepokepoke::

Lovers_End 8:10 PM

    ooo! yes yes, what would you guys like to do? i'd be pretty keen to do somthing eh, (even though we're from such different social groups!) ☺

NorthDaughter 8:11 PM

    true. ladies night out i believe is the theme...ahem, do you have a curfew?

Lovers_End 8:11 PM

    nopes, weeeeell if i'm sick i will. ugh.

NorthDaughter 8:12 PM

    they said something about.....::innocent expression::...getting drinkables too...but what! oh yeah that's the other thing. do you mind having a church buddy? ::lopsided halo::

Lovers_End 8:13 PM

    hehe, nopes, awesome/all good i say.

Lovers_End 8:16 PM

    oh yes and mental note: (as in i'll say this but you don't have to respond unless you feel it is completely necessary) I totally missed you today! lol dammit :P (as a mate...etc blah blah blah) and AHH sheesh, lots of stuff going on. I won't bother you about it all though!

NorthDaughter 8:17 PM

    i am a good non talker type listener. i promise to talk to you about my problems too, ok?

Lovers_End 8:19 PM

ok. ☺ well...right now i'm just sick-and kinda frustrated at things, and...you know how i really liked henry? well i made the MISTAKE of telling Nicole this--as she has the utmost ANNOYING AS ALL HELL habit of GETTING WITH the people that i like (fucking bitch....but i love her.etc etcccc). She got with him at MY house two nights ago...ugh. they aren't doing anything with each other now that Henry knows i like(d) him, which is quite nice of him, and he and i had a good ol' d&m (deep & meaningful conversation) about it so at least we'll be alright mates...☺ it's just kinda...sad.

Anyway, it's all over – just thought you should know! Moving right along! What do you want to now babble about in return? ☺

NorthDaughter 8:21 PM

ok, so we're playing this game are we? fine i'll babble and we can both give advice and our thoughts..sound fair? ok i called bernadette yesternight. she asked me if I want to live with her and tiffany(her new lover person) when i get back. apparently she wants us both etc etc. as in she loves tiff and still loves me too but i am sooo lost as to what to say

Lovers_End 8:22 PM

ahhhhhhhhhhhhhhhhhhhhhhhhhhhhhhhhhhhh!! wtf??

NorthDaughter 8:22 PM

i kinda suspected early on. she has this habit of polygamy speeches but you know...you try to ignore stuff...

Lovers_End 8:27 PM

oh really? that's horrible!

NorthDaughter 8:27 PM

indeed...and my parents tried to get me to go to my shrink again today...haha nice try

NorthDaughter 8:31 PM

dad said, 'why don't you go to your appointment' i said, 'i don't like talking to strangers, i don't like talking to friends even. i just don't want to talk..' he says 'so i guess if you don't talk willingly i'll just have to tie you to a chair and make you..' joking of course. stupid man.

NorthDaughter 8:31 PM

> i miss mis chicas. shit! ::plugs babblement hole:: forget that...just you know...talk or whatever..nothing important. as in no point in continuing..::smiles::

Lovers_End 8:38 PM

> i think you should come with me to my appointment with Dr. Snow sometime

NorthDaughter 8:38 PM

> ok fine, i'll whup some counselor ass

Lovers_End 8:40 PM

> sweet as, i'm sure he'd love to see you challenge him ;) he's awesome miss.

NorthDaughter 8:40 PM

> good then i will! prepare for trouble mistah...(and make it double)

NorthDaughter 8:44 PM

> whatcha doin? ::incessant child like tone of voice::

Lovers_End 8:47 PM

> hehe, cute! ahaha :P hey why don't you like your counselor?

NorthDaughter 8:47 PM

> she is insane. and she won't play with me. and i don't trust her, and she has no good motives, and i only want certain people to deal with me, that's why.

Lovers_End 8:48 PM

> fair enough. sheesh mate, you're on to it. ;)

NorthDaughter 8:48 PM

> i am? huh? what?

Lovers_End 8:49 PM

you're onto it, as in you could pretty much do what ever the hell you
wanted cuz you're brain just works that way

NorthDaughter 8:48 PM

i cannot do whatever i want, i have had this drilled into my head
recently. it's good to be a failure of a daughter, neh?

Lovers_End 8:51 PM

humf, well I've just decided that what I say about you (ie:
compliments) are more important than any other negative statements
people might say to you simply because i am waaaay cooler than they
are ;) so disregard all the things your parents say to you that is simply
not worth listening to.

NorthDaughter 8:57 PM

indeed. sure you are..::hides a smile::

Lovers_End 8:57 PM

i am!! hehe ;)

NorthDaughter 8:50 PM

p.s. i am not 'onto it' i just don't like counselor/psych people to treat
me as their patient

Lovers_End 8:51 PM

lol. hmm...god forbid you ever be....*gasp* haaaappy?

NorthDaughter 8:51 PM

who me? NEVER! ::evil cackle:: i don't need them to fix me.

NorthDaughter 8:52 PM

gasping...is that sarcasm i detect...::voice rising:: look you! i don't! i
just like quality time to play. thus the counselor, but she won't play.

Lovers_End 8:53 PM

lol, suck mate!

NorthDaughter 8:53 PM

suck why? huh? you gonna explain or do i have to use my amazing powers of tickle on you? did i mention them yet? or are we not at that stage or comfort....? ::flexes fingers menacingly::

Lovers_End 8:55 PM

i meant it sucks that she doesn't play (the councilor), and no, we are not at that   stage.

NorthDaughter 8:56 PM

mmmffffff ::blank face:: yeah i miss that too.

Lovers_End 8:56 PM

mmmmmfftt to what?

NorthDaughter 8:58 PM

i miss having a friend that i can have hold me and not feel...'uncomfortable'

Lovers_End 8:59 PM

who used to "hold you"?

NorthDaughter 9:00 PM

rose, rosalyn sometimes

NorthDaughter 8:59 PM

but you know me, im not really the touchy feely type..::attempts to smile::

Lovers_End 9:00 PM

raises eyebrow err? not the touchy feely type? that's not how i remember it.

NorthDaughter 9:00 PM

huh! ok miss....that was special circumstances

Lovers_End 9:01 PM

lol...hmmm, tiredness? hehe *grins behind hand* tee hee heeeee. do you really not have any close mates here?

NorthDaughter 9:02 PM

huh? no oh hell no. i have friends/acquaintances and shag buds. thus ends it. my only family and real friends are mis chicas. it's sad but i don't care. i love them more than anything. eight years can soften a person...neh? ach! no touchy feely stuff!! i don't want to talk about me anymore.

Lovers_End 9:05 PM

i was going to say that you haven't been here or known people long enough. otherwise I'm sure you would have many good friends eh

NorthDaughter 9:06 PM

doesn't matter. i am not trying to find friends... you goin out tonight?

Lovers_End 9:09 PM

I don't think so eh.

NorthDaughter 9:11 PM

my reason for not trying to find friends...i rely on my friends alot, they take care of me, etc. i won't be here long enough to solidify anyone ....but just long enough to want support....and mis chicas are branching out right now, they have each other....they are making new friends...and they don't need me as much as i need them...look hell..grr stop i will not babble!

NorthDaughter 9:14 PM

dad's making eggs and bacon..look at that. true sign of an american family..eggs and bacon at this hour

Lovers_End 9:14 PM

you're so good at babbling though!! ;)   yea, i know what you mean about support--and I do believe you just contradicted your statement of "people don't need others to talk to" cuz they really do huh? ok, well i'll be here for you, as i've said before, for as long as you're here-and when you go back home to Arizona i'll write lots then too, even tho you won't really need a supportive mate from new zealand...

205

NorthDaughter 9:14 PM

    i don't! i don't need support.

    so when do i get to play with da counselor?

Lovers_End 9:17 PM

    you mean play with Dr. Snow? in two weeks time mespinks

NorthDaughter 9:18 PM

    oh really? uhm you sure you want me there....do you have ulterior motives miss..because i don't want to be manipulated..

Lovers_End 9:20 PM

    no no, no ulterior motives.

NorthDaughter 9:23 PM

    hmmm you didn't talk to him about me already, right? ::vaguely concerned:: AHH! you can't warn him!!! you'll ruin my entrance!!! although i don't really want to barge right in you know...like be accosted by nurse attendant thingies and dragged off screaming VIVA LA REPUBLIC!

Lovers_End 9:24 PM

    i won't tell him you're coming, but yes i told him all about you...I told you about talking to him about our drive...but it was a while ago, sorry!! ☹

NorthDaughter 9:24 PM

    DAH! like what. do you even know..'all about me'? why should he care about me..why should i be a topic! daahhhh

Lovers_End 9:25 PM

    cuz you're cue

NorthDaughter 9:25 PM

    ehhmmm not likely. wanna tell me really this time? ::pokepokepokepoke::

Lovers_End 9:26 PM

ok, real answer (hehe): I want you to come because you're as spiritually odd as I am. ☺

NorthDaughter 9:27 PM

oh nelly.... ::backs off:: spirituality is not a shrink topic my dear

Lovers_End 9:27 PM

oh it's alright Dr. Snow is *amazing* he is also a super amazing Christian like my Mom and when I talked to him about everything spiritual between you and I he was amazing about it.

NorthDaughter 9:27 PM

it's a topic that results in strait jackets even

Lovers_End 9:28 PM

hush you. it's ok

NorthDaughter 9:28 PM

no it aint miss!

NorthDaughter 9:29 PM

my shrink thinks i have adjustment disorder. HA!!!

Lovers_End 9:28 PM

well we can go together, I'll go in first and then come out to retrieve you when I'm ready

NorthDaughter 9:32 PM

hehehe retrieve me!! i am not some newspaper to be picked up and slobbered on! ::blinks at THAT mental image:: i gotta run. callin you tomorrow before noon to discuss our impending activities with nellie and daisy, so be up miss. nighty night

Lovers_End 9:33 PM

AHAHAHAHAHAHA *honestly sat here laughing for aaaaaaaaaaages..ahahahahahaha*

yes can't wait. :D

****

Subject: rant

To: Jasper
From: Sage
Date: September 30th

hi. so i am going to rant. you talked about being disappointed in people not following through with what they promise (eg. Nicole and her whole taking over Henry dispite saying she wouldn't...) and here's my response. i never expect people to give to me, thus i am not surprised when they don't but when they do i am. this is a wonderful attitude to adopt it helps to save your opinions from becoming harsh and of course i am never harsh, oh no..::smile:: ehhmmmm lesse..so are you going to answer my questions now yes hmm? ok then....well i want to know (i know this came up already but hell must discuss it until its dead) why do you expect things of others that you do not expect of yourself? this may be a tad bit of projection on my end, because i do it too, but it slightly upsets me that a person with your 'moral standing' would do this perhaps unconsciously. next...oh damn i gotta go eat..well hmmf. ruin my rant. ok then talk later write back and so on and so forth

lots of love and big sloppy kisses ::smirk (got your attention):: -sage

****

****

Subject: (acronym)

To: Jasper
From: Sage
Date: September 30th

p.s. (this is an ACRONYM for post script)

you forgot to take your socks with you.....AND.....

'You just need vodka and honesty..'

(thank you New Radicals)

****

Tick, Tock

⚘ 1:21 AM

October 1st

NorthDaughter 10/1/00 12:07 AM

> hey...right so dad is sleeping downstairs at the moment..and
> well i can't. i am clenching my jaw so tight right now you'd
> think i'm in pain..god i am so scared. i haven't been this afraid
> since i was little...it's like god....damn i keep saying that don't i?
> Jesus though i can't help wishing you were here...i don't want
> to sleep i don't want to close my eyes....i am afraid....

The energy.   -- -- -- Hi, again.

The stretch of her across my face. Eyelashes flutter. I hear her silent plea, the
echo saturates my body. I feel her.

                      You are alone, with her.

and those
drawings.
those.
drawings. on
my wall.

```
       Black ink
strokes TUCK
         away
     aberrant,
        sickly
thoughts all
         lying
      secretly
   underneath
one another,
        hidden
    under less
     offensive
     material.
          They
      vibrate.
```

Peripheral vision – ceases to be.

Eyes detect mere pinpoints of light –attention focuses on invisible, hidden *dunamis*. Obsidian depth. It erupts in earnest and cools to a deep chill; too early it seems for light to beg it's presence inside.

Letters trip over themselves and bloody their knees

NorthDaughter 10/1/00 12:11 AM

oh god...i am just being silly aren't i? just silly. but if you get this before morning could you please call me? i am just a tad upset....don't care about father man because he is asleep...jesus i hate shaking like this...look i'm sorry i should just shut up and get over it..oh god i heard a noise damnit damnit damnit grow up must grow up, it's just my imagination that's all. I should stop reading such things before bed, the book wasn't scary....i loved the thoughts it provoked in me..ok calming now...very good. just leave all the lights on right...i hope i get some sleep tonight but i am beyond scared..i am going insane that's all right...tomorrow i will laugh it off you know..i will just pretend it was nothing..wonderful nothing i have no fear..no fear i saw your keychain you know. right focus on this place...

Ring, ring. Ring, ring.

　　　　1:06am

　　　　　　　　　　　　"Sage?"

　　　　　　　　　　　　"Jasper."

"Are you ok? I just got home from eating out with Melantha. I just read your online messages."

"It's so dark in here."

"Turn the light on."

　　　　　　　　　　　　"I have."

"Sage? You're ok now. Nothing in the...the book, yea, no, the book – nothing in the book can hurt you."

"The *book*?! Books can only push you so far! It's not the fucking book

...oh my god.

It's

looking

at

me."

Turning towards the center of my room, slivers of void shimmer and form the outlines of three figures.

Daemons.

Each stares at me in turn as they pace...and stalk a transparent image of Sage. Their eyes are creamy white orbs with pinpoint pupils – similar to the eyes of my nemesis, the Great White shark.

My stomach clenches and I recoil, buckling.

This all began the night you nearly took your
life.

Silent terror sweeps away my attempts to calm down. In a desperate effort to **hold   her,** I whisper, "You're angel is with you, now. She'll keep you safe."

Instant twist of pain.

Liar.

"*Bitch.* I do not have an angel, and you know it.

DON'T FUCKING LIE
TO ME."

Looking up, I begin to cry.

Their skeletal, muscular forms resemble that of rabid dogs standing six feet tall on their hind legs. Rotting black hide sinks into the apertures of their otherwise long, smooth canine skulls. Rancidity. Their energy closes in around the spiritual echo of

      Sage

   lying

      in a fetal position

  on the floor.

"*SAGE!*"

My knuckles burn, "*Sage!*"

           "Jasper? Please...I don't know how to get rid of them..."

Three wisps of breath.

    The phone fails.

I call her over and over and over again. No answer.

****

Morning.

"Sage?"

"Yea," Her voice is dull, distant.

"Everything alright?"

"I only just fell asleep – the sun finally rose."

"Oh, gosh, hey – I'm sorry for waking you up. I really am. I'll let you sleep. See you in a couple of days for our girlie night out with Nellie and Daisy, yea?"

"Probably - except Daisy's pulled out. Goodnight."

****

It's difficult, when you are possessed. When the
tongue of a leech will actually soothe your skin
instead of break it open,

        upon his lap your blood spills - a
therapeutic method of ridding oneself of untimely
insanity and eventual death...

        but it is all a fiction, my friends, a
delusion.

****

✍ The Woods

Everything reminds me of Sage. Dammit.

Breakfast. Talking. Every time the phone rings. She doesn't call me, or I her.

The night comes when I am *finally* able to go and see her,

you know,

all casual like.

I wear baggy jeans, a black choker, a black hoodie. I throw the hood over my head and stuff my hands into my pockets. Nellie lives just one block away. I ascend up and down the hill that's between us.

A quaint white trellis welcomes visitors. It frames the façade – a white halo that makes Nellie's house inviting in a fairylike, reserved way. Overgrown, beautiful flowers hold conventions in every corner. Colors splash around the front yard as if Jackson Pollack met Georgia O'Keefe and their love children played there, forever playing about her house. A cobblestone path leads the traveler from the busy road to the beautiful kauri door.

Raising my fingers, I ring the doorbell. A *'GONG'* reverberates back. The flower children seem to scamper, hide, and hush behind me.

The huge door opens.

"Jasper! Woo! Hey, Sage! Jasper's here!"

A blur of red finds its way into my nose, ears, and mouth: a feather boa.

Sage trills and giggles.

"Uhh, yea. Hi, guys." I use my hands to bat the feathers out of my face.

Sage's golden eyes.

Nellie's laugh rolls over us as she pulls a feather out of my hair, places it behind her ear and dances.

Not having lost contact with Sage's eyes, I set inside.

****

Nellie's *Room*

candles,

lamps,

incense.

Shadows sculpt *patterns* out of the walls. Every surface is covered.

Sage plunges onto a small cot that had been pulled out from under the bed, and Nellie flops onto her bed's pile of thin blankets. I settle away from them - several feet away - on the floor. Nellie whines and offers a spot next to her.

"Nah thanks, I'm good, eh. Hey, so you two ladies should know that I'm not drinking tonight. I've been super sick lately so I've decided to give drinking a miss."

Nellie whines anew.

I try to ignore her. "Yea, so what do you guys want to do?"

The whining stops and she takes a scandalous breath in, "*Well*, Jasper, are you bisexual yet?"

My eyes widen.

She squeals, "Well, I am!" She throws a twittering glance at Sage.

God.

219

"OH my gosh, Nellie!" I throw a pillow in her face, which makes her explode with giggles. "Considering all the guys I've dated, it seems I'm pretty damn straight, now doesn't it?"

Nellie coos as she falls off her bed and crawls into my lap, "Awwww...Jasper! C'mon now! You should date *me*! It'll be fun!"

Jokes aside, I retreat. She's a cute girl but Fuck No. I am not bisexual.

Sage bats Nellie off with her pillow and begins pretending that *she'd* be the better partner for me. My face mirrors Sage's violet heat.

"No, no, no, Sage, she would *never* want to be with *you*. You're much too butch for her! She'd like someone like *me*, a femme. It'll be **safer** for her, you know? Right, Jasper?" She turns to direct this question at me, her face flush with the affects of what I'm guessing is wine.

I don't answer.

Instead Sage does. "Oh, right, Nellie, like she'd ever be interested in you – someone with *no* experience, *no* direction and *no* future. I think she'd take a butch over *that*."

I freeze.

Nellie doesn't (or chooses not to?) notice Sage's tone. Instead she diplomatically collapses again – this time far away from me.

****

We've decided to walk down to The Gardens. Perfect. It's a beautiful night.

With the transition to the outside, my asthmatic lungs welcome the reprieve from Nellie's musky incense. Sage and Nellie are friends again. As moments build upon one another, they become more and more tipsy, more and more goofy, but less & less safe.

Drinks replace inhibitions...

Simultaneously, they ambush me; they link arms with me on both sides. *I am surrounded!* They begin to flirt with me again – unremittingly. *Damn this is weird.* I decide to play along – if I make a fuss it'll become a bigger issue than it's worth. I let myself smile.

. . .

Hysterically, the three of us snake our way down the super steep, winding path near Nellie's house. It spits its occupants right beside The Gardens, our most   coveted   of   social   spaces. Not a bar, not someone's house, but the woods.

We split up. I put my hand on my heart – *thump, thump. thump, thump.* – Good. I'm still here.

The girls spout outrageous anecdote as we throw our legs over the garden's knee high stonewall. Running off, their arms flail as if shipwrecked at sea, but with a certain rhythmic charm. Rave dancing. The sight would have been ethereal had Nellie had her light sticks.

A picnic table. I sit, deciding that I should just wait for them here. I put my head down on the table and view them sideways. *Hehe, their feverish dancing is even odder from this angle.* I muse about how significantly form and content can change with just a slight alteration in perspective. Closing my eyes, I rest in isolation for a while. The thirty minutes is bliss.

Sitting up, my head spins as the pressure equilibrates in my inner ear.

It is dark.

I hear them laughing nearby. Soon they join me and sit down. My smile soon fades.

Sage's aura is different.

(Is she angry?)

Her usual purple tones have intensified into a deep indigo and her outer edge is shimmering with shafts of pointed white light.

"What's up?" I casually ask. Maybe I'm making things up.

Nellie and I sit and talk quietly about a few topics but we eventually fall silent. It's real – there's something very odd going on with Sage.

Silence creaks, as an old crone's hand does.

I look around and suddenly feel very alone. Desperation seeps along acidic fingers. The trees that were once beautiful seem ominous, distant. They are unable to ease my instinctual

        need to Flee.

        I turn my head to face Sage. I need to be with her or against her.

        Wait and see what she does.

                Ok, then. Do it. I'm ready.

        "Nellie. What do you believe?" Sage, softly.
                The trees turn.

Nellie's lazy eyes trail along after Sage's whisper.

Ah. That's *where this is going.*

Energy b   n
        e   d
               s.

"Wha...?" Nellie asks.

"What Do YOU BELIEVE?"

Existential questions. Nellie - every ache in her body, confronted.

"Who are you?

    "What are you?

"Where are you going?

    "What will you become?"

"How are you going to succeed in life? What do you have going for you?"

Nellie shrugs timidly.

"Ok, I agree with you there. You Have *Nothing.* That's Right. You're lost potential."

1600s courtroom walls. Dirt floors.

What Sage really wants to scream is her **own fear** of
amounting to nothing.
Projection.

"I don't know about 'nothing'...I'll work something out, yea? Just go to different parts of this country, work there a bit, and wander around...y'know..."

"HA! Waste of your time. Going that route will amount to nothing significant.

"So I'm going to ask you again,

"What do you *believe*, Witch?"

The year is 1629.
'How did you cripple that man? And how did you make the local village's
water mill break down, Miss Isobel Young?

"What is your EXCUSE, Nellie, for not being ambitious? For being
so placid, so nonchalant, so lifeless, so *predictable?*"

'Oh, water mills just decay on their own do they? Ha. Nice try Witch. *Your*
reply is grossly 'contrary to the libel', that is, it goes directly against the
charge brought against you. No respectable court will stand for such
rubbish! You are found guilty.'

Miss Nellie's chest and arms are bound, inch by inch.

The knots are tight. She is to be tossed into the lake to see if she
survives the drowning. If she survives, she shall be burnt at the
stake. If she dies then, No, she was not a witch, but her death
shall serve the purpose of shading the villagers eyes and making
them believe that they are being looked after, that the
extraneous devils of their kind are being eradicated, one by one.

Just like Marion Cumlaquoy of Orkeny who was burned alive for making her neighbor's barley crop rot. Crops cannot be allowed to rot.

Or the tailor's wife who was murdered for making her neighbor's children sick. It is scary to have your children fall ill.

Or the witch that succumbed to her ultimate fate after quarrelling with an overzealous drunkard who eventually - in his paroxysms of vomiting - accused her of witchcraft. She promptly lost her life[6].

---

[6] Walker, B. (1983). *The Women's Encyclopedia of Myths and Secrets.*

****

Such actions we take to eradicate the most painful shadows of our own lives. It's a fallacy to think that torturing another will wash away your guilt, your failings, your mother. No amount of another's pain will spare you yours. No amount of yelling in the face of a failure will make your own failings sink unnoticed into obscurity.

****

Nellie is apathetic; her expression, catatonic.

Never   once   did   she   truly   retort,   correct   or   plead   with   Sage.
                                                            She   merely   sat   -
swallowing - sound.

I, too, am quiet throughout the trial and execution.   A
mere observer.

Diffusion of responsibility theory

> diffusion   of   responsibility   n.
> A REDUCED SENSE OF PERSONAL RESPONSIBILITY
> and individual accountability experienced
> in certain circumstances by members of a
> group, often leading to behaviour untypical
> of any of the group members when alone. See
> bystander effect, deindividuation, social
> loafing[7].

The brutal murder of Kitty Genovese in 1964.

I feel saturated and defiled by Sage's destructive energy; each billow of her dark light hovers in my eyes – I don't feel alone, I feel open and bleeding in the presence of the energy generated by one thousand people ~

I am struck dumb: impotent as to how to alleviate the situation. The one time I try to defend Nellie, Sage looks at me through pain-stained eyes, I feel the pressure of another, and I

hush.

---

[7] Coleman, A. (2001). *A Dictionary of Psychology.*

```
**********************************************************************
```

Sage rises, blessedly mute, having completed her undertaking, but no better for it.

Nellie is a ghost, condemned to walk the earth as a shadow. She has been drained, never again to be filled.

```
**********************************************************************
```

In linguistics, a **phatic** expression is one whose only function is to perform a social task, as opposed to conveying information[8].

The term was coined by anthropologist Bronisław Malinowski in the early 1900s.

October 2nd

NorthDaughter 3:39 PM

::yawns::

Lovers_End 3:40 PM

ditto

NorthDaughter 3:40 PM

::scratches head:: how is the you?

Lovers_End 3:44 PM

gooooood. ......so did you have a good night last night?

Lovers_End 3:51 PM

it was very interesting watching you interrogate Nellie.

It reminded me how you interrogate me. The main difference was she enjoyed it less. I've always appreciated blunt honesty ever since being bullied in intermediate school with gossip and hidden secrets. Now I'm just happy if you say it to my face. Nellie doesn't have the same past as me though.

---

[8] Malinowski, B. (1923) "The Problem of Meaning in Primitive Languages", in: Charles K. Ogden / Ian A. Richards (eds.), *The Meaning of Meaning*, 146-152, London: Routledge

NorthDaughter 3:52 PM

    interesting was it? well i am glad i amuse you

Lovers_End 3:52 PM

    amuse isn't the word.

NorthDaughter 3:53 PM

    oh wonderful, ok i'm glad i disturb you?

    i assume i don't but hell all things change...

    just look at nellie...

Lovers_End 3:53 PM

    I'm writing you an email about it. I'll send it after

NorthDaughter 3:54 PM

    ok. im talkin to rose surprise surprise. god i miss her

Lovers_End 4:01 PM

    why is it so hard to let go?

NorthDaughter 4:02 PM

    i don't know, you tell me?

Lovers_End 4:03 PM

    holding onto the person makes the memories more real.

NorthDaughter 4:04 PM

i   love   this   song

'Der Herrgott nimmt

der Hergott gibt

doch gibt er nur dem

den er auch liebt

bestrafe mich'

'the lord does give

the lord does take

does he give love

to those he forsakes?

punish me'

Lovers_End 4:06 PM

"does he give love to those he forsakes?" interesting line...

Lovers_End 4:06 PM

i think that people just need to step back from the bible and believe
that God is all loving. I mean, why be any other way? there are sooo
many different people going to hell, i mean - if someone wants to get
all crazy about the different condemning passages. I think we should
read Genesis, Romans, Revelations, and there was another
one...anyway

231

Lovers_End 4:09 PM

> so do you actually think that it is a good idea for Nellie to face up to what she is, and will be?

NorthDaughter 4:10 PM

> she will someday

Lovers_End 4:10 PM

> hmm, and what a sad day that will be.

NorthDaughter 4:12 PM

> i don't want to focus on it. i don't care about her

Lovers_End 4:12 PM

> well, shit. well put

Lovers_End 4:13 PM

> oh yea, and when you get the chance-write down a list of books i should read ok?...sorry egocentric, but fuck it

NorthDaughter 4:13 PM

> i might then

Lovers_End 4:18 PM

> you know how a while ago you asked if we were at the point where we could just lie around as mates n' that and it not be weird?

NorthDaughter 4:18 PM

> i do

Lovers_End 4:19 PM

> yes well, i do believe that i've gotten to that point with you.

NorthDaughter 4:19 PM

    why do you think so?

Lovers_End 4:19 PM

    hmm. I've decided I can trust you "physically"<--lol.

I just can't help but be attracted to your mystery...
the way you interrogated Nellie horrifies & drives me.
What an extreme individual, you are.

I like being tested...
privately.
...touching could start something interesting.
a way to innocently explore..

NorthDaughter 4:20 PM

    why ever for? you shouldn't, for what reason i mean

Lovers_End 4:20 PM

    i shouldn't? lol.

    i mean ...well...ok yea threw me off again.

    Let's come back to this topic later.

NorthDaughter 10/2/00 4:21 PM

    ok.

NorthDaughter 4:22 PM

why don't you help me?

Lovers_End 4:22 PM

because you don't ask for it

NorthDaughter 4:22 PM

you think that

Lovers_End 4:23 PM

well. are you asking for me to help you then

NorthDaughter 4:23 PM

NOT PHYSICALLY

Lovers_End 4:23 PM

whoa. holy shit, ok so that came out of nowhere

NorthDaughter 4:24 PM

did it? oh you really think that?

Lovers_End 4:24 PM

ok...so no, figure of speech, ie: i wasn't expecting it. anyway

NorthDaughter 4:25 PM

'everything you are falls from the sky like a star'

Lovers_End 4:26 PM

yes so you don't need anything do you Sage? nothing at all, you don't need friends, you don't need love, you don't need companionship, you don't need knowledge, or family, you don't need cleansing...you are strong in your weakness. is that right? what is your cell made out of?

NorthDaughter 4:29 PM

you won't teach me anything i don't already know..or maybe i just won't listen

Lovers_End 4:30 PM

there you go, at least you admit to it

NorthDaughter 4:30 PM

fuck you

NorthDaughter 4:30 PM

it was sarcasm i think..who made you miss superior i don't need your praise

Lovers_End 4:31 PM

right ho, well i'll see you later then.

NorthDaughter 4:31 PM

i don't need anyone's praise or help thanks...i was just pointing out a lack of motivation on your part, oh forget it. later

Lovers_End 4:31 PM

whatever

NorthDaughter 4:32 PM

yeah

"Komm mir langsam

    leg du mir die Kettan an

    und zieh den Knoten fest

    damit ich lachen kann

    Komm mach den Kaufig auf

    und ich bin sternenreich'

'Hurt me slowly

    put me in chains

    and fasten the knot

    so i can laugh

    open the cage

    bring me to the realm of stars

NorthDaughter 11:10 PM

    forget i said anything

Lovers_End 11:27 PM

    backing out of it now eh? EH? lol, nah that's cool. ok well i'll just be online...and reading (?!?!?!) so if you come on say helloooooo there ok?

    I went ahead and sent you your email (I wrote it before so it's a lot cheerier than this online conversation would suggest it should be). *sighs* this is LAME. I'm sorry that we've been fighting so much lately, but yea it hasn't been too bad right?

✍ FFFF ... (friends, foes, friends, foes...)

October 2nd

NorthDaughter 9:57 AM

> fight who me? never...

NorthDaughter 11:18 AM

> 'you grew up way too fast, and now there's nothing to believe, the reruns all become our history..'

****

Subject: Nellie

To: Sage
From: Jasper
Date: October 2nd

Hey miss prissy (hehe), how are you? Soooooo as you might have guessed I have some *dum de dum duaaaauuuum!* questions! As always, it seems! Ok, list style today:

1. I just have to say fairly honestly that your interrogation of nellie last night really threw me for a loop. I was intrigued by your bluntness and interrogation style (I think everyone needs to be confronted with the kinds of questions you asked her because it helps you realize the important things in life and where your greatest weaknesses are) but it just came out of nowhere, you know? But then I think, "Surely it didn't *really* come out of nowhere, surely you thought it through and there was a reason for it all?" So was it all nessecary miss priss? If so, why?
2. Why did you say that it'd be better to give up on Nellie altogether? Seems harsh.. :-s Don't we all deserve compassion?
3. Are we still fighting? ☹ I don't want to fight with you!!
4. If we're not fighting (fingers crossed!), do you still want to hang out with me outside of studying? I ask because well, uhh, ah! I don't know *(Jasper! Stop being so insecure.)* I just wanted to check. I can't read you sometimes - sometimes i worry that you don't want to be friends.

5. Nicole, Evette and Melantha have all mentioned to me recently that they miss me and they are a tad upset that I haven't been going out with them as much. It doesn't bother me really, just thought I'd mention it.

6. oooooo it is sooooo neat that we have so much fun together (when we're not fighting) I love being friends with you *gasps as she calls Sage a *friend* – oooo* ;) hehehee yay for last Sunday together! aaaaahahaaa I laughed SO HARD. oh my gosh. you are sooooooo funny. I love it. ☺

thinks for a moment it *is* odd how we ended up here, writing all the time and seeing a lot of each other. It really will go down in history as one of the weirdest moments in my life when you first asked to stay the night, totally out of the blue.

goose. oh and my beautiful golden kitty Platypus says "hiya toots". ;)

jasper

****

Subject: Re: Nellie

To: Jasper
From: Sage
Date: October 2nd

first of all 'i am not prissy!'

hmmm let's just say sometimes i give up on people because i KNOW they won't change until they realize what they've done to themselves (or others) or whomever, and there is nothing i can do to help them, and it pisses me off.. then again i don't care about people all that much anyway so why should i bother about their ultimate downfalls? i guess with nellie i am glad she is where she is. at least she can pretend and be blind to any sort of reckoning that may happen (soon, later, never) and i miss that: like i said i would love to be where she is again just for the sheer lack of responsibility. but oh well. no reason to bother with people who won't listen(and yes i know-'hypocrite' is carved on my forehead) and no reason to listen when you won't/can't accept it.

you seem to be worried that you and i are fighting. maybe it's just my perspective but i guess one rant isn't a fight. besides fights are just so petty eh? so you think i just want you for study? is that it? hmm ok then well i am glad we spent so many hours sunday night 'studying' because it's good to get all that work done...and wow it's good that i never talk to you about anything except vocab words...and damn look at that, hell obviously i can't stand you so i clear my schedule all for nothing is that it? (can you feel the sarcasm yet?)

::bows:: thank you

well my dear, 'friends' is such a strong word. truthfully i would prefer to not have any ties here, that makes it all easier later. not to mention one can survive without friends. but then the dichotomy that is me takes over and says: yes i want to be your friend... and then i beat it down with a stick ::beats inner self into submission:: the fish(bones) that I drew on my arm are falling to pieces..::sigh:: aint that life?

tangentially...do the drug comments have many purposes? i get the feeling that you are informing me of my future or perhaps warning me except that i won't be warned, and i won't heed advice (so similar to miss nellie is it not?) but that is because it is my spiral, and if i want to destroy myself then i shall. i have no problems being a slave.

so if your girls' comments about missing you don't bother you then why are you mentioning it? because you think i should or don't already know? i talked to morgan[9] last night, she just mentioned the same, but i told her that if she was studying for the university entrance here it would take up a lot of her time too.

yes i was thinking about our first sleepover too. it's odd, but i don't make friends unless there are dubious circumstances, or we end up unconscious together at some rave somewhere. you know i hated rose before i knew her. we were arch enemies for like a month...then we were best friends.. then i hated rosalyn because she was taking my rose away from me..but guess what friends again...rose i really hated because she was 'taking over' bernadette's life (or so i exaggerated) you know bernadette is the only person whom i have not hated first then loved later...i just loved her. but it's odd..my very first best friend, we were so close. then i moved...then she started hanging with all the druggies and gang members, and i became a social outcast for the longest time..and the next time i saw her...i was more friends with her mother than her. and she forgot me. but rose and rosalyn and bernadette are as close to me as is possible, bernadette maybe a tad closer, maybe not. do you ever go through life thinking one thing, and then as you look back you realize that it was all just a facade? yes, well it dosen't bother me that i amuse you, it bothers me that that is all i am there for. i love to make people laugh, but i don't want to be the group jester.

---

[9] Morgan

Morgan's the youngest of all the girls in our grade. She has four siblings and is the second youngest. She is often put to work looking after the baby. I stayed the night with her during our first semester at high school, and we had a great eight hour conversation. Later we had this awkward conversation where she wanted me to be her 'best friend', but I couldn't really be because I was focused on two other girls...silly high school stuff. It spun downhill from there. Yes, we still have these intensely close moments, and I do value her, but she's an insatiable gossip. Nothing I tell her remains quiet for very long – it totally sucks!

Let's see, what else. It's strange how little she seems interested in boys...although maybe it makes sense: I think she's jealous of me sometimes...I seem to date a lot more than her (actually, she hasn't really dated at all yet), and for some reason all the guys she likes end up liking me or Nicole. But then again I wonder if she's just asexual or something – or maybe she's a closet lesbian...?

240

::secretly types giving a certain feline a meaningful look::

(6807)

ahem anyway right so i've just babbled...know this: i am considering deleting it all just because i am like that. father is gone for the day (yay!) and i am going to lounge around online for a bit.

right.

sage was here->.

'you scream in silence but i can hear you..'

p.s. are we going to study today?

****

Subject: and whiskers on kittens

To: Sage
From: Jasper
Date: October 2nd

hmm...hey there missy priss. ☺ thank you for your email...wow, lots to respond to! wooo! fun!!! :D

we need a code for responding! since there are so many topics. i've thought about it and i think this will work:

>> lalaa sage's words, yea yea, what what ☺

then I'll respond normally. rite ho--forward we charge!

Your entire first paragraph floored me...

It amazes me that nellie didn't flick you off and tell you to go to hell. I mean i'd never want to tell someone to go to hell...but sheesh, you really scrutinized her. I see what you mean about it being annoying as all get out to watch someone waste their lives...just maybe a slightly different approach would work better next time. :P however, even as I write this out i remember yelling at steve to change, just screaming at him to give up the drugs, the grand theft auto, the sluttiness...over and over. it didn't work, but it was at least somewhat therapeutic.

i wanted to tell you something. i was pretty quiet during your interrogation of nellie (you might remember..) and i think i was because a) it was so shocking to watch you change so rapidly into such an intense person..and b) i was watching her aura with great fascination. she changed, very notably, as soon as (i guess) she realized what you had launched into doing. the colors of her aura retreated into the folds of her skirts and she became someone you didn't have access to. she seemed simply detached but spiritually, it seemed she had fundamentally disappeared.

ok, enough of this topic...i'll leave it be.

>> well my dear 'friends' is such a strong word.

this is a fair enough statement to make...but would you mind terribly if i call you my friend? ☺ we've dabbled a bit with it already (some days you're better than others! hehe) because I already consider you mine and i'm letting everyone know how awesome you are, and if you were to just leave me hangin' by denying mah friendship it'd look a bit wrong now wouldn't it? hehe ahaha...yessss okkkkkk we're mates alright?

when the time comes for you to leave...i hope by then we'll be able to say that we had a very rad as and productive relationship...ohhhhhh!!!!!!! missssssss!!!!!!! ☹ALRIGHT, fuck it-i'm no good at departures, so I'm not gonna think about it. anyway. you're never leaving alright? (shush you, don't correct me; leave me & my candyland dream alone :P hehe) Also, yea people can live without mates, but do you really want to?

>> do the drug comments have many purposes?

nah i wasn't totally aware of myself aiming them at you-i don't really think you have a huge problem with drugs, i mean you shouldn't do them, true as. And smoking (cigarettes)? well yes it is your life-and do what you must.

I'm lying, but because I 'have' to, to avoid encroaching on your personal space. Yay for me for being such a 'great friend'. Ugh! In reality, I hate drugs. **Hate, hate, hate.** They've fucked up tons of my friends and continue to make them into dorks to this day. Lack of motivation, jail time, stupid discussions touted as 'enlightened'. I don't want to see the brilliance of you, Sage, turn into a ghastly shade of unproductive, lumpy gray.

And cigarettes! Ugh! Disgusting. It's so hard for me to understand smokers. Cancer is NOT fun. I watched my Mother's very (very) best friend die horribly after years of excruciatingly painful lung cancer. The cancer got so big that it bulged out from underneath her neck and side. I was eight when she died. Mother still cries about it. Why people are so selfish is beyond me.

I know I can't control anyone – I don't want to. Too much responsibility (ah, Steve. dammit, why do women love males like this?), no matter how much I love them. You just have to give other people all the information you have and then let them live their lives. It sucks.

>> i have no problems being a slave.

this is one of the most powerful statements that i have read in a long time-but I have no idea why...do you?

```
      The idea of
    being a slave
       terrifies &
      thrills me.

    I agree more
with Richard von
   Krafft-Ebing's
    psychological
   classification
          of
   sadomasochism.

    I think of the
  concept entirely
      in terms of
        control.

  I reject that it
      is about
       cruelty.

    And yes, many
   individuals are
  dichotomous and
  seek out moments
     of power and
   powerlessness.

    It teaches us
        about
         Our
    boundaries...
```

>> so if your girls' comments about missing you don't bother
you then why are you mentioning it?

oh yea, so i'm getting used to all the curiosity surrounding our relationship, lol.
i hope it's not bothering you? lol. hmm, it's weird-it seems like people are
always up in my face about my relationships.

Now you wrote about your chicas, bernadette, rose and rosalyn, and well to be
honest (best way to be) i am not sure what to say. i think that you and
bernadette sound like you really have something special...it's annoying that she
is so far away!! ahhhh, oh bother. Right ho, i won't comment anymore about
her cuz: a) as you said, i am ignorant on how to deal with long-distance
relationships, and b) i'd end up being just plain protective of you. humf.

>> do you ever go through life...and as you look back you realize
that it was all just a facade?

yes. that's why i love my diaries. if i ever look over them, i see the progression
of growth all through them in myself. it's awesome eh. so whatever you write
now will be totally facinating later, whilst being theraputic (sp?) and nice to
write in now. it's a win/win situation - journals are. but yea still...annoying
how you know that your mind isn't completely mature or anything so you
might write stuff that is just totally fucking stupid...and you weren't aware of its
patheticness at the time...and everything. ahhhhh, ok it's nice to try and find
the best in everything i say. annoying as it might be.

>> i don't want to be the group jester.

Ok, so i think i miscommunicated something, cuz i didn't mean that you were
only good to laugh at. As i said lots last night-you are the most fascinating
teenager that i know at the moment, perhaps ever. Melantha is fuckin'
awesome too...hmm i wonder what it'd be like to get the three of us in a room
together? She's just so busy with her CD store job. But yea, both of you have
this intense fighting streak, like neither of you will put up with shit if you
believe in something. But then again, you are both good listeners...anyway. lol.
hmm, the point is you're awesome because of a great many things, not just your
crazy ability to make people laugh and relax by having a genuinely good time.
For example (ooo! are you ready for some PRAISE!? hehe)...

-you challenge people on their basic life assumptions, thereby helping people *think* – giving them the opportunity to be *more* than just be empty shells responding to their society in a blind stupor

*The [wo]man of madness communicates with society only by the intermediary of an equally abstract reason which is: order, physical and moral constraint, the anonymous pressure of the group and the requirements of **conformity**.*

- *Foucault (1972).* Madness and Civilization.

-you are open to everything while still being grounded in doing and thinking the way that makes you most comfortable which makes conversations productive, interesting and entertaining

-you're hilarious

-you're a wonderful listener, i feel like i could tell you that i was an evil alien that loves to torture buttons and sewing kits (because they're alive, alive!), and you wouldn't ostracize (learned this word when I read *Catcher in the Rye*) me. it's rare this feeling...i thank you.

-you're honest about most things...i am assuming about things that matter2u. ☺

yes so there you go. hmm. i'm in a truthful complementary mood at the moment if you hadn't noticed...tee hee ☺ i actually love building people up and holding up a positive mirror by which they can see their truly radiant selves.

lastly, i'd love it if you would write to me about your concept of spirituality. we've touched on it from time to time, but never really in depth since that first (insane) suicidal night when i told you all about me. what do *you think* (feel, know)? ...and you know? i'm glad we didn't kill ourselves that night. i would have missed the many other levels of craziness that we're now so involved in. ☺

leaves her computer for a moment...

platypus the kitty stealthily sneaks upon the keyboard while jasper is gone and types '12123968'...jumps down...and escapes a deadly attempt of murder...

signing off,

jasper!

I WISH I COULD RUN AWAY JUST LIKE THAT SENTENCE.

> "If we would build on a
> sure foundation in friendship,
> we must love friends for their sake
> rather than for our own."
> Charlotte Bronte

****

Subject: shit

To: Sage
From: Jasper
Date: October 3rd

dammit fuck, i love my friends so so much, but it's like wow – they finally came out and reiterated how they were missing me and thought that I was kinda spending too much time with you...and the horrible thing is that I was actually thinking that I hadn't been spending ENOUGH time with you and thought that perhaps I could get away with spending a little more time with you and maybe they wouldn't notice but now, not able to...dammit my sense of obligation to them is preventing me from what I want to do...AHHH this annoying umbilical chord...seems I've been born into a new type of hell knowing you, but the old chord doesn't seem to want to fall off...oh wow ok I've gone into a different frame of mind than I'm used to.

sorry – run on sentence.

wish I could run away just like that sentence.

Jasper.

****

October 3rd

Lovers_End 11:27 PM

> oh and i've been meaning to ask, do you really not like praise? like, really really?

Subject: Re: shit

To: Jasper
From: Sage
Date: October 3rd

i guess really you have to understand that no one is trying to prevent you, you just realize your commitments really...hmm that came out obtuse aye..ok scratch that we shall start again... thank you for giving me de musak ach! me=too happy-scary-...::yawns:: ok now i am making no sense. right so i realize you are being melodramatic about your friends. and really i know how you feel, but i try never ever to show what i really feel on topics, because i don't want to influence the decision, i don't want to seem...i dunno..'too excited' over things so i just sit patiently. and if things turn out badly well then i deal with it alone away from people. thus them not having to deal with my feelings if they happen to be upsetting. ok the praise question...i guess there is a difference between not liking praise, and never ever ...oh wait..that is me..sorry teehee well i guess my dichotomy(remember this word?) does require praise to keep going...but thus we stiffle neh? anyway...moving on.

you seemed to retreat into your shell today when i said that i thought i knew what you were thinking... perhaps it would be wiser for me to say(in the future if this comes up again) 'no i don't know what you are thinking' thus making life easier? do we need another hassle? but i figure i won't bother your thoughts..as you so adamantly claim..'my thought my thought!!' so i won't go there ok then? right oooo so thus i respond to basically everything we've discussed recently and here's my comment for the day:

```
                                  when you heard me
     say i knew what you were thinking, were you hoping that
                          i did?
```

-sage was here->.

"when you heard me say i knew what you were thinking, were you hoping that i did?"

. . .

God No, Sage...I can't have you knowing what I think of you, how my thoughts and feelings ripple and swirl every day, how my cheeks flush when you look at me. You impress me in ways I can't even describe in some dumb poem. Every day at school we all walk and talk amongst ourselves...&

I try to ignore my aches for you –

I AM IN CONSTANT FLUX.

I'm trying so hard to deny this... I looked at you, today, God...today...your skin as fiery milk, mirroring our memories, hinting at our potential.

You said you thought you knew what I was thinking. FUCK. It's not safe for you to know...to know that this idea is starting to saturate my mind, this thought...this droplet of truth -

****

October 4th

Lovers_End 12:06 AM

ok so this really sucks, i just yelled at mom cuz i didn't want to be here-
and i wanted to stay there tonight, ok fuck this shit, night. sorry to
bother you.

NorthDaughter 10:57 AM

hey miss, don't worry about it. there will be other times...maybe
NEVER ::laughs:: sorry j/k but don't get huffy. besides my room is a
mess.

Lovers_End 11:04 AM

huffy? HUFFY? aaha - make me sound like a troll or something

NorthDaughter 11:06 AM

are you? ::holds up a mirror::

Lovers_End 11:07 AM

hehe :D yay! trust you to come up with some smashing response to
ANYTHING, yay ☺ *grin* woo, getting in a better mood

NorthDaughter 11:07 AM

wonderful

Lovers_End 11:08 AM

☺

Lovers_End 3:37 PM

lol damn you

NorthDaughter 3:38 PM

>to hell?

Lovers_End 3:38 PM

>if you are so intent on going--then i ain't gonna stop ya

NorthDaughter 3:39 PM

>good. maybe i'll shake some shit up down there

Lovers_End 3:44 PM

>perhaps. or you might just rot and become nothingness...but either way

NorthDaughter 3:44 PM

>exactly slave to karma

Lovers_End 3:55 PM

>slave my ass, you are far too apt at manipulation my dear

NorthDaughter 3:55 PM

>who me? never....

NorthDaughter 4:03 PM

>bite me biotch teehee

Lovers_End 4:05 PM

>nopes, i don't go for VIOLENCE lmfao!

NorthDaughter 4:05 PM

>teehee poor you, missin out, it can be fun to tie someone...ack!..::smirk::

Lovers_End 4:06 PM

>   missin out? hmm, on nothing good.

NorthDaughter 4:07 PM

>   thanks for the support!!

Lovers_End 4:07 PM

>   ...ok so what am i missing?

NorthDaughter 4:08 PM

>   hehehe ::innocent:: no comment

Lovers_End 4:09 PM

>   hmmmm, yes well there you go

NorthDaughter 4:09 PM

>   hmmf i am not a graphic person miss

Lovers_End 4:10 PM

>   at least not outloud...*smirks*

NorthDaughter 4:11 PM

>   ACH! ::bright red::

Lovers_End 4:12 PM

>   hehehe, yes!! exxxcellent...*raises eyebrow in satisfaction*

NorthDaughter 4:13 PM

>   mmmf look you i am not here for your teasing enjoyment

Lovers_End 4:14 PM

>   who's teasin?

NorthDaughter 4:15 PM

>   ::blinks::

October 4th continued

NorthDaughter 7:29 PM

whoohoo i have found an answer

Lovers_End 7:30 PM

answer? err?

NorthDaughter 7:30 PM

jasper, look at me, fuck i really do believe in something shit...i can't believe i have faith again..oh my god.. like i said, read my latest email, my discussion with god

Lovers_End 7:31 PM

exxxxxxcellent

NorthDaughter 7:31 PM

jesus mary and joseph. this is so weird. what is today? too bad i refuse to write in journals other wise..hell must mark calendar. so im expecting a reply from you so i will check my inbox later okies? write back damnit

Subject: Re: and whiskers on kittens

To: Jasper
From: Sage
Date: October 4th

no soy una chiquita, soy grande (i am not a little girl i'm fat)

well, i guess you could mistake all of what i've thus far said about nellie as dismissal, because it is, but not to the degree you believe. i do care about nellie, but i know that she won't see until she is far gone, just what exactly was happening inside. i can't change her, and i won't try. but yes i suppose it would be hard for you to understand that because you feel so much, even with people you don't know. (dispute this if you want but it's true.)

ah. well how can one disbelieve in the spirit realm? no, i always believe in it, i just try to reason with myself sometimes, and perhaps that is the greatest delusion of all. now this is one thing i wanted to discuss, have patience with me. i believe that the devil, lucifer, satan, whatever...i believe that he is neither evil nor good, the same with god. my belief is that god stands for order and loyalty to a cause, and a system. order in chaos even. but i believe that the devil stands for loyalty to self, freedom of decision, self government, and opinion, freedom of belief perhaps. look at everything the devil 'said' or 'did' or 'caused to happen'..it revolves around doing what you want, for the sake of enjoyment, or because it feels right, or because it is YOU not god who makes your decisions. of course this puts god into a less revered light, which he shouldn't be, loyalty to a cause can be the one thing that makes your life worthwhile, and order is necessary at times (if not at all times), if you don't have a reason to live, then why would you? of course is living for yourself all that bad? for instance, if there was a war and new zealand was being attacked and you were called to war, would you defend your country, or would you (if you had the choice) escape to neutral territory with you family etc.? god in this case would represent the decision to defend your country. and the devil would represent the decision to escape to freedom and safety. thus serving yourself, not the order. you see i could never choose between god and the devil because i believe in my freedom and my life comes before everything (except those i love, but is that any different?) BUT i believe without a purpose, without guidance we have no reason to exist, we are not anything, we are pointless. this is why god is necessary, as well as the devil. i won't choose sides, there needs to be a balance don't you agree? of course i am insane so nothing i say makes any difference. by the way, i talked with god a long time ago; i told him that as soon as he told me why, i would believe. i'm afraid i may have an answer and it is scary.

i guess that yes, i confront people sometimes, but the only reason for that is because i believe they will listen and someday it will seep in and they will remember, maybe not who or where, but why, and what and how it affects them, and they start to realize their purpose. this is all speculation of course, as i have yet to figure out my purpose, or perhaps am ignoring it, but i can still believe can't i?

it's good that i make you laugh, if i had a choice though, i'd rather make you think..well, i guess all things must be balanced right? ::crooked grin:: it's true you know, the quote 'aint it sad to know that life is more than who we are...' he[10] must be god's advocate. do you think it's true? or is the purpose merely to discover ourselves in truth, perhaps we aren't even separate beings, beyond our physicalness maybe we are one body that has been shattered by the balance, and made separate, perhaps that's what we will find, we are all one, we are a single being. would that surprise you? all of our 'superficial' inhibitions, all of our assumptions based on smoke. you could never say anything about anyone else, except as 'I'. does that scare you? i am afraid to lose my individuality, that is the purpose of the devil methinks, to separate us into people rather than the 'masses'. god unites, the devil individualizes.

then there is that other concept i have to discuss because it has been floating around in my conscious for a while. the devil, by his definition(although how we can define such a being is beyond me), cannot create. he cannot 'make' anything. everything that is everything is 'made' by god. it all stems from him. so why do we blame things on the devil? why (even if we MUST make the devil into 'evil' and corruption incarnate) why must we say on one hand that god created everything, god is The Creator, why do then suddenly turn and curse the devil for tempting us, or trying to turn us to 'evil' acts...when it is obvious that god himself created temptation, and what is wrong with the devil using god's tools to explain to us, to show us more than one version of life? and if it is evil, then why would god create temptation, and evil at all? god is all powerful right? yet his creations are flawed? perhaps we aren't. i am starting to realize

---

[10] Quote by John Rzeznik of the band the Goo Goo Dolls.

that perhaps the devil and god are nothing other than the same being. that just as we are not only one thing, but many, so is god/devil. and thus together all of us are one being, we are the devil, we are god, we are all one. we think differently may be one argument, yes, but if god and the devil were one being then obviously it means one being does not have to be unified, that one being does not have to be made up of a single thought or self. thus i am you and you are me, and preposterous as it may seem, i am the devil, i am god, you are the devil, you are god. steve is the devil steve is god. i am steve you are steve, steve is the both of us, and so on. just as an example. do you understand what i am saying? we are so caught up in believing that god and the devil are opposites and one is one thing and the other is another, we don't see that it would make more sense for it to all be one thing entire. for us to be all one thing entire. besides what are we but physical matter? we are more, we have to be. but can we be separate? can we? or perhaps, can we be one?

-sage

****

whiskers on kittens

let's recap.

how can one disbelieve in the spirit realm?

    reason → a delusion ?

    God: Satan
    me: you: us: one

    Satan: Evil :: God: evil
    Satan: good :: God: Good

    God: order; loyalty to a cause; loyalty to a system

    God: order in chaos

    Satan: hedonism; loyalty to self; freedom of decision; self government

    Satan: freedom of belief ?

    our physical nature: shattered by balance: made separate

    superficial inhibitions: prevent contact with others
    superiority: illusion

you is to I as I is to you

      individuality lost, solidarity gained?

  individual ≠ masses

God: creation :: devil: craftsman

    God is all powerful right? yet his
    creations   are   flawed?
    perhaps we aren't.

Satan: God: me: you: them: together: unite

thought: fracture

belief: union

one being does not have to be made up of a single
thought or self.

              are we s   ep   a   rate?

or are we (one?)

* * *

"...why do [we] then suddenly turn and curse the devil for tempting us, or trying to turn us to 'evil' acts...when it is obvious that god himself created temptation, and what is wrong with the devil using god's tools to explain to us, to show us more than one version of life?"

Job   1:8   –   12,   21

The LORD said to Satan, "Have you considered My servant Job? For there is no one like him on the earth, a blameless and upright man, fearing God and turning away from evil."

Then Satan answered the LORD, "Does Job fear God for nothing? Have You not made a hedge about him and his house and all that he has, on every side? You have blessed the work of his hands, and his possessions have increased in the land. But put forth Your hand now and touch all that he has; he will surely curse You to Your face."

Then the LORD said to Satan, "Behold, all that he has is in your power, only do not put forth your hand on him." So Satan departed from the presence of the LORD.

[After Satan tests him...]

21 He said, "Naked I came from my mother's womb, And naked I shall return there. The LORD gave and the LORD has taken away. Blessed be the name of the LORD."

* * *

Lovers_End 7:36 PM

> yups i shall reply missy – i just left a msg on your answering machine sayin' that i would write back (maybe not tonight but asap!!)...have a nice night i say!! :D

259

NorthDaughter 7:37 PM

ok later then

Lovers_End 7:37 PM

lol, i'll be out till like 1am with the girls (we're going to this thing down on Pond street! apparently it's really trance music etc., which isn't TOTALLY my thing...but I'll love dancing with the girls!! :D hehe yay!)....but you could come online around 2 just to say hey... ;)

NorthDaughter 7:37 PM

hahaha nice try

Dear Reader,

While Sage was scripting out the above theologically explorative email entitled 'Re: Whiskers on Kittens',

I was about to have my

one,

my only(?),

one-night-stand.

sighs

Ce la vie?

Yep, anyway, I am just that classy.

☑ A One Night Stand (plus a game of pool)

Dark room photography is pretty damn cool, you know?

When a negative develops into a photograph, everything is in the reverse. Relatedly, when you start looking at yourself and discovering who you are, you may try hiding in the dark room. You pretend that you are the negative, especially if you fear development. Photographs just seem too permanent.

I personally rejected exposure...for years.

What path are you taking?

Now that I'm older, I know that there is often a stage of denial among closeted lesbian and bisexual women. Apparently, rather than be a woman who loves another woman (that would be way too simple. God do we love drama) we *react* by going out and sleeping with the next reasonable - if that! - male that shows us any attention at all.

***

Like a developing photograph...

a young woman,
who finds herself falling in love with another
woman,

dodges and burns,

& focuses on the black and white precursor to her
fully formed image

rather than allow what is real to exist.

***

AHHHHHHHHHHHHHH!

AHHHHHHHHHHHHHH. Bloody hell, things are just crazy. We do this; we do that – all to PROVE that we are NOT who we ARE!

Fucking Ridiculous!

If we're not who we are, who will be?!

Dodging light, numbing ourselves to the holes in our eyes – façade

"I AM Heterosexual, NOT Homosexual."

"I Like Males." "I Can Make Boys Happy, I Can Make Them Cum…This *Must* Mean That I Only Like Males."

Huh?

I followed this river of falsehoods, manifesting a true stereotype. At the time I didn't know about the stereotype – only of the sledgehammer-of-havoc inflicting merry little blows over and over on my internal identity clock. *Slam! Slam! Slam!*

I was feeling divided, you know, about the emotions cascading through my head. Every conversation with Sage was another compelling reason for me to love her. Just let go & love her. *Damn woman.* I felt irritated – how dare *feelings* take over, like impassioned activists? Like the PETA reps who rushed Calvin Klein's New York office in an effort to convince him that **fur is NOT OK**, my emotions were rushing in unannounced and fervently throwing faux blood all over the walls of my mind.

263

This tactic, along with the refusal to leave until a decision was reached,
inspired Calvin to cut fur out of his line for good.

Yes, they are controversial.
There will always be someone, somewhere,
who takes issue with you.
Move (on).
Controversy is healthy.

If only I had been an activist when I was 16 and falling in love with Sage.
I shouldn't have let my emotions have all the fun.
If I'd been this strong I would have catapulted my principles at the top of my
lungs by **SCREAMING**,

"FUCK YOU, SOCIETY[11]!
AND YOUR ANTIQUATED
IDEAS AND RATIONALE!
I LOVE THIS WOMAN AND FUCK YOUR JUDGEMENTS AND FEARS BECAUSE
THIS IS WHO I AM!"

Instead...

i went to a dance party. you know, the mature, intentional thing to do when you're trying to understand yourself. *rolls eyes* it was on the top level of one of the commercial buildings downtown. rave music split and rearranged our heads replacing their innocent growth with superficial notions of popularity.

droplets of sweat, sex, lipstick, grinding...little girls without a clue in the world parading around chatting up all the seniors from our high school. *Oh he thinks you are soooo cool!* ha. at the time i wasn't feeling too attractive, instead i was having a sorry-assed-pity-party sort of day, what with my total lack of ability to go after the person i was *actually* interested in - Miss Sage. sighs.

---

[11] "FUCK YOU, SOCIETY!" –While editing this section, my co-editor pointed out that this sentence needed a comma after 'Fuck You' and before 'Society'. We laughed uproariously – struck by the juxtaposition between the anti-structure sentiments of the passage versus the confines of modern grammar. It was *so* funny, in fact, that we felt is necessary to share our moment.

now, i won't share all the excruciating details. (how fun would it be if I told you *everything*? like wouldn't you be bored if i just prattled off about how Nicole was wearing practically nothing, three guys were fighting for her attention, Muriel kept doing this weird lopsided smile/mouth movement, and i think i stepped on an olive. see? not all that thrilling. i promise i'll be detailed when it counts.) i'll summarize.

in a chicory nutshell:

i kissed him,   the first stranger of my life.

       (or he kissed me),

following several more dances, i was gaily dragged off into a car full of his guy friends (perhaps this is where my fear of gang rapes was born...).

i fell asleep on his shoulder.

       groggily i woke up when we arrived in front of his pad,
                          an old victorian house.

       a decaying iron gate hung off its hinges.
       it was a funereal ground for flowers.

i got a bit nervous then,

       looking into the hollow eyes of the house.

once i'm in there i can't really say 'no,' – it'd be rude. like i would have led him on... anyway, i don't know where i am or how to get home. i just have to go through with it.

yep, i certainly did panic a bit in those seven seconds because in addition to

       considering my 'obligation' to this guy,

              i kept thinking about Sage: how all i wanted
              to do was to be with her...and how much
              everything in that single moment –

being with a strange male,

loving a woman,

not wanting to upset my family by being a
freak and so wanting to prove my
heterosexuality (ah!)...

freakin'
scared the shit out of me.

on top of all of this, i had the issue of not having my fuck toy
(steve, the sociopathic abuser) around because he was still
enrolled in his damn drug rehabilitation center, which by
extension meant i couldn't perversely prove my sexuality by
fucking *him*.

damnation. such *drama.*

so yes, i decided that i simply had to go through with
fucking...this...guy, this *stranger.*

well, his eyes reminded me of a doe's eyes, so at least he was cute, right?

i allowed him to drag me out of the car (what a gentleman!), and he pretended
to care about whether or not i was alright. we walked into his house, and i
familiarized myself with all the pictures on his walls – posters of bands,
cannabis, hot playboy bunnies, car magazine cut outs and skateboard company
stickers. the ceilings were super high, i remember that. you know, it's the little
things you remember.   they say survivors and victims of trauma often
remember the most insignificant details.

the girl who sees her
mother
die in a car crash remembers not
her mother's last breath,
but the
song
that was playing on the radio.

then, one thing led to another (as the cliché prescribes), and well...let's just say i wasn't...uhh, 'quiet'.

i also didn't require him to use a condom(!?!). insane. i've heard that stds are more prevalent in the states, so it's a good thing that i was being such a "wild thang" in new zealand, i guess. hmm, i wonder if the family planning clinics of new zealand will now come after me for saying such a thing. just for them – uhh - don't...fuck two people at once...unprotected. Yea. (not that i have experience with these – i hear they're the most dissatisfying fantasy to realize out there.) luckily it would be my *only* one night stand (i explain this so that i can regain a little bit of dignity...). however, my next paragraph is surely going to undermine any dignity i might have just acquired. ah well. what can you do?

the next morning rolled around. i got up and looked down at my stomach – i was happy to see that it seemed rather slim. hmm. alcohol-related dehydration. fabulous. prancing about the room, i tied up the silky string on my black pants and admired my ass in the mirror – you know, as you do. i was in denial about the previous evening's events. why worry about things you can't change? silly.

oh - the bed was empty. *i wonder where he is.* i think he was in the bathroom. i found my bra and top, put them on and then glanced back at the mirror. images can captivate you for hours.

i have a problem. while denial is one of my favorite sports, i can't seem to maintain it past a certain point. so while i was having fun with this mirror, once i turned away, i did start to feel a bit icky. this feeling was magnified, perpetuated, reinforced the moment i stepped out into the chilly hallway; gray walls, faded red carpet. odd stains bruised a coral colored antique chair that sat alone next to where my right hand paused midair. i looked down on its arm and a letter was balanced insecurely, half open. turning my head to read its subheading, i recognized it immediately. *steve gets these all the time.* it was a subpoena for getting a five finger discount, addressed to the guy i just slept with. *great. another fuck up.*

out of nowhere his *mother*, yes his mother, padded along in her robe & house shoes and greeted me with the crass comment of, "so i'm glad you enjoyed yourself last night, at least i'm assuming you did. you're a pretty loud ride aren't you." she withered down the rest of the hall, in striking resemblance to the falling wrinkles on her face and the deeply creased anal-mouth lines only achieved by the most dedicated of smokers. i swear she recovered her bathrobe from a fetid pool, it smelled so bad.

her comment hit home, nevertheless. it made me feel as shitty as i should have been feeling, considering it all. the boy eventually offered me coffee. i took it, drank it and somehow got home. the whole time i was like…well…

i would tell you something like, 'i just wanted to die and dissolve into the floor' but this story is already *so* cliché that i won't go that route. i basically wouldn't want all of the little old ladies at my church knowing what had happened. but then again maybe i'm not giving them enough credit. after all, they were flapper girls in the 1920s. .anyway, you've heard it all, right?

i'm sure you get the picture.

October 5th

Lovers_End 9:07 AM

oh whoa, you know how you said you wanted to make me think? yes well i must assure you now...you are definitely a thought provoker ok? you always have been. sorry i didn't point it out, i assumed that you already knew this. Awesome email-shit a completely new theory to me so i'll have to think on it before i reply...not to mention the fact that i am still trashed this morning, dammit! well intoxicated, whoa, i forgot that your head can swim this much

NorthDaughter 10:25 AM

indeed. ::grins:: ok then miss sleep, sober up and find me find me!

NorthDaughter 10:45 AM

btw i had an incredibly disturbing dream last night,
and **you were in it** as in co star ::grins:: (i wonder if it had anything to do with what you got up to last night? teehee). i wrote it down (thank god) oh and i am getting a journal as soon as possible. danke for your time (inebriation girl) teehee 'they all said she's just another groupie slut..' (from empire records – the movie!)

269

NorthDaughter 10:50 AM

> i may write more on the topics in the last email I sent because i just had a new concept as well..so you have to ADD it to the other one! BWAHAHAHAHAHA ::bows:: thank you

Lovers_End 11:47 AM

> oooooo, JOURNAL!!!!!!!

> Yayayayayyayayayayayaayayayayayayayayay AND I'm awake again! haha ok brb, i've GOT to get coffee

NorthDaughter 11:49 AM

> k teehee bouncy bouncy! ::bouncing::

Lovers_End 12:00 PM

> lol, cute! ehehehe. so how are ya? can you tell me about the dream on here? and if i forget anything cuz i'm still kinda loopy, i'll just re-read it laterz ok? cuz forgetfulness (whoa i cannot spell...or type...) seems to be a theme today...ahhh

NorthDaughter 12:01 PM

> always a good thing? i could i guess...::droopy:: are you sure you don't wanna come over and hear it? ::hopeful innocent:: ::hides a grin::

Lovers_End 12:01 PM

> aww, cue man. :D I might be able to make it over tonight yea? I'd love to hear it personally

NorthDaughter 12:01 PM

mmfffffff whatcha doin todaaaayyy? ::whiney kindergarten voice(just cause she's in da mood):: ::yawns:: blah blah blah yackity schmackity

Lovers_End 12:03 PM

oh goodness, you are sooo cute ahaha. I've need to vacuum, do errands with Dad and then an appointment at 1pm. what about you?

NorthDaughter 12:05 PM

stupid dad won't let me go out till i've studied and today i wanted to finish all the vocab and get right into the maths again – so I won't be going out it seems.

NorthDaughter 12:05 PM

'anna you're my obsession, i love you to the bones..'
'on my knees for you'

Lovers_End 12:06 PM

hold   up...rewind   back   to   the   vocab   comment: *gasp*
...finish....the..WHOLE....vocab??

NorthDaughter 12:06 PM

yes..? MISS "I AM TOO BUSY TO PAY ATTENTION TO THE SAT's" ahem!!!!!

Lovers_End 12:07 PM

☹ dammit I WILL succeed at this!!

NorthDaughter 12:09 PM

dammit eh? well damn this **"HELLO :D"** on my ARM written in PERMANENT marker by a CERTAIN jasper...grr...

NorthDaughter 12:09 PM

::bouncy bouncy bouncy:: and where are ya goin to today at 1?

Lovers_End 12:35 PM

Dr. Snow's. Dad's noticed that i'm not myself lately-so he's giving me his appointment, but you can still come next week with me right?

NorthDaughter 12:36 PM

hmm so who are you then?

i dunno if i should come should i?

Lovers_End 12:36 PM

who am i...? ohhh shyt, good question. who cares? yea you should come.

NorthDaughter 12:37 PM

i care

hmmmmm

Lovers_End 12:37 PM

do you now? *weak smile* that's really cool, thank you.

NorthDaughter 12:38 PM

hmmf don't tell anybody else though especially not jasper..

Lovers_End 12:40 PM

yea man, it's all good--safe with me

NorthDaughter 12:40 PM

excellent. and if i ever have any secrets to keep from jasper i'll tell you too. btw don't tell sage about this

Lovers_End 12:42 PM

sage? hmm ok then. yea well i don't think jasper was gonna tell you this...but she got mixed up with another druggie guy and i don't want to go down with her!! dammit! ugh, but he's "oh soooooooo sweeeeeeeeeeeeeeeeeet" etc. hmm

NorthDaughter 12:44 PM

oooh yucky, she seems to have a complex concerning them. it must be subconscious. well first things first..while she's asleep you sneak out make sure you have plenty of duct tape etc...and slide through his window...

_End 12:45 PM

ahhhhhhh

NorthDaughter 12:45 PM

::slaps forehead:: what are you insane? do you like molesting young boys at night!?! girl you got issues..

Lovers_End 12:46 PM

do not!

NorthDaughter 12:46 PM

YES HUH! i know your type missy

Lovers_End 12:47 PM

ugh. i am NOT a type

NorthDaughter 12:47 PM

oh? are you saying we can't define you then huh? well i was just gonna warn you, the counselors never send you straight to an asylum, first they try psychotherapy, then drugs, THEN 'hospitalization'

Lovers_End 12:48 PM

yea well shit happens. I'd kill myself before i went into some shit hole like that yea?

NorthDaughter 12:48 PM

it's a sort of warning sign when they prescribe 'chemical aids' to your diet

NorthDaughter 12:49 PM

are you on drugs though? ::worried::

Lovers_End 12:49 PM

nopes

NorthDaughter 12:49 PM

::phew::

NorthDaughter 12:50 PM

rose was on drugs

Lovers_End 12:50 PM

    really? that sucks

NorthDaughter 12:50 PM

    antidepressants...eh sort of...i was horrified

Lovers_End 12:50 PM

    sorry to bail right at this moment....

NorthDaughter 12:51 PM

    no you aren't..::grins::

Lovers_End 12:51 PM

    lol cya

NorthDaughter 12:51 PM

    bye

Lovers_End 3:14 PM

    hey miss...i just replied to your email and i'm coming over soon whether or not you're ready for me dammit!! :P

✍ Black Copper Kettles

****

Subject: black copper kettles

To: Sage
From: Jasper
Date: October 5th

gidday gidday, it's Monday afternoon-the first day BACK at school (notice the insinuated connotation of 'back' as in the regression to a lesser existence...ugh!), drat splat! I so love the holidays. (It's so strange having 'year-round' school, isn't it? Can't believe we don't have three month summers like they do in America...but it's nice in other ways, too.)

I owe you a response to the email you wrote on nellie and your theory of God and satan. Here we go!

just off the top of my head - remember how you proposed the idea that 'everyone is one'? Well, if everyone became one in thought-like everyone was 'for' one set of things, like "goodness" for instance, i wonder if that would make heaven on earth? Or, conversely, if everyone became satanistic would we destroy the world? hmm.

dammit what is that word!!!!! that means insecure and stuff...ahhhh, cuz i wrote a poem-well rather a phrase down a while ago, and it is about patheticness of being insecure (something i'm wrestling with) etc...and it would be so cool to create a word (neologism!! right??) that provokes thought as opposed to words that everyone knows and kinda looks at like 'd'urrrr'. lol, what??

Nellie...

I finally understand...

like she's an example of a few billion people that are going to live shaded lives, and will only be able to realize what they have wasted when death comes...i suppose people that see, or half see things are already half dead? hmm, weird assed statement eh. ignore it if it's too confusing

>> because you feel so much, even with people you don't know. (dispute this if you want but it's true)

yay!! i love this...well most of the time. i love *feeling*, empathizing, emotions-it makes me human thankyouverymuch, and don't you try and say you don't feel the same way about people! I know you do somewhere...or maybe i'm just making this up because i am so determined to believe that there is light in everyone.

Regarding spirituality, I'm soooooooo glad that you believe in the invisible layers that exists all around us...and perhaps in us?...hooray, it's wonderful to hear.

damn woman, i don't know if you realise...i hope you do anyway, that you have such a complex mind miss! I love reading your beliefs because they are just so compelling. Yes I believe in a balance at all times-i think that should be our motto. yes yes, quite good. (unless you have some strong feeling that we shouldn't, or don't deserve a motto, in which case let me know.) hmm...seeing as how you are so brilliant, i think if you decided to open everyone's eyes to their true potential and all of the things they are doing to prevent their potential from blossoming...you could do it. i believe in you. then your lessons would ripple out and touch thousands of people's lives. hmm. Enough(!) with me stroking your ego tho-you might start taking it for granted.

Your definitions of the devil and god are interesting. I see truth and value in your theory and I agree with you. But what about the satanic, demonic side of the devil? and the holy saintly side of god? you mustn't dismiss these...as you actually mention i think. *rereads that part of your email* yes you did-ok, that's good. It's weird cuz your words are incredible-and yet i am still trying to find fault, now why is that? to make this email longer? no, i don't think so.

I guess it's just (WHOA!! JUST GOT THE ANSWER TO MY QUESTION AT THE END OF THE LAST PARAGRAPH!) that i am scared of ever letting the 'devil' get into my life in any shape or form. Yes i believe in supporting yourself and your own desires-with caution of course...because you need to think of consequences if you expect to be successful in this life and not have to be reincarnated for yet another life of confusion-but AH to just let him in... my whole life has been spotted with some of his little 'tricks' if you will, and `personally i don't care for them.` get me? There have been people that come over complaining of sleepless nights for months on end...and none of the insomnia drugs work, and they are afraid to see counselors or shrinks because they think they are possessed...and i can tell you now, call it what you like-but these people are definitely tormented. They come over to my family's house and i sit quietly in a corner as they speak to my mother, only one of three spiritually (spirituality and religion being different) tolerant people in Wellington. They don't know that i can see the 'demon'/'cloud of shit' whatever around their head, or sometimes heart, or feet...or stomach or whatever. I don't know what it's name is, just as we don't know God's name (did you know that in jewish mysticism books it says if someone utters the true name of god, as in his actual 'name' that heaven would come to earth? or all good would appear, or something? sweet thought) yes so...i dunno why i am telling you about this particular example, sorry if i'm boring you to tears, i actually thought you might have an inkling of interest in this sort of thing...but yea you might not as well, so i'll let you answer for yourself huh? basically, you can't ignore true evil – as ive seen it with my own eyes and respect it's presence. Mom has invited me to do several exorcisms, and no – they don't quite look like they do in the movies. far quieter.

we also can't forget to truly recognize God's light.

by the way, while yes, i'm telling you about people with sleepless nights who are tormented by something other than a physical ailment, i don't necessarily equate you as 'one of them', aka i am not pointing an accusing finger at you. it's true that i've sometimes wondered if you are or were possessed (eek!) but because I have no clear answer, let's go with 'innocent until proven guilty'. i think you're just sensitive to the invisible world and because you haven't set up boundaries for yourself (we should talk about this sometime – but maybe in a few weeks since school has just started up and classes are a'slamming). so yea, you do appear to have many sleepless nights and to be tormented by night terrors, but there are many different reasons why people wouldn't be sleeping, and not like counselors at the same time, ok?

me.

****

☑ ABSCONDER

October 5th continued

Lovers_End 8:07 PM

    hey chickie, lovely hanging out today and hey by the way I am not telling anyone but you, and maybe Melantha when she gets back from her family holiday, about sleeping with a guy last night ok? cuz well...I don't think my other mates would really be interested in knowing...ok not the right word interested', but yea :P lol, yay ok see ya later then.

October 6th

Lovers_End 8:55 PM

    hey lovebug! ☺ i hope you have an awesome night--i'm going into town with my boy and Nicole and Evette ☺ yay! And i'll probably come over tomorrow to study yea? would that be ok? it SHOULD be...hee :D catcha

October 7th

Lovers_End 1:11 AM

    laaaaa deeeeee daaaaaaa sowhatchaupto? huh? huh? HUH? hehe, ahahanah sorry (not!), that was a conscious attempt at being annoying...did it work? hehe ;)

    yay!! so i rang the boy. Evette, he and i then went out and played pool, sheesh he knows SOOOOOO many people, he knew all of the guys at the pool house and we knew most of the chicks (Brittany was there)...ohhh!! miss! he's so sweet :D yay. druggie...but sweet. lol ;)

me=happy i say....riiiight so i'm buggered to all hell so i'll write tomorrow, nighty night.

Lovers_End 7:07 PM

hey miss cue, ☺ i just sent you a kinda morbid letter...so if you're in an awesome mood, i'd wait a while before you read it. ok? ok. :D yay see ya missy priss....hehe ;)

****

Subject: tears

To: Sage
From: Jasper
Date: October 7th

read this at your own risk...(corny i know – but everything about me is starting to seem like a joke.)

so no bullshitting around. i'm just so fucked up, you know? so yea WHATEVER i had a fucking fine time playing POOL. i mean, c'mon people – what the hell?

What I didn't tell you (or anyone else) is that when the boy and i were walking along together and Nicole and Evette were quite a few paces behind us, he told me he had been caught doing grand theft auto and was going to have to do some jail time(!?!?) but it wasn't as bad as his mate who had been charged with yet another case of statutory rape. i just kinda smiled and nodded. What the FUCK am i doing? Do i really need a guy in my life to 'like/love' me to get along well enough that i don't throw myself off a bridge or something? For fuck's sake..

i've   been   doing   one   of   my   crying sessions...DAAAAAAAAAAAAMMMMMMMIIIIIIITTTTTTTTT   i just...want to be...loved! or something! fuck it!

and Mom...if she knew *sniffs* that her little girl was, as you jokingly quoted, 'just another groupie slut' (thank you *Empire Records*) what would she think? feel? i just don't know, at least the computer screen is kinda pretty when it's all blurry.

☹ tears.

Subject: Re: tears

To: Jasper
From: Sage
Date: October 7th

from what i see of you and your mother, it is this amazing relationship that i can't even begin to understand. you said that she is your advisor, you confidante, your friend...and she is there for your support. and not telling her is like denying her the right to be supportive. i know if you sat down and talked to her about this, if you really talked, and explained, you'd feel alot better. we rely on people for a reason(pay no attention to any and all hypocrisy).

the ego, without it we would be gray wraith-like figures surrounded by a thick gray mist that we could not penetrate for our senses would be dulled to the point of unobservance..ok so this is a rant. the point is, yes ego is vital. it just shouldn't run your life (and despite my constant comments to the opposite, you are not egotistical).

so right now what you have to do is **decide** why you like him, why you feel so good around him. and then you have to decide if those things are worth whatever may happen. i've noticed alot of times the bad outweigh the good, yet people still go through with whatever...mostly young people. but then perhaps there is a reason for that, we think it's selfishness, but is it really? because as you look closely at older people you see them hesitate, you seem them look closer, or perhaps we see them falter. they call this wisdom(as do we) but we have this life, what if it was our last? we have to experience everything we have to feel and live and if we don't why did we even bother in the first place? i don't call it wisdom, i call it inhibition. some of the wisest people i know are teenagers.

like i said, this is your life, he is an experience in himself. it is your decision. oh, and if you let ANYONE's opinions cloud your true feelings(including mine) that person needs to be removed from your considerations on this (or any topic) aye? i try to make my opinions look like jokes so as not to cause you to listen too closely to them. i'm sorry if it has affected your outlook on this so far. oh

281

and if you can't see anything bad right now, if you can't honestly see an issue, then why are you hesitating? are you just worrying? feel jasper. act don't react.

thus ends my advice (as shit as it was danke though for listening to the babble)

huggels

-miss sage

****

To: Jasper
From: Sage
Date: Monday, October 9th

so i need to respond to an old email[12]

of yours, miss jasper, and then i have some other thoughts too. your concept of noting quotes with />>words here/ and then babbling about the content of the quote (and i don't mean for 'babbling' to be negatively connoted) is a wonderful idea.

as in:

> >> hmm...hey there missy priss. ☺

AHHHHHHH! i am not prissy!!! thank you. hehe

hmmm as far as you 'telling everybody how great you are(I am)' bit...why bother? i mean they will have their opinions and unless they are 'easily turned' they will continue to believe in them. besides i think you only see in me what you want to see, otherwise that statement would change.

> ("i only hear what i want to.." (sorry good song))

you said:

> >> Also, yea people can live without mates, but do you really want to?

---

[12] She's referring to my email entitled 'Subject: and whiskers on kittens' and it was written on Oct 2nd...yo, yo.

i say: erg! woman grumble grumble graaa mlaaa etc. and no i don't. but i don't want friends who aren't in it for the long haul, i don't want 'acquaintances' my friends are a small tight knit group, and they are people i'd die for.

i guess really the 'slave' comment was focused towards the concept of becoming a slave to karma...my goal used to be to destroy my karma entirely...but i guess it has dynamified (haha i made a new word) into fucking over this whole 'purpose/plan' concept dammit.

::at this point she takes a moment to surreptitiously(haha vocab word!!) sneak a type...404 678 831.....winks once at her kitty Platypus cohort and then disappears in a flash of smoke! (ok so maybe she dosen't do the smoke thingie but we can all have our dreams right?)::

ahem, anywhoooo hehe, yay for secret messages for kitties!

right so i got my first close look at Melantha today. hmmmmmm sorry no comments as of yet, my data is incomplete therefore making my diagnosis inaccurate (basically i don't know her thus not gonna make any public judgments. aye...) hmmm so i thought about everything ya know? like whenever we touch something we leave this strand connecting us together..and no matter how far we step back from it, we could never see the entire web..maybe that's God's job. i think it is enough just to see the connections.

drat, my pen exploded. ok then, to plan B. i am a duck.

::blinks at [my evil twin]sandy...:: who asked you to join in anyway? miss if you ain't gonna help then you can just leave.

::nods:: that's right. anyway, back to email. so i decided just to prove i can write ever so much more than you. as such, i shall top your 'allegedly massive' email by spouting mere babblement and DOGMA. (a bonus to that would be if my inanity(not insanity) is contagious and you are infected bwahahaha!!! ahem.)

so. ladidoo. ok then i'll write em as they come aight? (teehee that phrase was originally bernadette's so there miss, and she older than you by 2 months and 12 days..) ok so today i wandered around, you know? it was odd, i guess i am just sick of people. oh and my journal idea seems to be unable to take hold. i just can't actually write myself out onto a paper, and if i only write superficial stuff, then there is no point. i also forgot to put my journal in my room at night, thus not wanting to wander out and get it. hmmf cannae 'elp 'er cappan. she's loony.

so, you made a comment about loving more than one person. yes i am going to pry ::grins:: can you honestly fall in love so often? can one person fall in love often enough to fall in love twice in one lifetime? or perhaps twice in one year? someone (i think it was nicolas, my gay friend) told me that it's not love unless it is reciprocated. they have to love you back. i guess that means i've been in love once. and could i ever even contemplate loving anyone else that much? i doubt it. yes this is my most upsetting and the one basic topic i won't go into voluntarily. but lately ive been goin with the concept of facing yourself and thus making oneself stronger. except if i let it, i can despair enough to feel that this approach is a pointless exercise. isn't it? you know what? it's sad. after this unholy test of doom, we're gonna go back to being ourselves in our own little worlds, and someday our memories will fade to the point of not caring. you know, we never went to see that movie. not that it matters.

so yes my mood has plummeted. reason? sure. this is most likely just a lovely mood swing based on the moon. reality: if you believe that you are less empathic than i thought. hell, i am sick of trying to figure stuff out ya know? it's like, why bother? no matter which answer you get, it's always gonna hurt like you are dying. i always talk about death don't i? it's because i am too afraid of it to turn my back to it. if i wanted to die i would sleep without a light on at night. if i wanted to die i would explain to myself the truth.

ha ha. yes. lies the fruit of all that is evil? when i speak about facade i mean how a person can be so wrapped up in their own lies to make sense of who they are. they probably didn't even know who they really were to start with. the sad part is one day, they will find out. someday they will open their eyes and guess what? the truth will kill them.

yes i attacked nellie. should i not have? should i not have given her fair warning of what she would become? yes. forget it, i won't meddle in your lives, is that it? god, if somebody had only helped me when i needed it. it's sad when you can see just what you could have been and that the only reason you can never be that is because you are too weak. yes, let's talk about the weak ones. not the ones who are led, not the ones who follow, no, the weak ones are the ones who aspire, the ones who dream, the ones who dare to believe in something, the ones who dare to disagree. they are the ones who are exposed to their fatal flaw. the flaw of their Maker. somehow something went wrong and now the small fracture line has become a fissure, the stone is crumbling, it is time to cut the loose ends.

do you ever stand at the top of a hill facing into the strongest wind you have ever faced, and just want to open your wings and fly away? i know why man has no wings: they dissolve the moment we open our eyes.

'i wanted more, than life could ever grant me..'

i wish to be blind.

I WANNA FLY GODDAMNIT! 'pink ribbon skies, we never forget, i tried so hard to cleanse these regrets, my angel wings are bruised and restrained....'

i gotta go, i'm tired. sorry. try to ignore my babbling, but i am just so tired. i'd delete it if i only could. i'm sick, and now i do want to die. sorry but i just have this hanging over me. so what?

tonight i sleep in the dark.

i only wish i knew you.

****

October 10^{*th*}

Lovers_End 11:12 PM

    i'm dreading

    the day

    that you will

                    `move away`

after your dad is all done working here.

i mean, ok, friendships end or end up diluted by other things sometimes...but perhaps...

    it's just different with you. anyway good night.

October 11ᵗʰ

Lovers_End 6:51 PM

> eeeeeeee! traaalalalaa..yay! we got to hang out tonight again! you are sooooooo cue. you were definitely in a 'dark, cloudy mood' **rawr**, hehe, but twas ok! i just bounced around anyway! lalalaa!

> This nonchalant approach comes from Dr. Snow – he always taught me to hold my own; carry on being happy, even in the wake of black moods or 'suicidal' friends.

NorthDaughter 6:52 PM

> oi ve.. stop the madness...i'm so glad you're happy, you are right? cause i'd be worried if you weren't....lord woman you are like the happiest thing ever..hehehe thing is a complemement miss

Lovers_End 6:54 PM

> yea, happiness comes with being the daughter of my parents. *smile*

NorthDaughter 6:55 PM

> i see. good it's good then miss.   i   hate   upset friends..even though i tend to fill that role aplenty

Lovers_End 6:56 PM

> well i love ya, upset or not. ☺
> yay!

NorthDaughter 6:57 PM

> mmmmfff love is overrated.

Lovers_End 6:57 PM

> Love isn't overrated.

NorthDaughter 6:57 PM

> mmmmfff

NorthDaughter 6:59 PM

> look, isn't it sad how i expect frankness in my relationships (unless we are adversaries) yet i won't be anything but subtle; i test everyone, 24/7 i am testing...i need psychic pals...

Lovers_End 7:01 PM

> yes, i think that if there was a person next to 'hypocrite' in the dictionary (as the saying goooooooooes!) it might very well be you.

> it would be interesting for you to being frank all the time (because yes, you did ream nellie, but that was a rare occurrence – you are always testing, testing in a super subtle way)...but i find it's part of the beauty of your personality to be understated, it adds to your mystery, gives people the impression that you aren't just a surface person...if you get what i mean ☺

NorthDaughter 7:03 PM

> am i just a surface person? i hate being misinterpreted,

yet if someone knew my thoughts all the time, i would probly die..yeah i guess it's sort of better being alone in my thoughts....kinda i guess

Lovers_End 7:03 PM

re-read my message dear, and read what it says not what you are insecure about please

NorthDaughter 7:04 PM

huh? which? HUH ::blank headness::

Lovers_End 7:05 PM

the one about you being subtle...go to 'message history' and scroll to the message

NorthDaughter 7:05 PM

fine fine nagging woman just like a wife..::grumbles::

Lovers_End 7:05 PM

blinks and freezes ....yes..

wtf? her wife? why the hell would she use...'wife' in a convo to me?!

NorthDaughter 7:06 PM

freeze err? OH SORRY WRONG PERSON you are jasper not my pretend wife kimberley teehee

Lovers_End 7:07 PM

kimberley?? as in from school?

NorthDaughter 7:07 PM

yea sorry and hey i don't see nothing in history it cuts the message in half sorry i'm sorry ::huggels::

Lovers_End 7:09 PM

☹ hey mespinks i'm gonna cruise eh.

NorthDaughter 7:09 PM

> yowie, ok then have fun...not too much though, don't do anything i wouldn't do aye...

Lovers_End 7:10 PM

> hmm. yea. k see ya

NorthDaughter 7:10 PM

> later jasper

NorthDaughter 7:36 PM

> i guess it's like, am i so transparent? sometimes i feel like everything i say is double meanings attached to it, and everything is loaded....but then i see other people attempt to be subtle, and i see right through them, and i get worried that i am too, thus becoming more abstract and difficult to realize...the only problem is i can't always control my face, and my eyes, bad thing i have noticed. oi ve woman. too confusing this is. ::smiles::

Lovers_End 10:57 PM

> well sounds like your observations are gonna get you somewhere if you act upon them and change things. I'm not gonna tell you how to change, you're old enough to figure issues out for yourself, unless you ask for help-and then i will give advice. But you gotta be up front and say it ok? ok. *copies sage and stifles a goodbye phrase because it would remind her too much of sage leaving soon* cya-jasper.

> > *I'm refraining from giving you advice, Sage, because Dr. Snow always says it's vitally important to let teenagers, myself included, make our own damn decisions...we can consult adults and wise mentors – like him – but it's part of becoming an adult to fuck up, learn and redirect.*

However...(ha!) if I did allow myself to overstep and give you advice, Sage, I would totally be on my knees begging you to ease the abstraction of your mind and see the world in shades of light instead of shades of gray. You writhe and squirm under life, always in pupa form, always analyzing and waiting for life's worst traits to leap out...I want to slit you open – prematurely - and let you fall, fall to the ground to wither and dehydrate, you're always scared of taking a chance to believe in anything remotely good – you're a quintessential pessimist wrapped tightly in a dark green sleeping bag, just barely breathing under all this sand.

Lovers_End 11:00 PM

if you could have one thing in the world,

what would it be?

cliché I know, but a good question-hence it being a cliché.

⚘ FRAGILE FORMATIONS

****

Subject: random question

To: Sage
From: Jasper
Date: October 11th

tell me, why is it that when someone likes another person...and the other person is totally aloof and non-responsive, or only a tiny bit responsive, does the person seem to be totally enamoured with that person? but when the person that the person is liking all of a sudden starts to communicate and resipracate some of the loving the first person was expelling...does the first person all of a sudden get all wierd and back off? sheesh it sucks. sooo annoying!

****

To: Jasper
From: Sage
Date: October 11th

jasper i honestly don't know. ::sighs head on arms:: life just sucks that way? so which boy are we talking about now? you realize that if one of 'em hurts you i'll have to kill him. ::attempts to smile:: sorry old habits die hard. oi ve. i HATE phatic communions. DO I LOOK LIKE A GORILLA????!!!

i guess for me, if i were to like someone and then they suddenly showed interest in me (yes, as *does* happen once in a blue moon, shush you) i would fall back on my preference for solidarity instead of launching into vulnerability with them and offering myself to be the chopping block. (this is just me rambling ok, just an OUTSIDE OPINION ok? i have no idea who you are really talking about so it's impossible for me to be exactly in tune with whatever situation you are referring to.) personally i trust very few people, and they have the power to literally kill me. this is scary.

292

i also think that when a person becomes overly insecure, they'll typically just back off or freeze up or whatever....i mean just as an observation.....dammnit..sorry gonna curse whenver i stifle a thought that i feel i should voice, but won't. sorry it's cruel but HELL. thank you. oi VEEE me and my bottled up issues. i think i need a big stick to let some pressure out ja? anywho not gonna overload you aye..im not someone who makes you deal with their problems....i want to help but i dont want to recieve help..ahh hypocrite aye....ok yeah so thus comes the stutter joy.....AGGG gonna shut up now, gotta go run away anyway cause me is not in a particularly happy mood. by the way(btw)! we are starting off our SAT examination weekend on friday the 13th during a full moon in a CAR in a MOTEL thank you. my point is made.

me myself and sandy (evil twin...)

****

Subject: hello you. <--hmm... 'hello you' seems inappropriate at the end of this blunt email so: 'hello' will do.

To: Sage
From: Jasper
Date: October 11th

hi there, so you're cursing and stifling thoughts you feel you should voice, but won't. right. well lemme see...how to start off? oh to make an impression that'll wear off eventually...ok, who gives a shit, how's this: WELL COME ON THEN!!!!! PHUCKIN' SPILL YOUR GUTS OUT GIRL!!! HELL YOU SAY WE SHOULD LIVE, SO FUCKING DO IT!!!!! right, how was that? or maybe... Yes so Sage...if you want to trust someone, or rather need a friend to trust in new zealand-i'll be glad to be that mate for you. Someone to use as a tool to help yourself get by a little better. You're a huge part of my world at the moment...and i'd like to think that that'll stay that way for a while, but shit things fucking happen. anyway. I'm here for ya babe-as the saying goes. ugh. It's weird cuz i have this HUUUGGEEE urge/mission feeling for you to be happy.

But then again...i dunno! It's like good to be sad n that once in a while right? as without the extreme lows, you don't get the highs right? right. I really have no idea how i am doing here, or if i'm communicating the things i want to. You are not transparent...at least not to me, and i presume your chicas. *glazes over* I don't know how've you done this. Spun this web of thought around the earth and then settled yourself as the spider in the middle. Awaiting what you are waiting for. Shit mate, it might just be the sleepiness talking, but it also kinda feels   like   i'm floating...ahhhhhhhhhhhhhhhhhhhhhhhhhhhhhhhhhhhhhhhhhhhhhhhhhhhhhhhhh hhhhhhhhhhhhhhhhhhhhhhhhhhhhhhhhhhhhhhhhhhhhhhhhhhhhhhhhhhhhhhhh hhhhhhhhhhhhhhhhhhhhhhhh I am SOOOO tempted to erase all this, perhaps i will after getting it out? shit for real-right at this moment, i have no idea what i'm gonna do with this email.

..

today you seemed like you didn't want to listen to anything i said-or interpret it correctly rather. It made me feel like if we lose each other on this thin wave length-a spider's delicate work-it'll snap and new strands will be built with other people...and ultimately our connection will be lost. i suppose change isn't nessiccarily bad...no i'm getting off the topic here. damn it, I suppose my mind just might not be up to yours huh? if that's the case then do let me know won't you. The email i sent you just before this one wasn't anything to do with a male. Sorry if i'm seeming at all diffident, ← (vocab word) *small smile*, it's just one of those things-i don't feel like i'm in a pathetic mood so if i sound like it-don't be phased by it.

you said this: "then they just back off or freeze up or whatever....i mean just as an observation.....dammit..sorry gonna curse whenver i stifle a thought that i feel i should voice, but won't. sorry it's cruel but HELL. thank you. oi VEEE me and my bottled up issues."

what were you going to say? anyway, i suppose i have a billion more things to comment on, but i must filter them out first, and we've got a million years to live after all, right? hmm, obviously not.

****

Subject: goodnight

To: Sage
From: Jasper
Date: October 11th

also, after today when you just turned off listening, it's made me really scared that...well you're just never going to listen again. ☹

goodnight.

****

♂ THE SATS

It's a sunny morning. We're outside, just outside of Sage's gated courtyard, standing in her driveway. My Dad just dropped me off 15 minutes ago.

Tomorrow we take the SATs. We have to drive out of town to take the exam – there are only two cities in New Zealand where 'official' SAT tests are given to American immigrants living here.

> "Jasper? I'll never stop listening to you.
> I'm sorry about yesterday – I had a lot on my mind.
> You'll always be important to me." She murmurs the words into my hair as she passes.
> My heart stops for a single moment; I didn't know she was behind me.
> I gulp...
> & avoid eye contact.
> Instead, I nod - a casual, friendly, noncommittal nod.

Sage's dad, Louis, is traipsing around making sure we have everything we need for our two day trip. I absentmindedly place my backpack and sack of snacks into the backseat, where apparently both Sage and I will be riding. This is strange to me because it means that her dad has to sit up front by himself. I never let Mom sit by herself – she feels too much like a taxi driver if I do.

"Is he going to be ok by himself up there?"

"Huh? Yea, sure. Why wouldn't he be?"

My mind flips back to the impending exam.

> K...
> Wow...
> I can't believe
> I am going to be taking the SATs tomorrow morning at 10 a.m.
> All those hours...attempting to study...
> attempting not to be...

"Everyone ready?!" Louis hollers. He's over six feet tall, sinewy and the obvious source of Sage's natural intelligence. He has light, wavy brown hair, and he seems to oscillate between goofy kindness and a darker, angry side.

296

"Am I ready for *this* exam? Not really..." I shyly whisper.

Sage grins. I melt.

We all get in the car, and Louis honks the horn. Sage's younger sister Edith comes running out of the front door and piles in with us – we'll drop her off at school before we head off for the night. She'll stay with a friend. Edith is three years younger than Sage, but their eyes, noses and mouths mirror one another. It's their bodies that are so fundamentally different – Sage is butch, edgy and masculine whereas Edith could be on the cover of a Seventeen magazine.

* * *

The drive is fairly uneventful...

Except:

1. Sage *lies down* on me in the *back seat* where her Dad could *SEE US* (oh my god), which makes me totally freak out,

    &

2. Louis nearly kills us.
                        Hmm...

    He distracts himself with one of his own stories (he keeps on turning around and gesturing wildy, attempting to emphasize his final punch lines), and he ends up driving the wrong way down a one way street. Nice! Sage has to call out for him to notice.

Finally we arrive at the motel – much to the relief of my introverted side. She is in desperate need of some alone time.

Indeed the city is gorgeous – the flowers are simply prolific – and I love running around & exploring the complex on my own. Sage and I then find each other & have a loony ol' time on one of those huge trampolines.

* * *

"Ok, he's coming."

Steve is going to be outside in just five minutes, to 'say hello'.

"He's already snuck out of his rehab center. It's only, like, 30 minutes away from here."

I'd emailed him a week ago telling him of our travel plans...and he gave me a phone number to call. He'd actually answered. He had had to tell some girl to be quiet in the background, which made my tummy hurt, but I couldn't complain – I was just sleeping with him when he was in town, not dating him anymore.

"Ok. Again, you'll have to sneak out. Dad won't want you walking around alone in this city without a chaperone."

Undeterred, I say, "Weird. We are all 16 years old. Anyway, yea ok, I sneak out of my own house all the time. It's all about confidence. No worries, mate." I'm pulling on my shoes and making sure that my hair looks good. Makeup, too...black, black, black...

Moments later, my heart starts racing with the old, dull thrill forever associated   with   Steve.
I slip out of our motel's front door when the TV really starts screaming. I'll throw rocks at our window when I need to come back in...it's awesome that Sage has agreed to this.

* * *

The night is cool. I make my way across eight lanes of traffic and wait at a bus stop.

Five minutes tick by. Ten more. Six more.

My mind begins to chip.

Why aren't you spending this time with Sage?

I don't want to 'need' her.
I'm scared of being too attached to a lesbian.
Finding Steve here will help me –
it keeps up appearances
&
I can make out with him.
Feel the lips of a guy...
Yes, but Sage is so much more fun.
This is silly. Go back inside!
She'll be glad to see you.

No, I said I would wait for him.
Just because he can be a flake
doesn't mean *I* have to be.

Oh right, like you owe him anything!
He's one of my best friends!

Ha. Funny concept of a friend – he fucks you & leaves
you &
all you do is sit on this wall and wait for him?!?!!?!

I'll just wait a few more minutes...

Ha. Yea, that's always the way.

* * *

...Why did he say he'd be there so much earlier if he didn't mean it?

He always lies.

       He does not always lie.

Yea, fine. That's what makes it difficult.

      How can he lie to me?
     I've put so much effort into him...
      & my family has too!
    We fostered him for so long...
      before Mother got sick.
       For about a year.
   Mom & Dad nearly divorced.
      Why doesn't love count?

He's a borderline and/or has a sociopath personality.
Nothing you do will help him.

     Well, I guess that makes it inane me
        expecting
        anything
        from him.

You're finally making (some) sense.

* * *

   Steve twisted me into loving him so intensely that no matter
   what anyone said, I loved him.

   He was my project, a broken child I saw myself being able to
   rescue.

      Me, a momma bird – or a psych patient.
   He manipulated my entire family during
   the year
   he lived with us.
   First he stole $1000 from my Mom's credit card. then, then,
   then...

    Mother responded by taking him in as a foster child.
      She takes after her own mother,
      who loved people unconditionally.

Mother kept working her 60 hr/wk ministerial job.
Then she would stay up till 2 a.m. to teach Steve his
correspondence classes, after he was expelled.
It nearly destroyed her health.

She paid for him to see Dr. Snow for months.
She thought we could all 'fix him' too.

Dad didn't object, then.

Steve cheated on me over 50 times during the year we dated.
I became friends with each of the girls - a meek attempt to
defend my position.
I thought if I was nice to them, they would stop.
Ahahahahahhaaa.
Wrong.

```
He taught me how to steal,
how to be an alcoholic,
how to fuck without inhibitions
& how to FEEL PAIN.
```

```
"...you feel so much, even with people you don't know..."
```
* * *

He arrives.

I let him hug me, excessively, but...

Something's off.

The same thrilling, dysfunctional and neurotic emotions I usually get from
seeing him are...absent?

Huh?

Oh *shit*. Not Good.

* * *

So here I am. Sitting on a wall with the guy I so desperately wanted to rescue all these years. I push him off me. First true time.

"I just don't feel like being fondled and pawed right now. How are you?"

He thinks I'm playing. He begins to pout.

I look across at our motel, and I notice that Sage's light is still on. I want to go.

"Steve? Yea. I'm going to go, ok?"
    Why did I have to ask for permission?

He tries to get me to stay. "Aww, don't do that. You should come fuck me in my buddy's pad...it'll be sweet, Sweet Pea..."

I disentangle myself from his sticky fingers. Without meaning to, I RUN back to the motel.

Darting into the first floor hallway, I catch my breath before casting the 1st stone.

* * *

Bedtime.

"Hey, Sage? Thanks for letting me in."

"Yea, no worries. Did you have a good time?"

"Uhh..yea. I dunno. It's weird. Like...things are changing, but I'm not sure I want them to."

"Hmm. If you want to talk about it, let me know."

"K. My first line of attack is to change (my clothes)...so I'm going to do it in there, ok?" I throw a gesture over to the tiny closet in the corner.

"In there? You sure? I can leave, you know."

Pause.

I grin. "No, no, that's ok. I'll just…" Now giddy and playing, I squeeze myself into the tiny closet and take care to close the old fashioned wood door without locking myself in – there's no handle inside. Peeking out of the narrow gap, I keep an eye on her as I bang into the walls of the closet so many times that by the time I come back out, both of our faces are bright with laughter.

* * *

The SATs. Adorably we don't take the tests in a massive school hall. Instead we take the tests in a little Kiwi lady's house officially ordained as the examination venue. We take the test with three others American teens living in New Zealand.

Throughout the examination, I find myself daydreaming about Sage. She's sitting in the front row, me in the back. We'd stayed up pretty late last night laughing and talking…so I can't find myself to really care about this test. I'm just *happy*…hmm…I s'pose I should do a few word problems..

Sage is to happiness as strawberries are to satiation.
Sage is to Jasper as hard work is to hard out play…hehehee…

I giggle.

* * *

After the exam, we all stand around and make small talk. Well, Sage & all the adults do, anyway. Louis seems particularly interested in talking to the little examiner lady. Observing, I watch as our examinations are sealed & addressed – set to be sent off to the States for marking.

WHOA.

…Ah, well. Never mind. The main thing is you get to hang out with Sage today & for the rest of the (delightfully!) long trip home.

* * *

"ohhhhhh,   *tell*   me   what   you   want,
what you reaaally, reaaaaally want,

just   tell   me   what   you   want,
what you really, really want..."

"OooOoOoOooo, Spicegirls! Ahahaha, classic!" I'm shaking my butt from side to side, *YEA!*, following Evette's ballad at the top of my lungs. Nicole is trying to be sexier than we're caring to be...hahahahaa...guys in chairs nearby keep looking and laughing with us. *FUN!*

Taking a break, I weave through the crowd, intent and delirious.

Bodies are water molecules, I - oil, ohhhhhhhhhh yeaaaaaaaaa...

I ask someone for the time...YES! Tis TIME! Hooray! FINALLY! I can officially go and retrieve her – like a puppy! – she'll be all done with her shower now.

Oblivious to eyes, I dance out of the basketball court that skirts the party hall. It'll only take me five or ten minutes to run, skip & fall all over myself on the way to her house.

* * *

I ring her doorbell.

I decide

it would be excellent

for her father

to answer the door and

take me up

to her room. OoOOooo and...

then!

then!

then!

perhaps she'll still be *changing*...oOOooOoo...

My skin flushes. I giggle.

Me = Goofball Goose. Yea, yea, baby, yea, yea..

I am such a different person when I drink! Woo...

My fantasy is short lived.

Drat splat!

Sage answers the door – fully clothed.

Ah, well. Maybe another time?! Hehehehee!!

I go to move inside.

Instead – blast it - I am barricaded off. "Ohhh, nope Jasper! We don't need to stay here – I'm all ready!" She bounds past me and opens the gate. *She probably thinks I'm too drunk to be around her family. Dammit.* Turning back to look at me on her front steps she comments, "Ah, you're looking mightily happy. Had lots to drink, yea?"

I resist the intense need to pout. "Well...*maybe*..."

She laughs and pulls me down and out the gate.

"Oh, I soooooooooooo wish that I could just Speak My Mind! Wouldn't that be cool?!"

I slap both of my hands against my mouth.

"Yes...most ideal...what's up, Jasper?"

My eyes wide, I vigorously shake my head side to side. *Nothing, nothing! Nothing at all!*

She raises her left eyebrow and smirks. "Yea, alright. Ready?"

* * *

The party spans three grades – sophomore, junior (us), senior and even includes the drop outs

oh, that could be me, could be me, could be me — do-dah!

Sage and I are separated against our wills – we are pulled in two different directions by our crazily opposite friend groups.

Later, I rise up, up onto my tip toes to look over the party...

hmm...where is she?

I scan the dark, yellow-lit basketball court and spot her – in a crowd on top of a grassy bank. Everyone in the group oscillates between having oh-so-very serious faces and hysterical laughing, but I...can't...tell........why...

I crouch down and move closer, unobtrusively stalking the group (or so I convince myself).

Eventually I reach the outskirts of the group. I can't see Sage from here. Peeking through shades of hair and crushed corduroy (my least favorite fabric), I find her again. The stench of beer reigns supreme here – in harsh contrast to our group's vodka and orange.

I spot her. But then she..she..? starts kissing someone.

Then someone else. And a third. She kisses girls and boys, girls and boys. They all spin the bottle but it is Sage, my Love, that meets the most lips.

What?

I blank out.

****

Brittany dangles herself across my shoulders, "Hey, so Jasper! I don't mean to pry as it's really none of MY business, but I do want to make sure you're ok – you were dating that boy a while ago, right?"

Ok, if you think you're butting in, just go with that – back off...please.

"Uhh...yea, sort of."

"You should know that he had a hickie necklace on just a few nights ago. I think he's seeing his ex-girlfriend again."

A stone falls gracefully onto my toes, trapping me in silent torture. What a familiar feeling.

"Really? Well, that's ok because he and I really weren't serious at all; we just hung out one night." *One very odd, long, loud night.*

"Oh, ok, no worries then!" She relieves my back of her Barbie doll weight and spins off to find her latest male 'conquest', to suck her own power dry.

THE SABOTEUR

BY CAROLYN MYSS

"...[T]he purpose of this archetype is not to sabotage you, but to help you learn the many ways in which you undermine yourself. How often do you set new plans in motion, only to end up standing in your own way because of the fears that undermine those optimistic plans, or you begin a new relationship and then destroy it because you [can] imagine a painful outcome?.

The Saboteur's fears and issues are all related to low self-esteem that causes you to make choices that block your own empowerment and success." [13]
By recognizing this archetypal pattern in ourselves, we can begin to note when we are starting to disempower ourselves.

My legs are captive. I must sit.

****

"Ready to go home? You are definitely welcome to come stay the night. It's been a while." Melantha and I have been hanging out for the last hour. Thankfully, she showed up after her work and removed the stone from my toes. I haven't laughed this hard with her in months, it seems.

"Umm..." I glance around to see if I can find Sage. I can't get this desire to go home with *her* out of my organs; skin. It's like alcohol – no amount of toothpaste will rid the smell from my body, for it seeps out of every pore, every laden motion...

I spot her from several feet away because the party is thinning out. It's around 3am.

---

[13]   Myss,   C.   (2002.)   *Sacred   Contracts*.   Harmony   Publisher. Online reference: www.myss.com/library/contracts

I close my eyes and ask her to come to me. I feel my aura stretch out, find her light and draw her in.

Sage? Please come if you want to.

Within moments she heads straight for me. I'm shocked with how quickly she reacts, or how well timed this coincidence is – depending on your perspective. She too, asks me if I want to stay the night with her.

Five awkward minutes.

If I go home with Sage, this will be the first time I don't stay the night with Melantha after a party where we are both there. We *always* hang out afterwards.

If I go home with Melantha, I will miss Sage more deeply than I'd ever admit.

You're a Strange girl.

Melantha finally makes the decision for me. "Well, Jasper – whatever works for you. If you want to stay with Sage, stay with Sage." Her voice has a slight edge to it, but I convince myself that it's ok to take her words at face value.

She begins her long walk home, alone.

GUILT.

But when Sage links arms with me, delight spins throughout my life. I forget to be worried about Melantha, spin the bottle, the boy. I am with *this girl.* Relaxing into her, Sage and I turn down the street, and find home.

```
************************************************************
```

Subject: yea so.

To: Sage
From: Jasper
Date: October 15th

hey chickie, ☺ thanks for having me stay last night, twas a good walk n' that. Ahh, the magic of suppression when it came to hearing Brittany tell me about how the boy has hickies all over his neck...it's not like we're going out-but still. i dunno, it did kinda hurt but yea.

ok so...this is gonna sound really wierd-but when you were getting with all those people-shit i hated it. Dunno why, ok well yes i do. Green-eyed monster! It's cuz well, i've thought about things like: if you were a guy, sheesh i would have jumped you a long time ago, but you see you're not. *She's not.* so nothings gonna happen like that right? right. But still kinda fucked me up a bit. So yes, that's   why   i'm   not   really   letting   you 'play'   with   me...

> – ahahahaa i just imagined someone
> else reading this (er? weird thought) and
> then by accident reading this all wrong....ok
> so to anyone that reads through these letters
> later (why am i saying this?), let me explain.
> 'play' here just means funny tickling stuff,
> NOT 'play' as in 'hey baba, im a sleaze, can i
> have a play?' hmm, yes so aaaanyway hehe –

...i'm not letting you play with me anymore cuz well it's crossing the boundary of more than friends, and well we are just mates-and cuz nothing more than friendship will ever happen, i feel it would be alot easier on me (sorry if i'm being selfish) if we just stopped things like that. Sorry if this is sounding harsh at ALL cuz i'm really not trying to be. Just trying to be matter-of-fact and not fuck round so as to get my point across. right ho, so love ya missy miss_jasper


```
************************************************************
```

NorthDaughter 12:10 PM

ok i lied. i will tell you my answer to your whole `'if there was anything in the world that you could have, what would it be?'` question – if you answer a question of mine in return. the one thing (i am assuming i only get one) i want is my perfect soul mate. surprise. it sucks but there it is. and i will probly never find them so why should it matter? oh yeah and i want to pass this SAT test. ::grins:: alright now you tell me, what is the one thing YOU want most in this life? (or any life for that matter)

NorthDaughter 12:48 PM

yes so actually scratch the bit about soul mates, i lost my faith. i guess really i would like to fall in love with the RIGHT person. thank you.

Lovers_End 2:35 PM

yes so true love would be awesome. Or even just a relationship that makes you feel good 95% of the time eh, that'd rock. ☺ Also, my wish: for my parents and sister and i to all die at the exact same time, so that none of us ever has to miss one another..... ☺ yes.

> *I wrote, rewrote and rewrote this reply. I chose to send the safe answer, and it is true: I'm petrified of living without my family...but this is not my single most paramount wish.*

> *I wish to be real. I wish to love with honesty. I wish to take you in my arms and cradle your lips in mine, I wish to make an impact in your life. I wish to make love to you — to know what "making love" to someone really means. I wish to stop growing up so fast, to take time to be innocent, take time to be a 'girl.*

Lovers_End 2:38 PM

the boy rang me before, (yay!) hmm, yea so i told him that i had been hearing some things about him...and he's like, 'like what?' and i told him that i heard he had hickies...and he went quiet for a few seconds, then said "yea i can't deny that". *ok, mental note: he didn't lie!!!! YAY!!!!! ohmygoodness, it sounds fucked but yayayayayay!! :D* because Steve lies to me ALL the time, this is huge for me!! and so i asked him what was up with that-and it *did* apparently happen with his ex. he broke up with her two weeks before he was with me-so yea, i understand why he did and all that, and am sweet as with it. ☺ I understand cuz Steve's my ex...and well hmm, enough said. So i asked the boy if he's going to go out with her again, and he said no cuz they just have too many differences, and they shouldn't have let it happen etc. cuz of that. hmm, so I said that us just being mates while he's going through all this will be cue shit n' that, so yay. ☺ We had a really good time talking-and i told him how i was gonna ask him out n' that, and how that the idea of doing so is funny isnt it? (because it makes no sense for him right now – it would have gone all wrong, lol) and he's like...you think the idea of asking me out is funny, lol--ironic.

ahhhhhhh, ok waaaay to many details--over all i am really happy with him now, being friends for a while will kick ass-the way all relationship thingmees should start out. ☺ yay.

Wow.

NorthDaughter 4:23 PM

::blink:: i fear for my sanity at this point

Lovers_End 4:24 PM

whys that?

NorthDaughter 4:24 PM

apparently i am a slut, via morgan's opinion...kinda just blinking at this point.

NorthDaughter 4:26 PM

actually pretty pissed off right now. not at anyone in particular, just life in general.

Lovers_End 4:26 PM

how horrible for her to say that!! lies!! "slut" is just a stupidly provocative word... ☹ but i'm sorry. Just cuz Morgan didn't get any!! hehe ;) (don't tell her i said that, i was just joking...well, sort of)

NorthDaughter 4:27 PM

yeah. i didn't shag anyone, i couldn't then anyway. but right now i'm feeling

`self destructive`

enough to.

Lovers_End 4:27 PM

`self destructive enough to shag ?`

NorthDaughter 4:29 PM

yeah, i don't randomly shag people unless i want to fuck myself up, which is one reason why i don't understand the concept too well.

i love/ed bernadette...

nicolas is upset, because he had hopes to get with his friend (guy friend) and he got stuffed (rejected), so he's in a dead mood. and he is in love with the guy. god damn this is a cruel world aye?

Lovers_End 4:29 PM

yes. Mom says that being homosexual is one of the hardest life's to choose for that very reason. ☹ she says...

313

NorthDaughter 4:30 PM

>   PLEASE   i don't need that at the moment.

>   Lovers_End 4:30 PM

>   sorry.

NorthDaughter 4:31 PM

>   no i'm bitchy right now.. oh and mark dosen't want to go out with me
>   apparently (thank god)

Lovers_End 4:31 PM

>   lol, whoa-how'd that come up?

NorthDaughter 4:31 PM

>   morgan is updating me...

>   *Oh Mark must have been one of the boys Sage kissed last night. How
>   profoundly odd that I have to process her kissing males. MALES!!*

Lovers_End 4:33 PM

>   oh okies, right ho. oh yea and kimberley came on and wanted to know
>   the gossip...so I told her I basically knew nothing.

NorthDaughter 4:33 PM

>   oh joy. yeah that's fine....so are you happy then?

Lovers_End 4:33 PM

>   by the way: mental note: only believe half of what morgan says, and
>   never tell her anything you don't want at least one other person to
>   know ok? she's actually quite good at making you feel comfortable
>   enough to tell her somthing personal...but whatever you tell her
>   NEVER stays under wraps – she's all tricks ok??

NorthDaughter 4:33 PM

>   i see. ok then.

NorthDaughter 4:37 PM

>..oi ve kimberley is attacking me...

Lovers_End 4:38 PM

>go onto invisible if ya like

NorthDaughter 4:38 PM

>no it's now or tomorrow i'd rather not have to deal with it tomorrow then i have to look at her.

Lovers_End 4:38 PM

>ok, fair enough. hey, so you got my email then? i'm sorry...if i had known you were upset i wouldn't have sent it today.

NorthDaughter 4:38 PM

>that's why i'm upset now that you mention it.. ::weak smile::

Lovers_End 4:39 PM

>what?

>ohhhhh. <-----feeling small..

NorthDaughter 4:40 PM

>don't. this is me attempting not to turn to drug therapy..::grins::

Lovers_End 4:41 PM

>*becomes an officer for silence*

NorthDaughter 4:41 PM

>::laughs:: you silent? teehee....::yes lighten the mood::

Lovers_End 4:42 PM

>   i need to go to sleep soon.

NorthDaughter 4:43 PM

>   ok you should. i thought you were going to earlier

Lovers_End 4:44 PM

>   yups. me= had shower, yay :D

>   well i'm sorry about everything...

NorthDaughter 4:44 PM

>   why?

Lovers_End 4:44 PM

>   just cuz.

NorthDaughter 4:45 PM

>   yeah. well don't worry i have no heart anyway right?

Lovers_End 4:46 PM

>   whatever you say dear. be right back – I can talk a bit longer.

NorthDaughter 4:47 PM

>   ok

Lovers_End 4:49 PM

>   boo

NorthDaughter 4:50 PM

>   boo to you

>   obviously i take it we aren't going to talk about stuff

Lovers_End 4:52 PM

which stuff, and if you want to initiate a conversation then go ahead.

I just don't want to start it – I'm the one who sent the email in the first place.

NorthDaughter 4:53 PM

actually i feel like getting drunk. how many times can one do that at school before they get expelled? besides i have taken the SATs so screw high school.

Lovers_End 4:55 PM

yea...cuz that makes sense...er :P

NorthDaughter 4:57 PM

it does. i guess.

don't yell at kimberley.....

Lovers_End 4:58 PM

lol, don't yell at kimberley? would you like me to? hmm? hmm? hmm??? i just messaged her "you arn't hassling sage too much are you? ☺ lol" yes, that is exactly what i said in the ways of defending you thankyouverymuch. ;)

NorthDaughter 4:59 PM

your enthusiasm is frightening. or maybe it's just me right now. this is me little curled up ball of fluff....

NorthDaughter 4:59 PM

she said you 'told her off'

Lovers_End 4:59 PM

well, i just quoted exactly what i said which in my books it's hella not telling   off,   lmfao.
No kidding.

317

NorthDaughter 5:00 PM

>ok. yeah so i need music now. sorry if it seems like i am not listening. i am. but i'm just censoring my responses

Lovers_End 5:01 PM

>okies..why?

NorthDaughter 5:03 PM

>you didn't answer my question...are you not listening?

Lovers_End 5:05 PM

>what question? and yes i am listening...if i didn't answer it that means something probably, but ask me again. but i'll brb cuz i gotta fold clothes

NorthDaughter 5:07 PM

>i asked if you were happy. i asked last night, i asked today. i guess if you don't want to talk then i can live with that. maybe i shouldn't spend so much time with you, then maybe i could care less.

Lovers_End 5:12 PM

>ok, so yea there was a reason for me not answering, it was a basic principal of being supportive. you weren't feeling too good, and so i'm not gonna sit here and babble about how good i am cuz that would be rude doncha think?

NorthDaughter 5:14 PM

'i'll tear my heart out, before i get out....pink ribbon skies, we never forget, i tried so hard to cleanse these regrets..my angel wings were bruised and restrained....'[14]...smashing pumpkins

NorthDaughter 5:14 PM

well damnit woman when you don't tell me i get worried

NorthDaughter 5:16 PM

'my eyes feel like they're gonna bleed..' hehehehe such a funny song..'that's the point of delirium..' cool....

---

[14] **Today – Smashing Pumpkins**

Today	is	the	greatest	day	I	've	ever	known
Can't	live	for	tomorrow,	tomorrow's		much	too	long
I		burn		my		eyes		out
Before			I		get			out
I	wanted	more	than	life	could		ever	grant
Bored		by	the	chore	of		saving	face
Today	is	the	greatest	day	I	have	ever	known
Can't	wait	for	tomorrow,	I	might	not	have	that	long
I'll		tear		my		heart		out
Before			I		get			out
Pink	ribbon	scars	that		never		forget
I've	tried	so	hard	to	cleanse	these	regrets
My	angel	wings	were	bruised	and	restrained
My		belly			stings
Today		is,		today		is
Today	is	the	greatest	day	that	I	have	ever	known
I	want	to	turn	you	on
I	want	to	turn	you	round
I	want	to	turn	you	on
I	want	to	turn	you
Today	is	the	greatest
Today	is	the	greatest	day

Today is the greatest day that I have ever known

319

NorthDaughter 5:18 PM

folding clothes still?? ok then

NorthDaughter 5:27 PM

you know, i have no problem when i make a decision and bad consequences (or ones that i don't like) occur, but damnit i didn't choose to be the person i am, i didn't decide. i didn't say 'make me this and this and this', i didn't say i want to be brown eyed..i didn't make that decision. yet i have to deal with the consequences, it isn't fucking fair!

NorthDaughter 5:41 PM

well i am gonna try and call bernadette right now. have fun. goodnight if you aren't online later.

Lovers_End 6:05 PM

sorry didnt come back in time to see you...i'll be on around 9 again probably, so if you want to be on then sweet as, if not see you tomorrow.

oh!! ...ooo it's raining heaps isn't it!! :D yay! :D I hope it continues through tomorrow!!!

I need to do something for her – she's hurting and in part it's because of me. What should I do...?

I know! I run out to the car and swish into the driver's seat. *A present - I'll buy her a present.* I turn the car and windshield wipers on. *Music. A CD.*

Rain.

The street lamps offer identity consultation to the droplets; their light defines their outlines. I grin, despite it all. *God , I love Rain.*

And I miss thunderstorms.

* * *

Taking the neatly wrapped CD out of its little paper bag, I exhale pure cotton-candy happiness. I prance out of the mall, alone and satisfied. Giddiness trails along my lips, and I squeak.

Yea, people sometimes call me mouse. Or a hummingbird.

Driving back home I consider waiting to give it to her. Maybe I should just sneak it into her hand at school assembly tomorrow morning...

> *I'd like to take her away from all of this – for us to go out*
> *together into the middle of the sands and*
> *be wise old spiritual teachers.*
> *Students would intuitively be called to us.*
> *We would visit with them in their dreams, real or imagined, &*
> *connect, transform.*

> *I feel destined to*
> *fall   in   love   with*
> *the one that most ignites & catalyzes my*
> *spiritual gifts.*

322

Hmm...Go give her the present today! I can never be patient in these situations – once I get an idea to spoil someone, I've gotta do it right Now! Haha, lol. Passing my house, I race the car to the top of the street.

Heart quavering, I muse, *I wonder if she would ever like to marry me...* oh my goodness, I wonder what Sage would say to all this.

> *This is SO silly. You're thinking all of this even before you've even kissed her!*

> *It's because she's so brilliant, so challenging, so damn androgynous and*
> *beautiful,*
> *she simply rocks.*
> *She would be such a good, loving partner.*
> *I would be so thrilled to be blessed by her by*
> ***being given permission(?)***
> *to love her for the rest of our lives.*

Jasper.

Reality check: *You will Never marry her, you will Never discuss these thoughts with her and you will Never kiss her. Just Stop.*

I sigh. Forgiveness, please.

To: Jasper
From: Sage
Date: October 16th

You bought me a CDDDDDDDDDDDDDDDDDDDD!!!!!!

::bouncy bouncy bouncy::

depressing lyrics, but hell all the music i like is depressing. hahaha had to get up early to catch the bus today so i am listening to it and typing to you teehee god it's only 7:40am oi veeeee oh and i had a dream about this ghost spirit that was like insane and he trapped me cause he thought i was his sister, or lover or something...and the thing was ...he was like bound by his own conceptions, like he thought he couldn't go through a door thus he didn't do it when i locked him out of the room with the phone..that's all it was at the end. just a room with a table and a phone. weird huh? but anyway...our water heater is dying and it needs to be fixed asap and the car is going into the shop as well so i have to walk or get a ride anywhere today. yucky and maybe tomorrow as well. hmmf sorry i haven't been writing too much lately, too much to think about right now, but don't worry i am making it up in journal writing ::grins::

anywho good song on now, so i gotta go...::huggels (just cause it's a cute word- even though I am NOT):: later

-sagey

October 16th

NorthDaughter 4:52 PM

hey, so mom just e-mailed me. the house she is living in is in the high school district that rose and rosalyn are zoned to and go to school in...so if i did go back to school over there it would be awesome because i could be with them..oh and my mom got a truck apparently hmmf weird. ok, must go shopping with da padre!

****

October 18th

Lovers_End 10:22 PM

hey miss, hmmm...the boy wasn't home when I called him, 'hurumff'. i hate that feeling of wanting to appear laid back but feeling really desperate to see/talk to someone. maybe im projecting these feelings onto him inappropriately because it really has to do with me wanting to see someone else, but i can't say who...i can't tell. my head is so chaotic!! anyway i hope to see you on here in a few minutes-laterz

Lovers_End 10:28 PM

i want mah sagey!!!!!!!!!!!!!

Lovers_End 10:44 PM

oh yes, so im writing you this interesting email....ahhhh-beware
it's kinda fucked.

Lovers_End   11:17 PM

oh fuck, i just sent the email... im dying inside
at the prospect of you totally rejecting me... ☹
cries please sage...

Subject: truthful juicy spilling guts out stuff...

To: Sage
From: Jasper
Date: 18th October

yea so hi...hehe got your attention with the subject did i? 'excellent.' :)

i'm normally not at all possessive about people...but that night at the party i ended up being exceedingly jealous of you and Nellie...and hmmf i dont care if you say 'it means nothing' missy, cuz well jealousy isn't about whether or not it means something to the other person, it's if they aren't with you. get me? right – in a purely friendly way...ugh. anyway

when i ran to your house to retrieve you all i could think of the whole way was, "i really want to see her...go a little faster Jasper, almost there..." etc. and it was kinda disappointing how quickly you wanted to go to the party cuz i wanted to see YOU not everyone else...but it's fair enough-you didn't know what i was thinking and to keep you away from your friends would have been selfish-so it was fine. :) Melantha was heaps of fun, etc...i'm not trying to make you feel guilty-i'm just spilling some thoughts out that might be of interest to you(if they're not, sorry-and let me know).

yes so then when we went back to your house after the party...i didn't want to leave you at all...

AHH!!!! weird!! i have these kinds of 'not wanting to depart' feelings with GUYS.

umm & im sorry for being detached that night, i stepped back when i re-realized you are your own person and i really have no right to want or expect anything from you.

...i guess writing this email is me trying to sort out some stuff about my feelings.

ok, so here's the deal. IF you were a heterosexual chickie-i wouldn't think twice about any strong friendship feelings because nothing romantic could come from them, ya know? but because you are open to queer stuff it's gotten me thinking lots-and the fact that you're easy on the eyes doesn't help things.

i mean, Melantha and i had this intense emotionally dependant relationship where once we stayed the night together for a weekend, we proceeded to stay EVERY weekend with each other for the next YEAR. yes yes, with maybe two weekend nights missed in that. all my other mates were sooooo shitty with me...but i didn't care for some reason. Melantha and i challenged each other, supported each other completely and had heaps of fun laughing our asses off. but we were just mates, ya know? so i know that i could-and probably am (cuz i like males)-confusing some things when it comes to this intense relationship with you.

i just don't know what to do...which sucks quite frankly. I hate being out of control...(unless it's in a sexual way, ehehe *giggles*...ok ehem. down girl. lol ;)

i could never have an open girl on girl relationship-ever. just wouldn't work for me...and the fact that the girl wouldn't have a penis...ahhhh!! :(wierd. i think girlfriends are there for emotional and spiritual growth-and unbelievably awesome relationships-and guys are there for the sex. that's it & when Evette and i find a guy attached to a brain...we'll marry them.

Gender stereotyping can be one result of abuse.

i've been thinking so much lately...it's a turning point. i have to admit this one thing...*cringes*...i *have* done stuff with other girls. *ducks...* yes, I haven't ever

actually *kissed* one of them-that was true-but i have done things with touching.....ahhhhh this is sounding wierd...but you're one of those wonderful wonderful people in life that people can open up to and know that they won't be judged on every little thing. right, so...

****

✍ AADITA

It started with Aadita and Sarah. Slumber party. We're all 12 & 13 years old.

328

Aadita was beautiful. Indian, tall, slim, a killer laugh. She was a Scorpio. Leaping onto her bed, we launched into a pillow fight. Sarah splatted her in the face with the largest pillow, and I burst out laughing. Sarah was your typical cutie pie – blonde hair, blue eyes and a face that was simply...ordinary. Aadita held something over and beyond Sarah, her dark eyes demanded intense attention, regardless of whether she knew it or not. I found myself wanting to touch her...What? Why? Where will that get you? – it will get me to her - shh...she's watching you...

Aadita then got this crazy idea. "Hey! Why don't we try to hypnotize one another?!" Sarah and I looked dubious. "No really! We'll do this. It'll be fun." She dashed out of the room. She and I were the leaders of our group, so naturally Sarah would have to comply. Hmm. Was I interested? Sure, anything. She came prancing back.

We followed through and played 'hypnotists' with a piece of string attached to a coin. Then Sarah decided she wanted to hypnotize Aadita and I, together. In the true spirit of the game, we squinted our eyes half shut and began talking about the boys we liked. Sarah poked fun at us, telling us we were faking it. Then, true to her classically early bird form, she went to set up her bed on the floor. We'd all agreed that Aadita and I would have the double bed that night. Aadita way lying in the bed as one usually does (head near the headboard, feet near the end) while I lay down diagonally, nearer to the bottom of the bed. We were both already under her huge comforter. Sarah jumped up to turn off the light, and as her supervisory presence disappeared as she lay down, Aadita placed her legs over me.

The room was painted in a cloak of blue. It was late, and the night spilt new, unabated moonlight into our space. We were in her parent's guest bedroom, which was on the bottom floor of their house. Magnificent bay windows stretched along 180 degrees. The curtains were open.

Sarah muttered something as she drifted off to sleep (she often fell asleep midsentence which was quite the party trick), and Aadita and I continued to play. Her legs. It was easy to ignore the occasional touch of her hand, graze of her foot or comforting gesture when we were in public, being watched. But here...talking had ceased, and I was finally forced, able, to notice. Humming; she was making my body burn. Thoughts of morality left my heated mind and I began to beg myself to have the courage to reach out and touch her. Again. Again. More. Please. I lifted my fingertips...but let them fall; there was no way I'd actually have the courage to be the initiator. I sighed and allowed myself to remember the last time I touched her. Massage night...her body was so much tauter in comparison to mine.

Aadita began to speak again – and my heart impaled itself. She was still speaking as if she were in a trance, but at a whisper.

It's incredible how a whisper can command so much of your being in comparison to an overtly audible word.

So far tonight our trances had only lasted approximately two minutes. This time, for an entire hour, we never threw off the cover of this guise. We were free.

We continued the game of talking about the two boys we liked (Kitt? Mike?) although I let her do most of the talking; I was so devoted to her. She murmured, "...how beautiful you are." Her voice dripped over my body. I found myself paralyzed. Then the oddest thing happened. She initiated it – I swear. Her index finger found my arm, and it quivered there, in anticipation – as if she were asking for permission. I think Sarah had gone to sleep by now. Had she? I held my breath. Yes, I could hear her breathing deeply, asleep. Truly. It was just Aadita and I now.

I stretched, a movement that could be considered as either intentional or innocuous, letting my skin touch hers, a secret message of absolute permission.

Her left hand slipped under the sheets and towards my thighs. 'Lucky thighs' I thought in a disconnected way. This couldn't be happening. Not really. I looked up at her. Her skin lay bare of any sheets. Her right arm lay across the comforter, her neck, her face...her finger made contact with my skin, and I forced myself to be silent. I arched into the comforter, imagining her there – on top of me, kissing me.

The trance. We are only in a trance.

Thank you.

Exploration. My thighs, my hips, my side...up and up. Ecstatically stunned it took me a few moments to return the favor. Timidly, I placed my fingers on her tummy. She pressed into me, affirming me, wanting me, welcoming me. Elated, I followed the heat of her skin up her body.... We are in a trance, in a trance *dammit. Aching to reach her mouth; I craved her. She became my plaything, my object of affection, and I hers. She touched my lips and cradled my hand, which radiated the joy that burned inside.*

At 13, we knew nothing of what making love really meant. I only knew that I would dream of tasting her for years, throughout each relationship I would have with another immature, but cute, boy.

She traced the outline of my lips and rested her hand against my cheek.

I smiles into the softness of the duvet, nudged her fingers with my nose, and slept.

****

whoa, Mom just came in the room...

sheesh you don't have any idea how fast this window went down... :-s

ok when I was 12 or 13, I did this thing with a chick when we got into a hypnotic 'trance'. it was fairly harmless, we just pretended to be each other's boyfriend, but then we ended up touching each other a lot more than i ever expected us to.

i really fell for her...which scared me cuz i **really** don't want to be gay-or even harder, bisexual-cuz Momma says bi people aren't ever really happy cuz they want both, which doesn't work out if you just want one partner, and not to share.

Mom lived in the 1960s & 70s and was surrounded by alternative lifestyles. Life was pretty hard for her during this time. Her first husband, my sister, Crystal's Dad, wrecked havoc on my Mother's life. Soon after they were married, his bisexuality took center stage and he discovered his lust for men. Mother was so desperate to keep their marriage alive; she allowed her whole world to be controlled by his desires. She was codependent, then.

Codependency:
A set of maladaptive, compulsive behaviors learned by family members to survive in an emotionally painful and stressful environment.

It got so bad that he would call her on his way home & let her know that a male lover was coming over for dinner so that he could his 'fix'. He'd tell her to put on a pot roast & take Crystal out until he was ready for the two of them to come home. Then she'd do it.

Her husband's argument was that she *had* to let him fuck men or else he'd have to leave her, as he couldn't be satisfied with just a woman. He had to have both. And so her concept of bisexuals was born, and hence (one of my many reasons for) my lack of enthusiasm about being bisexual, myself.

332

Massages. The most hidden, erotic memory of my elementary school years. Somehow(?) I'd always end up having the opportunity to massage one of the girls I had a crush on...one in particular – Leah. We'd literally give each other massages through the night, just hours and hours and hours on end... she'd let my quivering (always, always quivering) fingers stroke the inside of her panties as I pretended to focus on her inner thighs. She didn't seem to mind that I would linger there, neglecting the rest of her body. She would always do the same to me.

the thing is tho-this girl was really slim and she had no chest by that time, so it was kinda like she had a guy's body...ya know? and i've always been such a sensitive, randy freak when we'd give each other massages...i tended to get carried away dammit!!!

i worry...oh god do i worry! oh fuck, what if me liking her flowed out of my sexual abuse thing?? i wasn't in counseling yet...omg, what if i totally fucking violated her? 0_o *horror stricken* ahhhhhhhhhh *shrivels into nothingness*)

☹

I just don't know.

The abuse. Damnation. Why does it always have to reduce my feelings to this? I mean, maybe I just like girls and guys because I like girls and guys. Surely I'm made up of more than those two years.

333

Dad says that teenagers question their sexuality all the time. I guess he's right...??

nighty night sagey....sorry to drop this all on you - a person that's got herself all figured out, pretty much...i totally admire you. nite.

me.

ps. Just read through this email...I think chicks will always kinda have a thing with other chicks...like when Evette found out that you were gay-she asked me in this kind of totally interested way, "how does she know?" like she's asked herself the same thing. And i read somewhere about how chicks check out other chicks cuz they are looking to see why they look good-and who they are with, and what they have to look like to be with them...etc ya know? A curiosity thing...and the fact that some chicks are hot is just part of appreciating beauty. thank you. good night.

ps. HELP! and please don't be selfish in advice...i don't quite know what i mean by that, *I mean please please help me. Please don't just tell me I'm gay because it'd work for you. Please just tell me...tell me it'll all be alright. Help me. I don't understand any of this.* but that's what i am saying...hmm. err? crazy crazy crazy Jasper, signing off-...

****

October 19th

NorthDaughter 7:12 AM

    'we can go there tonight, we can talk until dawn..'[15]

DaughterNorth 7:21 AM

    ugmo, is it morning already? ::blink blink::

DaughterNorth 5:06 PM

    hmmf it's gonna take me ages to finish this e-mail so why do you keep peeking/popping on and offline? just come and talk to me

DaughterNorth 5:47 PM

    oh yeah! my email is SO much longer than yours...I whupped some ass YAY! hmmf later babe

DaughterNorth 6:25 PM

    fuck fuck fuck, i should not have written so much god damn it! ok now i am really screwing everything up aren't i? yeah stupid brain thanks a fucking lot...

DaughterNorth 8:57 PM

    uhm....goodnight then

---

[15] Mellissa Etheridge, 'nowhere to go'

```
*****************************************************************
```

To: Jasper
From: Sage
Date: 19th October

::stretches and grins cause damn this is a good song::

well, would you like me to run away? cause i can if you want-but i'd rather not. i guess i could tell you that since alcohol is a mood enhancer the fact that you had this obligation to be around me(!)…it could have made you feel more than you did. too bad, i don't think that (or want to) so consider that an empty statement, unless it makes you feel better.

it's kinda funny that you should email about this because i spent that party constantly dragging nellie, or anyone else off with me (with a convenient excuse) to find you. and something else-i wanted you to feel jealous. ::breathes:: yes i realize that soon the tables will turn and I will be the one who is scared of losing you (not that it hasn't already crossed my mind). ok and THAT is a huge thing: i ALWAYS want to hear what you have to say.

i hate not being around you, i have fun and stuff, but i guess it feels like something is missing, and it isn't even a something, it's a jasper, i miss you, lots. but your friends are so important to you, and i know how much time i steal from them, and i realize that since we're finished studying for the SAT exams together you really have no reason to hang around me so much. i mean, i never study for exams, or very little, at least for the ones in new zealand, yet i was studying away (or attempting to) just to spend time with you. yes so i know she's thinking 'alrighty then miss psycho…' and gets her bat out..oi ve..look at this, this is my journal metamorphisized into an e-mail.

ok your statement right here, "i realised that you are your own person and i really have no right to want anything or expect anything from you."….it took me so long to deal with that concept with you, it's like..'just let her go, let her do what she wants..it's her life not yours..' and so on. i do get possessive about mis

336

chicas back in the USA because i can't even consider life without them, which is why i could never really stay here for very long, i can't live without them. there is this short story i loved called 'searching for satan' (not what you think) and it was about this group who were bonded so tightly together it didn't matter if it was sexual or not because it was a soul thing...but anyway..it was amazing the love they could express. as usual i thought about it for ages. in my journal i wrote; sex is for reproduction, love is for the soul - yes i know, cliché, but the fact that i thought of it through a pattern of my own rather than finding it on some bookmark means something right? or maybe not. ok then i think about me and sex, and i realize that it can't be just for reproduction because if it was then i should have no problems letting people close to me, rather than worrying about their pleasure and happiness. i would just let them in. so now i get to ask you which seems more right..and damnit if this ends up being a BALANCE thing i will kill me somebody...grr...anyway (yes off track teehee) by the way I AM NOT PURTY nor am i attractive, no any other goddamn word you can think up cause it sucks hugely that i am not, and saying that i am just makes me remember that i'm not, and i lose that little delusion of myself.

regarding your intense friendship with melantha, i know the feeling. when mis chicas and i all split up for high school, i had to see them every weekend and i had no time for anyone else because if i wasn't near them i felt, well a lot like i do when you aren't around actually. empty, lonely, depressed...anymore adjectives i can think up? and if it sounds cliché then fine so be it, but that's how i feel, and i can't control my emotions, i can only control my words.

yeah, it's so funny, i skipped that anatomy page in biology class because i wrote 'right now i really wish i had a penis'. it's like, yes let's avoid the person, and focus on the genitalia. yes sounds bitter, but i actually am sick of it. what i want most out of any relationship (and this is what i was talking to my nicolas about) is someone who can hold me, someone to talk to, someone who loves me, and i can feel good with. i am not disregarding sex entirely because yes i realize it is a fun thing and so on..but it isn't like THE ONLY THING, ya know? nicolas was like, 'i can't masturbate thinking about him, i love him so much..' yes i realize that might shock you, it's just to aid in my point making. but if it comes down to it, sex is sex, and it is generally similar being with a guy or girl (this i can attest to) except that guys know what is good for guys and girls know what is good for girls...and so on..and like i tried to point out subtly in an online conversation of ours i didn't choose my body, i didn't choose my physical form, i had no choice, and it kinda sucks, cause honestly it would be easier to be a guy, especially with the way i am. although i don't particularly have penis envy or want to have a sex change or anything like that, because i know how awesome it is to be a woman. lord i hate emotions and social stereotypes.. i don't think being bisexual will make your life any more difficult, i think it has more to do with your concept of fidelity than anything. i mean even when you are in a heterosexual relationship, if you cheat on him with a guy, then you have done a 'wrong' and if you are bi and you are with a guy and you cheat on him with a chick, then you have done a 'wrong' and the same goes with gay relationships, cheating is cheating, monogamy and bigamy don't have anything to do with gender. sorry i'm babbling so much.

hmm i keep thinking back to our sort of conversation on being attracted to the person rather than their gender, or whatever. i actually believe that, i mean i'm crazy about lots of people (attracted i mean) but it isn't 'guy' or 'girl' it's 'john doe' or 'jane doe' and i guess i can't call myself a lesbian, although when it comes down to it, only about 20% of all my sexy people are guys so lesbian is as close as it gets. so now i ask what is so damn frightening or scary or wrong about being attracted to a chick? what are you so afraid of? just reading this e-mail of yours is like watching a person try to make themselves sound rational while they think they are going crazy. although yes i went through this when i found out i was attracted to a guy. but damnit-i am just annoyed at fate and life right now.

and last week when you wrote that you didn't want me to physically 'play' with you anymore it really hurt. lots. it's probably the most painful thing you have ever said to me. i conceive(right word?) intimacy with people i care about by touching them, i try to make them feel good and happy, and then it's like 'bugger off bitch i don't want your kind around here'. and yes i am attracted to you (how could i not be?) but i don't talk to you about stuff because having a friendship with you is more important than that. if i scare you away then i'm scared i'll fall apart. and no i didn't want to (or believe) that i could care so much about you in only a little time, but it's like here she is, that's where she's been hiding..i've found her....yet there is nothing i can do because you have your own free will, and thoughts and concepts and feelings and you still care lots about your past partner, steve, and i do still love bernadette, just not like i did, not so intensely. .and the last time i told someone i was falling in love with them, was rose and notice why i have no self esteem anymore. and i can never take losing someone, even now i can't deal with losing bernadette, the only thing that's holding me together right now is you. and you keep pointing me north when i stray (eg. drugs) and it's like, i leave to go back to America after this lovely little stint in New Zealand next july, or whatever..and goodbye Jasper, nice knowing ya, and then you slip right out of my life. yes i realize NOW that you are gonna be running away shortly, and hell it sucks and i might not send this...but i know i will, because i do value truth, and i want you to know how i feel, but i can't help feeling scared about it. but i want you to know, that despite how i feel, i am damn good at suppression ::half grin:: and i am not spending my days thinking about attacking you, because for me sex is a toy, and i don't want you to be anything like that. i have too much respect for you, and i care too much. yeah see this is why you shouldn't be so jealous of nellie because i doubt anything will come of it, and i don't particularly want anything to. of course i'm probably damn transparent anyway so this is all obvious shit, sorry for babbling about it. it was so odd, when i called bernadette, i spent 40 minutes talking about you to her. she thought it was cute...i don't want you to run away. i made a decision a while ago to not talk about my feelings with you..(just like with bernadette..and that lasted two years) and now look i've gone and fucking done it. joy. just please don't close up to me, because i need you in my life, if only as a friend.

-sage

ps. you have blue eyes.

♄ RELIEF AND ODDITY

****

To: Sage
From: Jasper
Date: October 19th

hey chickie,

I really liked...ok loved your email. thank you. I don't have enough time to respond enough to give your email justice, but i did want to say that i miss ya missy-you not being online n that.

I think cuz we both kinda have other people on the sides at the moment...me=the boy, you=Nellie-we shouldn't really try out anything just yet yea? Cuz i like him...but the thing is-I do really like you...but shhhhhhhh don't tell anyone ;) cuz well i am not sure if i am confusing friendship with like quite yet. I suppose something will eventually show me...

****

To: Jasper
From: Sage
Date: Thursday, October 19th

oh hello miss! i have to go to school now, but i had a lovely sleep so i think the day will be brighter today (no light on - yay!) right so aloha see you later

-sagey

ps. you should probly tell me if i am allowed to hug you in real life...i hate taking liberties... ::grins:: mlaaaaa MOLEST!! ahem anyway...i am a good girl teehee ok NOW i gotta go!

Subject: you're fucking awesome

To: Sage
From: Jasper
Date: Thursday, October 19th

damn man...you have no idea how awesome it was to finally hear you say some of the stuff that you always avoid...thank you. i really want to write back right now...but i can't cuz evette's here and wants to check her emailies...and so i guess i'll get back to you...right? right. ok night missy

Jasper

♕ THE APPOINTMENT

Sage *knows* how to play chess. (Haha, what a nerdy opening line.)

Sage and I have a date with Dr. Snow after school today at 5pm, so we have an hour or so to play. Nicole is going downtown, too, so we decide to walk together. Passing up the school buses and the craziness of parents, we step onto the soil of the path that leads all the way downtown.

"Jasper and I have played chess at Midnight Expresso a lot. We could go there." Sage's voice is light and open. I smile into my scarf – summer's on its way but I'm a sucker for hanging onto snuggly clothes.

"Good call." I hum.

Nicole's competitive nature gleams. "Sure, that sounds like a good idea! Maybe we could take turns playing…"

"Oh, you and Sage can play." I offer, happily slipping into my space of beta female. It's best to learn how to follow & eventually lead from behind (says Nelson Mandela).

* * *

I follow Nicole and Sage into the café. We crowd around one of the tiny tables next to the red, billowing velvet curtains. We can see right into of the adjacent art gallery. Asian umbrellas spin softly on the ceiling of a visible exhibit.

After ordering our coffee's, I get up and find the chess game. The board is old and threadbare – an odd accessory to such a posh café – but obviously well loved.

"Here we go!" I cheerily announce. It feels so good to be around Sage…EEEK! I grin widely to myself, eeeee! :D My heart jumps remembering our most recent, candid email exchange, & so I beam at her. She's smiling her soft smile at me. *Melt!*

I grin as Nicole announces she is ready to start. The first piece is moved.

Now here's the odd thing.

Sage is this incredible chess player, alright? And I suck royally at chess (why bother with learning a stupid game when you can be adored by a boy?).

So here are our truths:

Yes, perhaps I'm biased into thinking Sage is great because of my poor chess skills (as any set of moves that capture my pieces over and over again will impress me)...but seriously!

Sage is really good...

and when she plays against me, she's relentless!

She always makes me laugh uncontrollably (no kidding) when she beats me...hands down...All The Time. It's fun!

But here, in this new situation, and with all of these things in mind, tell me if you think this is weird:

Over the next 45 minutes Sage *lets* Nicole win. Let's her. Every time Nicole succeeded at sacking one of Sage's pieces, Nicole would clench her fist with triumph, glance up and then demurely throw out a girly comment in a diplomatic attempt to build Sage back up.

Sage would then look at me with these soft doe eyes.

Melting, I would allow her in.

In our moments of connection,

she communicated a new depth to her I hadn't let myself see.

Nicole just needs to succeed, to win, to be the best in the class. She fears all else because her Dad obsessively reminds her that she *must* make up for their failings, *must* prove to him that he is a good Father, *must* be a good little girl. She tries, she really does, and she succeeds – on the surface. She is on top of all her classes, a flute player, the captain of our netball team, gorgeous, kind, outgoing, etc.

The only subject she is poor at is art.

Her Dad is a painter.
It causes strain.

So Sage sits back and pretends to be oh-so-distressed by the fact that Nicole is winning. The game ends relatively quickly. I cock my head at Sage just as Nicole begins to squeal with delight at her victory.

343

Smiling, Sage nods at me, her message clear.

* * *

"So, Dr. Snow is really cool ok? You can *ask* anything, *tell* him anything or *do nothing at all*, ok? He won't mind. Ok, it's just up here." We finish our ascent up the hill at his office's doorstep. I lead the way in.

"Why, hello, girls!   Tea with lemon? Milk?" Dr. Snow's older secretary is seriously sporting her pixie hairdo.

Following Dr. Snow into his office with tea in hand, I wait to invite Sage in. I need to introduce this session in private.

A brief discussion later, the three of us occupy one room.

* * *

Sage has sunken deeply into the confines of the poofy black chair that sits just under one of the two massively tall, vertical windows. Her hands hide underneath the cuffs of her school jersey; her arms tightly cut across her abdomen. Her chin rests one inch away from her collarbone. She is talking, though.

"Let's see. Sage, if I might be so bold, which I can be, I believe, since you are obviously a sharp, no nonsense woman, I wager that since you've been moving all of your life, you've lost your concept of 'home'." Dr. Snow's words are like apple cider – warm & spicy.

"My home lies with my friends."

"Ah, not your family?"

"They are my family."

"Well. I am sorry you're no doubt missing them.

Sage and Dr. Snow carry on without me for 25 minutes.

Dr. Snow eventually turns back to me. "Jasper,"

"Yes?"

"So you shared with me an account of the car ride you had with Sage, near the beginning of your friendship. You mentioned in private, before, that you wanted me to bring this up once I got to know explore life with Sage here, some. Can I address this now?"

He looks at us both, waiting.

"Yea, that'd be great – but only if Sage's ok with it...like, I wanted to hear you opinion as to why it was sooooooo intense, you know?!"

Sage looks a tad paler, but nods.

"Alright, well here we go. Sage – correct me if I am wrong here. Now, if I am not mistaken, the reason your relationship is so intense is because Sage is constantly testing you, Jasper; forcing you to articulate *why* you believe certain 'truths'. This was seen clearly in the car, when she challenged your every belief about God, yourself, your boundaries, etc.

"In my humble opinion, she does this for several reasons.

"One, it's a form of relationship she has learned from others – no doubt she too has experienced the deconstruction of all that she believes, and so she does this with you now.

"Two, by focusing on you and throwing you off balance, you are too busy catching yourself to look too deeply into her.

"Three, by challenging and questioning you about topics that interest her, she is able to learn more about how compatible she is to you as well as learn more about herself and how her thoughts and beliefs are progressing. All in all, we have a very intelligent young woman here, and it's a delight to know you both."

Our final few, remaining minutes drip by with our last drops of tea.

****

October 20ᵗʰ

NorthDaughter 10:06 PM

> ::pokepokepokepoke:: 'ello love. ok then hope your talk with the boy
> went well. sweeeepy time nighty night moon
>
> sagey was here->.

****

Subject: hey chickie ☺

To: Sage
From: Jasper
Date: October 20th

hiya, how are you missy? :D I can't write long (ahhhhh!!!!!!!) cuz I am at
melantha's house...hehe YAY! ☺ I'm super thrilled and relieved to be here
because i was getting all weird thinking that she and i were somehow growing
apart. it's hard with her not being at school, because i feel like the one person
in the world who understands me is just not there, except for maybe you (eek!)
but you and i are still so new...anyway, it's nice to be with her at her house. ☺

So we had a radically(!) aweeeeesome day!!!! :D The Matrix is on and I'm doing
mah art assignment...and Melantha just said she'd look through her photo
albums for pictures of town for mah 'folio. ohh!! :D so sweet! :D yay me=likes
MAH NEW BRACELETS!! i got them in town today when she and i went
shopping after the Dr. Snow appointment! hehe yay! :D

Thank you for coming to the appointment with me, and thank you for playing
chess with Nicole: it gave me an opportunity to watch you...wow i keep
realising your talents when it comes to people...you're all that and a box of
chocolates man! lol..rite! hehe ;)

In another vein...but still talking about us being downtown today before we
went to Dr. Snow's...It was wierd...wasn't it? Like I really wanted to be with

346

both you and Nicole...but i just felt off...but i've been spending the last several hours just kinda trying to figure out WHY it was so weird...you know, musing in the back of my head (subconscious! woo!) so let's see...

OH SHYT!! I JUST GOT WHY IT WAS ODD...ok weird for me anyway (i dunno if it was for you)....yayayay now that i know WHY it means i can CHANGE and feel better about the situation, or make sure it doesn't happen that way again or whatever (hooray for psychoanalysis and it's power to change one's life for the better!), ok so the reason...lol ;) Yes so here it is: when i am with you, you challenge me and excite pretty much everything in my body in a completly new and wonderful way...and then when i am with Nicole I feel all superficial and fun and 'girlie'. ya know? ;) hehe yes, so it's super weird to try and be both things to both people at once. thank you, thank you. *bows* I officially rock. I love that dr. snow has taught me how to psychoanalyse myself – man it helps sooooo much if you just understand yourself, piece by piece. the mind is so powerful! and oooo hehehee...'no no! no time for autographs...;)' hehe yay, awesome.

Hey yea-thanks for your concern about Melantha...it was sooooooo fucked how when you asked me about her earlier (before she called me and we were able to hang out)-cuz a rock landed upon my chest and wouldn't go away-i was so near to crying. I was just so worried that our time together as very best friends had moved into a different space...it's hard for me to take change when it comes to the people i love most. She means the world to me-even if we are on different paths.

hey-i love you sweetie, you're wonderful and i thank you for coming into my life...and no i havn't been drinkin'. ;)

only driving...ohhhhh...

                    i love.

sometimes i think the freedom one experiences while driving like a bat out of hell is on par with breathing, and then i ask myself which one would i rather always have access to – to be able to breathe or to be free – and they seem one and the same, don't they? ehem. I'll go home early tomorrow after staying the night here so that i can catch any phone calls and get da alchomahol for our PARTAY. ☺ oh yes...you said in you last long letter that you loved your chicas and so that's why you couldn't not go back to america...and yes i totally agree that you have huge ties back there-and i would never want to influence you to not want to return to them ok? so don't let me. that's so cue that you had a nice sleep!!!!!!!! way to go sagey...hehe ;) I'll catcha later miss because Melantha is now just milling around and I should go be with her...;)

love ya,

Jasper

****

Subject: yups.

To: Sage
From: Jasper
Date: October 20th

hey miss...im aiming to start replying to your big email because melantha is in the shower, although i'll have to go as soon as she gets out...oh shit! she's already out! oh no! it was just a five minute shower! blast. ok, this will be short again, then. ☺ sorry. urg, lol.

Well you're little speil in your email that said:

>> i guess i could tell you that since alcohol is a mood enhancer the fact that you had this obligation to be with me..[the alcohol] could have made you feel more than you did.

hmm. this bit of your email made me smile at least...hehe. although i do disagree. ;)! so yes, i don't think i felt anything i wasn't already feeling towards you just because i was drunk, i think the opposite actually because when im trashed my inhibitions are down so im more inclined to be honest with myself and those i care about.

lol ok melantha's here-laterz

****

Lovers_End 11:20 AM

> my talk with the boy? err? i didn't talk to him last night cuz i went out etc...not that he rang lol

NorthDaughter 11:21 AM

> oh poor you. are you ok?

Lovers_End 11:22 AM

> yay! my melantha rang instead and we went out...:D

NorthDaughter 11:23 AM

> so i hear ::grins:: just read your emails. good

NorthDaughter 11:40 AM

> ::grins:: are you doing ok then? i was worried because i had a dream that you decided to never to tell me anything about how you were feeling, and you just kept on bottling up pain, and i got really upset. yes i realize the hypocrisy. but it sucked

Lovers_End 11:41 AM

> yup yup im awes. you?

NorthDaughter 11:42 AM

> eh. i exist at the moment. writing an e-mail but might not send it now, dunno yet

Lovers_End 11:43 AM

> *whimpers* noooo write it...whoever it is to, they'll be glad to hear from you ☺ ;)

NorthDaughter 11:44 AM

hahaha. last night i wrote a long one to rose. and then i quoted her song to her after that....cause it came on...and then all this stuff. but yeah i dunno. i was going to write about the appointment with dr. snow (look at me so open today) but now i guess i still want to know how you felt/feel about it. and so i wont

Lovers_End 11:46 AM

i ain't doing no exchange, if you want to talk about the appointment and how you felt about it, do it.

NorthDaughter 11:47 AM

nope. obviously there is nothing to comment on.

Lovers_End 11:47 AM

if you say so.

NorthDaughter 11:48 AM

::attempts to tear hair out whilst banging head into desk:: it appears so

Lovers_End 11:48 AM

raises eyebrow in mild amusement funny how it takes people a while to learn..

NorthDaughter 11:49 AM

bite me. i don't need no education ::stifles a laugh::

Lovers_End 11:49 AM

☺ okies

NorthDaughter 11:50 AM

ach! ::blinks:: MLLAAAAAAA ::sound of annoyment (new word):: so we are never going to talk again is that it? well fine ::haughty teenybopper air::

Lovers_End 11:51 AM

missy, you must understand that you have more knowledge
than me-therefore you starting things going will surely coast the
conversation in a proactive direction ok?

NorthDaughter 11:52 AM

i have no knowledge damnit. i thought we understood that
concept. ::laughs:: it's like kindergarter meets college professor
here.

Lovers_End 11:54 AM

with who being who? do you think

NorthDaughter 11:55 AM

you know more than me. this is a lesson but it pisses me off
dammnit. it's always a good thing to have communication
problems because it means we're afloat on different rafts and
we can learn from one another. but yes. you ask me to give and
yet you won't promise to give also

NorthDaughter 11:56 AM

'der hergott nimt, der hergott gibt..'

Lovers_End 11:57 AM

i don't need to. You know i will.

NorthDaughter 12:00 PM

anyway it don't matter cause i am writing the e-mail anyway. so
ha! wait a sec....::blinks looking very much like a blonde who
dosen't get a joke:: hehehehehehheh errr? how did i walk into
this?

Lovers_End 12:02 PM

lol, well that's fine then. ☺

NorthDaughter 12:04 PM

i feel sometimes you are just using me for my e-mails. ::hides a grin:: although you STILL haven't replied in full to my long email..not that i'm poised on the line between sanity and life or anything..::blinks:: now that don't make sense..sanity and life? errr? right ooo

Lovers_End 12:05 PM

yea cuz things keep on interrupting me! :P
well sanity and life go together concerning you...*grins at surprised look on sage's face*
comments in raspy voice: "exxxcellent."

NorthDaughter 12:05 PM

DAMN YOUUUUUUUUUUUUU!!! ahem

Lovers_End 12:06 PM

hey dork, that last message had alot in it...just so you know to disect that one if it's of any interest

I gotta go do chores for Mom...might be back on in a few-but if not i'll ring you or sumthin' laterz ok? or not cuz mah day is fucking packed.

NorthDaughter 12:08 PM

ok then dork hahahaha yeah no i already did i'm paranoid matie. anywho. ok then see you later at da gardens (yay!) and stuff. have fun. say hi to amy for me, tell her to bring alcohol if she comes or cigars cause we are short on them at the moment. oh by the by you could bring your miss kitty shot glass to da thingie party/gathering tonight? hehehe how cute! anyway. back to e-mail? might send it in a couple of days, nowhere near finished and after tonight i'll be sweeeeepy zzZZZzzZZzzz...hehe. bye now

Lovers_End 12:10 PM

    oh yea and p.s. I don't ever really study either-it was just to be around you...lol, just on that note-laterz.

NorthDaughter 12:10 PM

    ::blinks::

Lovers_End 12:11 PM

    blinks eh? keeps all the crap out of your eyes anyway. hehe ;)

NorthDaughter 12:12 PM

    uh..... voiced pause?

✍ *MOTHER*

****

Lovers_End 1:29 PM

  u there miss?

****

NorthDaughter 1:43 PM

  hmmf? uhm talked to nellie and morgan, morgan bought foodstuffs and lots of mixes uhm and nellie would buy alcomohol 'cept she has no one to do so, but if you call her later or something she could give you money(if you aren't too busy) to buy her some. right so that's my update for now, danke chica

  ::poofs in a cloud of red smoke::

****

parasite screams, i call it love, but i know better. it reminds me that i am...

sick

...i feel sick. again. I Have To clear my head...

oh my god.

jasper, you are fucking insane! fucking trash! Always fucking this, fucking that, I HATE YOU! and you swear too much! it's disgusting! An indication of a FUCK UP – someone who knows NOTHING, no adjectives, no adverbs, no artistic way of expression...Stop fucking loving a CHICK you stupid DYKE – as in DIE oK? fuck you.

Stop crying. STOP IT.

or don't.

actually, it suits you – it's draining away the rest of your crappy existence so no, i've changed my mind. hate yourself, loathe yourself, cry your bleeding eyes out. your decision to love Sage is going to destroy your family – you'll never be able to tell them but they will find out, and the shit will dissolve in your face. i'm so disgusted by you. after all they've done for you – you've fucked around doing chores all day for your Mother, your MOTHER! who loves you unconditionally and who almost DIED a year and a half ago – and now you're ready to shock her back to death? how irresponsible are you?! She's your best friend! She is the only one who has ever given you consistently good advice, and SHE says that all bisexuals are depressed, dissatisfied and lost. Alright fine, it's based on her own fucked history, but surely it applies or else she wouldn't have passed it along to you, she tries to be objective...and you're going to kill her. By being you – after all you've already done with being such a fuck up in school, you're going to fuck a girl.

Trash.

1 ½ years ago

I am 15 years old. My 16th birthday is on March 20th.

I'd just finished a late breakfast of stale toast and decaying strawberries. I forgot to notice their taste, the mere act of chewing comforting in its tradition. Dr. Snow appears at our sliding glass front door. Flowers arch beautifully behind him. His treasured wife sits still in the car. I pad over on bare feet to slide open the door. "Hi, Dr. Snow. What's up?" I smile at him. Surely he doesn't know what is going on. I must keep covering up my decomposing resolve – I have to be brave; I must keep chewing.

He smiles a little, his lips buried deep beneath his thick white beard. *What an oddly muted expression compared to his boisterous grin.* He is serious, it seems, and he kneels in front of me. Dad isn't home; he's still at the hospital.

"Jasper, I have some bad news."

I don't reply. Numbness begins to lock down all of my senses. *He wouldn't kid about anything serious – this has to be real – wait, What? Don't jump to conclusions yet, you don't know what he's about to say.*

* * *

10 hours and 36 minutes earlier

Friday night

Mother falls asleep early, at 9:12 p.m. She is ill, but no one knows with what. Her lower back hurts, a lot, too. She thinks she might have twisted it while gardening. So far this week she has consulted her general practitioner, a chiropractor and two doctors at the urgent care clinic. None of them have been able to give us a definitive diagnosis. "Get some rest," they tell her, "if it's musculature, it should repair itself over a couple of days, and at worst, a couple of weeks."

I tip toe down the hallway towards her dimly lit room. Her door is open so that we can hear her if she needs anything. I take care to avoid the creaking boards under the carpet, *two steps on the right side, three on the left, now diagonal slide...*I reach the entrance, stand in the doorway and look at my Mother. Her bed is perpendicular to the door; I can see her entire form from head to toe.

Cream curtains are pulled tightly shut against eggplant-toned walls, like the blankets bundled closely around her quietly perspiring face.

My body begins its shift to the space that awakens sight: I will be able to see her (spirit) now.

                    My eyes slip out of focus; the room bends;
                                    a tribute to Monet.

I lift up, out of my body.   I am weightless.

                    What do you see? Focus.

                         Her form.

          What is...

different

               strange

          unusual

                    off

          wrong,

disconcerting,

                         about it? about her state?

--what makes it THE most important element of this moment?

I cock my head and urge God to materialize the
vision prickling behind my eyes; to allow the
energy pulsating there to

    reveal

    its

    significance.

Moments tick, one * two * three.

Her aura is dwindling. It usually glows at least
a foot from her body, but now...but Now I see death,
her life's outline is close to her skin; her
spirit is dissolving into nothingness   –

the   radiance   of   my   Mother
is
          gone

                                                     ?

I throw myself violently back into my body and lunge.   *BREATH?*
Is she still breathing!

    Yes, yes – she is still breathing. But this makes no sense. Why, if she
    is breathing, is her aura all but departed?

My question is answered inaudibly in the tingling space around my head. I have the serene sense of someone whispering in my ear. Its voice is tender as it cascades atop the cusps of gently swaying leaves that tease a glassy river. It murmurs,

`She's dying.`

A compassionate warning.

`Go.`

I desperately whisper in my Mother's ear, "Momma? Momma?! Are you ok?" At first she does not respond. I place my hand on her forehead. `Fever.` "Momma?" She looks at me, her glazed blue eyes awash in pain. I see balance slipping away; I see every primal fear of mine bubble up like oil atop dark oceans –

"I'm getting Dad. You need to go to the hospital, right now." *Remain calm, Mother has always taught you to remain calm in a crisis – it's one of the talents she gained from by being a psych nurse years ago.*

CALM...

I do not wait for her to respond, but on my way out she asks me for a glass of water. I throw over my shoulder, "Yes of course, Mom. Be right back."

I find Dad upstairs – he is working on his computer. "Dad? Dad? Come with me." He hesitates, but I am insistent. I run ahead and find Mother water and then stride down the hall. I pause in her doorway and turn to face my Father. She has fallen back asleep – the water can wait.

"Dad? I know you don't normally see the things I do, but I know you respect me for what I do see. For the sake of argument, look at Mother. Do you notice anything different?" I restlessly gesture with my free hand and wait. I want him to see what I see, because I'm scared.

He peers in. "Well, no Baby Bear. What do you see?"

Gathering the energy that surrounds me, I exhale light, "I see death. Her aura is shrinking – it's only an inch thick around her body instead of the usual foot to six feet. Seriously. She is dying. We *must* take her to the E.R. *right now*."

His eyebrows knit together. Time. He has never been asked to do anything based on a spiritual premonition. He is the solid base, the eye of the hurricane, the earthly bound member of the family. "Jasper, can we wait until Monday? It is the weekend, and there are going to be tons of people in the E.R. I don't know how long it would take for us to be seen, and it's already 11 p.m."

My heart sinks. *No!* "No, Dad. I'm not fucking with you. She is dying right *now*; her illness won't wait three days."

He ignores my profanity; Mom and Dad are used to my mouth. They know I sincerely prefer for us to be 'candid best friends' instead of the nauseating option of authoritative parent and submissive child. "But how do you know this, Baby Bear? It all seems a bit odd to me. She seems fine, if her fever is getting worse, let's get her a cold washcloth to put on her forehead, and I'll go buy some flu medicine."

Dumbfounded, I stare at the person who claims to be my Father. *How is he not responding to me?!* "Dad. You're talking crazy – she doesn't need 'over the counter' medicine..."

The bed creaks. Our attention flicks to where my Mother is now sitting up, her hands beside her knees, pain painted across her delicate face. She is pale, paler than I. "Jasper, honey – what do you see in my aura?"

I stand riveted. I watch her aura, now the color of charcoal soot instead of brilliant blues and greens. The meager outline shifts and forms once more around her body. It is odd seeing a human without the usual swirl of color – odd. Really, really odd. I hand her the glass of water, and her hand shakes. "Mom, you need to go to the hospital right now." I purposefully ignore the question. I look pointedly at Dad.

She takes a little sip, coats her dry lips with her equally dry tongue and asks again, "Ok, can you tell me why, honey?"

I know what she is asking. *She has always been supportive of my visions.* My chest constricts. "Mom, it's your aura...it's fading."

She looks at me intently, despite the apparent agony of her sitting position, and I know she believes me. *Praise God.* "Well, Kevin, we need to go. Please hand me my robe."

* * *

Early Saturday morning

Dad comes home around 3:12 a.m. I am shocked to see him alone. "Dad! Where's Mom?!"

He looks tired. "She's been admitted into the hospital's Intensive Care Unit or ICU. Just before I left, they were about halfway through all of the tests they plan to administer. We'll know more tomorrow." He bypasses me and disappears down the hallway and into their room, closing the door behind him.

* * *

Three hours later

Without waking me, my Dad leaves for the hospital at 6 a.m. I wake up at 10 a.m. and wander around the house looking for him. *Empty.* It's then that I eat my stale toast, rotten strawberries and end up opening our front door for Dr. Snow.

"Dr. Snow...what do you mean, 'bad news'?"

"Come with me. I'll fill you in while I take you to the hospital." *The hospital? How does he know?*

"Ok..." I settle into their backseat. Dr. Snow's wife is in the passenger seat and promptly turns around to comfort me: `anxiously expressive`. Dad had asked him to give me a ride to the hospital. Riding in the back of Dr. Snow's car becomes one of the most horrific memories of my life.

Without me having to ask, Dr. Snow begins to explain the situation, "Your Mum has septicemia, a very serious infection caused by the bacteria Staphylococcus aureus. She has succumbed to septic shock[16]. Three of her major organs have failed so she has been emitted into ICU. She will be having surgery tonight, to remove a double helix of pus that has formed around her spine.

"It's serious, Jasper.

"I know it's painful to hear, but you need to know this. They are very concerned."

Shock crashes through my body – weavers of glass. I attempt to close down all of my emotions to find that peaceful space of simple numbness, but one emotion remains: fear. *I can't lose my Mother, my most precious friend, not today, not this year, not this young. She is everything to me: my lifeline, my protector, my mentor, my best friend.*

---

[16] Septicemia is a major cause of death in intensive care units worldwide, with mortality rates that range from 20% for sepsis to 40% for severe sepsis to >60% for septic shock.

             Even now,
        ten years later,
        a furor of fears
             returns
whenever I see headlines of others' demise:

Toddler   Starves
after Mother Dies

A mother and her 21-month-old

> ★ ★ ★ ★ ★ ★ ★ ★ ★ ★
>
> ### Child's   911
> ### calls ignored
>
> A lawsuit was filed Monday by the family of a woman whose 5-year-old son called 911 to report his mother had collapsed and was told by a dispatcher that he shouldn't be playing on the phone.
>
> The Mother died.
>
> Robert, who turned 6 last month, sat and played quietly with a Spider-Man action figure, the laces of his black shoes dangling untied under the conference table.
>
> ★ ★ ★ ★ ★ ★ ★ ★ ★ ★

son were found dead in their Omaha, Nebraska apartment. The child lived at least two days after his mother died.

Mother Dies of Septicemia

A new mother died of septicemia within hours of giving birth. The mother was unwell with a high fever...failed to notify a doctor of any concerns...The woman developed septic shock and was sent to hospital...She died during surgery due to heart failure secondary to the effects of blood poisoning.

Mother Dies from Septic Shock

...a 45-year-old woman died in Mayo General Hospital after she suffered a cardiac arrest when she was being prepared for surgery...the cause of death was due to systemic septic shock.... She died at 6.30 p.m. after she was admitted to hospital suffering from **back pains**.... Staff expressed their sympathy to her husband, their children and her family.

I say nothing.

My...my?

Jasper, your worst fears have materialized.

I don't even thank them for driving me to her. They are faceless chauffeurs; ghosts flying me through thick streams of mud. They are heeding the call of a death knell in their cataclysmic carriage. *Cataclysm: 'A violent upheaval that causes great destruction **or** brings about a fundamental change'. Which will it be, Lord?* I want to grab the reigns from their fingers, ride to my Mother, kidnap her and take her to a place infused with the Lord's energy and watch God heal her. I want it to all go away. I squeeze my eyes shut. I feel saliva drip from a silent scream so painful that I fear my body will implode. I want the Snows to be taking me to the beach where we might have a picnic. I want to call my best friends and ask them to go out to dinner with me. I want to curl up on Melantha's floor and watch stupid movies until 4 a.m. I want everything to slip away and form a new reality, a new reality where my Mother is not about to die.

"Jasper, she's on the third floor, ok? We'll just go up together, and I'll ask permission at the front desk for us to see her..." his voice is meaningless. Atop   a cliff,

```
Her aura wasn't lying.
          She IS dying.
```

He pulls up in front of the hospital. Disregarding all plans, I throw myself out of the car – attempt to slam the door shut, but fail – and hurl myself into the lobby. *Sliding Entrance Doors, People. The receptionist. A chaotic excuse for a carpet. A steel fountain. A weak woman in a wheelchair.*

People are staring at me, their eyes rich in sympathy...I shut them out. I clutch at my burning face, the tears having whipped scars across my eyelids, down my cheeks and into my mouth, I am screaming, crying, every cell in my body is pleading to be her surrogate, *please let me save you, somehow, don't leave me – not now...*I frantically press the elevator button, *tick, tick, tick.* It's blatant lack of concern an open insult to my heart, I heave myself at the stairwell's door and wrench it open. I find solace in the mind numbing echo of my feet slapping on metal stairs...

Mother

She is delirious. The infection is unraveling the threads of her mind: neurons cease to speak, to be known; neurotransmitters collapse into great hidden pockets. Sickened by their plunge, they reside there, useless, forever.

I crave the moment when she will come back to life, when she will come back to me.

She has lost the simple (simple?) ability to know how to piece together who she is, *who she is to me, who she is to us.*

She's lost the ability to identify her location by the symbols in her surroundings,
white   walls,
two high windows that ripple out the associations of a miniature town one
used   **to**   *walk   around   in,*
an   IV   that   speaks   secret   concoctions   to   your   heart,
wheelchair   access   sign,
a private bathroom.

As my hand touches her clammy face she jerks and then softens; the familiarity of my long, slender fingers a confirmation that I am indeed her daughter...

```
            I must Protect her.

            Be here now.
```

I sit for many minutes envisioning God's light flowing through my hand and into   her.   *Heal   her.*
Heal me. We are One.

368

Dad is sitting on the other side of her bed. The Snows appear to pray, extend a loving handshake to my Father and to hug me. Then they whisper their goodbyes.

* * *

She is thirsty, but she cannot drink before her emergency midnight surgery. We sit with her, her hands occasionally floating midair attempting to make contact with an imaginary water glass drifting there.

"*Dad*," I whisper, "Can't we help her somehow?" He shakes his head – his opinion of life is to follow the rules. I, rebelliously, believe the opposite.

"Her lips...they are splintered and bleeding." At my words, my Mother turns her head languidly to face me. Beneath wisps of limp, frosty hair, her eyes are glassy, feverous. She appears surreal.

Her parched throat forms an anxious, primal word plucked from the distant depths of her mind – the mind that once existed without infection, the mind that used to create, the mind that used to be my Mother,

> "water? Water? water..."

Screw this. I walk over to the sink. I tear down paper towels from their container and fold them into tiny squares. I wet the squares and walk back to Mother and place the artificial promise of water on her tongue. She sighs appreciatively.

38 wet squares later, nurses come in to retrieve her to go into surgery.

A long night.

Numbness, n um b ness, do-dah-day…

Maybe the squares will kill her? The moisture? Will it?!

* * *

Crystal, my sister, is my savior. Eight years of sub specialty medical training qualifies you.

Yes, she was in the States. Minor detail. She called the morning after mother's four hour surgery – you know, serendipitously (or providentially, depending on your beliefs), and Steve answered the phone.

Crystal is now considered to be one of the USA's top eight most qualified doctors in her field. Incredibly, even as we waited for Mom to get out of surgery, Dad hadn't thought to call her.

Why?

         `Denial?`

         `Fear?`

         `Preoccupation with 'the details' of`
         `'moving through' the tragedy?`

Once she got a hold of Dad in Mother's hospital room, she closed the conversation in sixteen minutes, & booked her flight in much less.

* * *

The first moment I see my sister, she is marching towards me. We are in the hallway just outside of the ICU unit. Relief rushes me as the mini waves do in the healing baths of Rotorua's hot springs...

She is in business professional attire. Nodding, she swings past me and enters the unit in full force. I follow quietly behind. She rounds up every relevant medical person and asks to be debriefed, immediately.

In response, I go to find my Mother's hand. Crystal soon joins us, her face now ashen, softer, falling. She looks at me and her eyes splash with tears. Then, finally after her 8,000 mile, 32 hour journey, she, too, finds our Mother's hand. The two of us begin to weep together.

Then Mother opens her eyes and looks at Crystal. She becomes frantic.

"Crystal? Crystal?! Why are you here...here...why here...why...am I dying? I'm dying aren't I, aren't I, *CRYSTAL?!*"

* * *

Crystal & I fight, viciously, about Steve.

At this point, he was still living with us off and on...but Crystal was now mandating that this arrangement be *eliminated*. She was horrified by what had been going on. Mom, Dad & I had kept the stress of   Steve   a   secret. It wasn't like our family to do this.

Secrets...

Crystal was the first one to truly hold me accountable for staying in such a dysfunctional relationship...

So because of her, I finally broke up with him...

but   I   still   dragged   it   on   –

At least it was a start.

* * *

In the midst of late nights spent sick worrying about Mother and trying to get Dad   to   express   his   feelings,

I see a radiant white, blue & green angel watching over Mother.

The angelic figure cares for Mom throughout her experience. I paint the angel in watercolor and pastel. I tape the picture on Mom's wall at her request. She wants to be able to see who is looking after her.

* * *

Mother was in the ICU for one week, in a 'regular' hospital bed for three more. She was then at home off of work for three months.

Throughout the first month, Mother was delirious at best and psychotic at worst.

"Their tones waxed loud,
Their looks were evil.
Lashing their tails,
They trod and hustled her,
Elbowed and jostled her,
Clawed with their nails,
Barking, mewing, hissing, mocking,

Tore her gown and soiled her   stocking,
Twitched her hair out by the   roots,
Stamped upon her tender feet,
Held her hands and squeezed their fruits
Against her mouth to make

The infection destroyed parts of her brain and the damage manifested itself in memory loss and paranoia.

her   eat..."
- Christina Rossetti

Crystal, Dad and I were called in almost every night to soothe her, outside of visiting hours, because she claimed to be trapped inside of the movie *Enemy of the State.*

She felt like she was Will Smith's

character –
being
watched and

HELD

hostage by a SINISTER HOSPITAL *torturing her* in order to pry out her   'secrets'.
She would clutch us with shaking hands & fiercely whisper details of the conspiracy theories surging treacherously through her MIND.

It was hell, misery.

I will never take her for granted. Ever.

She lives.

Now she gives lectures to classrooms full of medical students recounting the psychotic affects of her illness. She jokes about her choice of characters during the paranoid time of her illness: Will Smith from *Enemy of the State*: a buff, sexy, 30-something, black man versus who 'she is' (according to her!): a 'dumpy', middle-aged, white woman. Ha. She also notes how several years after her illness she went back and reviewed the nursing records. Interestingly, there are notes about one particularly peculiar hallucination: A large blue elephant that stood at the end of her bed several evenings in a row.

Not letting the peculiarity of the report deter her, Mother looked up to see where such a blue elephant might reside in a world religion. Indeed, she found the blue elephant Ganesh, the Hindu God of healing. Now she carries a blue elephant around with her everywhere she goes, and in these lectures she comments on how *curious* (and wonderful) it is that even though she is a 'Christian', the Hindu God of Healing found and nursed her. The class always laughs and asks tons of questions after this.

I personally find it hard to really find the humor in all of it.

```
****************************************************************
```

Lovers_End 4:37 PM

i dont suppose you'd mind if I killed myself? hmm...is that an
echo of hypocrisy i hear in my own voice? hmm? yes yes, I think
people that bitch and moan about dying are pathetic...well all
more reason for me to hate myself at this moment, me being
pathetic and all.

I love ya chickie-i've been crying for an hour now...hmm. It's
been good i guess. cya


```
****************************************************************
```

```
********************************************************************
```

NorthDaughter 7:01 PM

    if i will it hard enough could i make everything stop hurting?

NorthDaughter 7:01 PM

    i love you Jasper

```
********************************************************************
```

"Jasper, honey? Are you alright? You look like you've been crying." Mom peers at me, concerned.

"Oh what, me? Yeah, I'm ok Mom. Just want to go to the party; it's definitely dark enough outside now. Can we go?" She doesn't give up on the topic, but there will always be a tangible – if silent – part of me thanking her. *She cares. She'll always be the one who cares the most.* Only the physical barrier imposed by my exiting the car forces her to stop coaxing me, as she pulls up in front of The Gardens. She has good intentions – she's made it her life goal to ensure that both of her daughters are happy. I just don't feel like talking, as surely she doesn't want to know just how fucked up her baby girl is. She's always told me that I can tell her anything...*anything? No, not about Sage. It's your first major secret from her, ever.* A slight smile taped to my face in order to quell instinctual, maternal worry, I wave. I can see her apprehensive expression even from here. *It's ok Mom. I'll be fine. I'll be fine.* I lift my fingers to form 'I love you' in American Sign Language, and I nod to her. *You should know that you are one of the most important people in my life. I'll look after you; I'll be ok.*

One skill carefully extracted and maintained from childhood alongside bike riding and how to cook spaghetti – simmered, not too much salt – was convincing myself of the veracity of falsehoods. It's served me well. I step over the garden's wall and crunch onto the first few feet of the stone path. I hear Mom honk, and she leaves me. I ignore the emotional tide sucking at my stomach. *I don't understand why I go ahead and walk into situations like these when I'm feeling like this. It's like I'm on automatic pilot or something.*

Faint laughter trickles into my ears from hundreds of feet away. My head throbs, an indication of a migraine yet to come - a symptom of the last hour of sniveling I just inflicted on myself. *You'll drink, and it'll all go away.*

The woods sharpen my senses; I am alert. A bright moon glistens on red leaves – shiny tears in the corners of crying-ravaged eyes – as I cross the threshold from manmade path to overgrown brush. Giants rise above me on all sides, their smell intense and purifying. I walk. My long skirt is pulled and tugged by twigs, *stay with us, Jasper, you're safe in our forest.* I welcome their scratches and long for their thorns to reach every inch of my body, to break open my skin. Distress, seep out and be absorbed by them.

The skirt slung around my hips is from last year's formal. It has a very different character now. What was before the maddening superficiality of silkiness is now an assemblage of stray threads & rips from running, *running* as hard and fast as I could....

The skirt is appropriate: `it is fit for me, a child who longs to` `escape;` `to` `be` `real;` `for` `a` `child` `that` `longs` `to` `be` `discovered` `for` `her` `wildness, truth & creativity.` I pull out my bottle of **cheap vodka**. It's all us kids can afford.

I wonder if Sage is here yet. What does she smell like? Does she smell of the surrounding trees, does her skin pull your skirt as the twigs do, seeking, pulling, pressing... Can she sense me? Can I dissolve into her? Will she take me in...save me from this fabricated 'reality'?

Flash. Shadow. Heart pounding. I hold the bottle tightly in my hands. Awareness emerges. Was I thinking out loud?

Surely not...

"HEY, Gorgeous! What's up?!" the poster boy for braces: Steve.

"Shit! You stupid fucking asshole! You scared the crap out of me!" I want to thwack him across the chest in defense, but instead start walking again. He follows.

"Yea, well, it was easy to hear you coming, you were loud enough! What're you muttering about...?"

"Oh, shut up and...wait, what?"

`Redirect.` "What is *that?*"

"Oh, it's a video camera! Cool, eh?" He holds up the contraption proudly. A young boy in overalls, who has just caught his first fish. The fish wriggles. Grin widens. The camera looks expensive.

"Steve, where did you steal that from?"

Laughing he splashes my face with disregard; he bolts off without answering.

What an idiot I was to even mention this gathering to him – I hadn't expected him to turn up. He was *supposed* to still be in rehab, but he managed to swing an early release. He's a smooth talker. Sociopaths are.

Laughter.

Slam. "Hi sweetie!!! OOOOoooOOoooo! Look, everyone!! Jasper's here!!!" Nicole's trill carries over to the group of people already drinking, and I glance up at the moon. High in the sky, Nicole is going to have to go home soon – her dad never lets her stay out as late as the rest of us.

Ironically, the cocoon he wraps tightly around his daughter will compel her to
rebel far more severely than any of us ever will.
Crumpled.
For now, she is his precious
goody-two-shoes,
and not a single drop of alcohol has touched her lips.

"Hi, lovely." I murmur.

Softly wading over the grass, I see her. Sage. She smiles back, a coy, tender expression. I make the obligatory rounds of saying hey to everyone, but my eyes only see her. She's sitting cross-legged. Her baggy shirt rises up to meet the stunning beauty of those amber eyes. I melt to the ground. Begging myself to break eye contact, I notice the bottle from our illegal shopping trip still grasped in my left hand. Reaching into my bag, I hand Nellie the bottle I bought for her. Without further ado, I bring the bottle to my lips and swallow.

* * *

Giggles.

Weeeeeeeeee!!!!!!! frolick! frolick! love love loooooove!

Sage is playing chase with me. We are making right fools of ourselves. "You'll never catch me!" I squeal. As I turn to look at her, I dash into a crew of people from our party. Careening casually off of one of their shoulders, I feel like a six-year-old again. Alive, fresh, uninhibited, free. *This is why you drink.* She slams into me as she rounds the same blind corner, and I burst out laughing, "EEEeeeeeek!!!"

* * *

Blur.

I can't see. Are those people?

What are you doing Sage? Come find me.

"Hey, Jasper..." the voice fades. That wasn't her.

> *Kiss me.* My eyes obey emotion and close. I stand still, swaying slightly. *Vertigo.*

Hurry. I run through my mind's eye and find her. Delicate, yet strong, she can take care of me. Save me from these thoughts, these memories of....*kiss me.*

She's here, somewhere. The ground gulps me down more and more with each step; I am on the verge of disappearing into the familiar blackness of liver poisoning. That blackness is always there waiting for me; the deceitful lure of a black web – easily touched. Akin to the blackbody radiation of physics. A darkness that absorbs all energy that approaches it. There is nothing inside the blackness except black, black nothing. To me, this is tantalizing; to me, this is the   abscence of   having   to fight.

If only I could find her before I fall...please God, please, let me find her...

Sage!

Yes, yes   `violet light`! I see her sitting on a retaining wall taking in the scenery on her own.

Thank you...

Sage, come with me.

She looks up. Her eyes are dark, secret. She slips down to follow.

Thrilled, I take her hands and scamper off.

We must be quick! Before anyone finds us!

Adrenaline pulses in my palms.

More people!

Squealing, I drag her to the only place my feverous mind thinks will be empty – the outdoor bathrooms. A labyrinthine entrance, she trips a little in my rush. "I don't want to be caught!" I exhale as I slam my back into one of the walls, letting go of her hands. "I mean...we're running from them, right?"

we're finally here.

our breathing whispers off the walls of our crepuscular, twilight-loved hiding place. panting. black slipping into moments of grey cover our secret, our demise. a fluttering curtain of mauve, lavender and shadows materialize in my whirling mind and form an embrace of transparent light behind her. fear dissolves, a distant unimportant concept. i feel her near me. my heart lurches – we are together. for the first time, truly together. the moon is here, and i am grateful. it reveals her to me. Her eyes remind me of how my love for her is the only silver of truth in this crazy mind. Breathing, she steps towards me. instinctively I lift my hands perhaps to touch her, perhaps to protect myself...and she places her forearms under mine. Shaking. heat. my breasts lift against my shirt, and i find myself leaning into her; each sense of mine wants to Entangle itself in one of hers. She comes closer, her arms and hands still.

Our lips are inches from one another now. She looks up at me. We share each other's breath; neither taking enough to live, sanity slips away.

Her eyes. Looking into mine, we fold into one another, unflinching. I allow my breath to cease.

She kisses me. The dark solace of closed eyes. A timid appeal for love. Jolting, exquisite experience. All pain ceases. White heat soothes old wounds.

Trembling. Softness. The softness...the sacredness of our first moment. My entire body burns in response to this wave, and I need her. Intensely, I love this creature, this woman. Lost. Gone are the walls, the perceptions, the fear, the desperation, the falseness, the resolve to press away. This is real. Tipping my head I press in deeper to take her mouth more fully against mine.

LAUGHTER. It cuts.

...?

Laughter, outside...ohmygod...

An electronic hum... a male voice, "What the - what the - *fuck*?"

The sheer curtain of our moment falls.

I dive into the darkness of her shadows. We cease to touch. `Cowering, the shining red light from Steve's camcorder breaks the sacred depth of our lair. The light blinks`

    `once,`

        `twice,`

            `three times`

as he continues to stare at the shadow he has identified as me. He is wrong – I am just left of his stricken stare. He knows nothing of this sort of love. I press my cheek into the slippery stones and close my eyes against the accusations of damnation raking its nails along my lungs.

                        `i silently cry.`

Stepping back, he looks once more into the recorder to see if he has caught

my first kiss.

I was 'his'...but now I have changed, for him; I am no longer innocent. It frightens me more than him. Not speaking, he deliberately moves away and leaves us.

* * *

Screaming.

Poisoned. All of us. Crazy shrieks of maniacal laughter stream across the grasses in a mock display of false normality. I am fading into the scene once more... what? where...? someone grabs my hands.

"Ready to play?"

Fear laces my casual laugh. "Play? Whatever do you mean?"

"You know what I want. Seems you need it too – after your little stunt tonight." He begins to drag me through the forest. I am weak from the poison – I can't flee...I flit in and out of the trees, helpless bystanders. Tripping, I can't see anymore. I am trying to remain alert, but my lungs are failing me. My heart hammering, he is taking me...somewhere.

A labyrinthine entrance. Stone. *No! Not here!* I throw out my free hand and grate black colored fingernails against long, betraying walls. I look up and plead with them, *please, help me escape him – not here, not here...*

but they are speechless.

Disassociation.

Cold breathing down my neck,
I drift back and I feel my skirt tear. Clawing my hips...

My Desperation attempts to embrace the blackness of intoxication.
Eyes glued shut, mascara drains from my lashes and I become unrecognizable
- a masque of dirt and makeup.
I try to lift my finger to clear my lashes, but I find my wrists held captive, high
above my head, my fingers numb from obstructed blood flow. My back is
shoved against the stone wall, the same cold wall I felt only hours before
leaning forward to touch Love.
The stench is overwhelming, now. Someone has recently
vomited in here.
A rabid un-neutered dog unconscious of repercussions,
Steve stares at me, inches from my face, breathing.

He steals – does not share – my breath.

Ready for this?

I cease to be.

Crack.
My ribs whip against the wall, my face crushes into traitorous stones.
Captive,
I do nothing.

He thinks I will enjoy this.

A marionette, he positions me.

Seconds.

I hear him sigh in pleasure as his cock thrusts into me, away from me.

My drunken hysteria swirls into slippery messes of misery and confusion.

I sense a trickle of moonlight fall across the stone brick nearest

my aching eyes.

Why is he doing this to me?

Black tears fracture the slip of moonlight, bending it to a new, perverted, but

more real? form.

I can't stand it being real.

Disassociate.

Flung from her body, all feeling ebbs. Blood rains down her leg, the one true

kiss of physicality.

Scarlet ribbons of painted bruises, no voice, a dysfunctional slave.

Love *and* sex?

a dream.

* * *

Learned helplessness. A puppy inserted into cruel psychologists Kamin and Wynne's "shuttlebox", I have *learned* to accept his sadism, as he inflicts emotional shock, after shock, after shock...

The Stockholm Syndrome. I convince myself that I like it – that I like him – that I like this.

I sink against him, motionless, but he does not let go of my wrists, nor does he even hug me. He wishes to make sure his ownership never slackens. I am leashed, tagged, enslaved. He is 'protecting' me from Sage by providing me with heterosexual SEX. He zips up his pants and tightens his belt against his razor hips.

whatever.

         * * *

                                        Ah, the beauty of knowing you are
                                        expendable. The intoxicating rush of
                                        self-destruction overwhelms and
                                        thrills me. I am going to die,
                                        sometime, and this calms me. In
                                        some countries, the rainbow is a sign
                                        of death instead of hope. Everything
                                        is relative. For me, death is a
                                        rainbow – a pathway of colored light
                                        anxious to take me away...

                                              take me away...

* * *

My head lolls to one side, I'm a torn puppet that only wants to be a 'real' girl. I sink in and out of sight. Swooping down, around, higher and higher and then plummet...all is a chaotic black and white film in   s...l...o...w   motion. I am nauseated. Everything aching, I just need to sink into the grasses, to crumple and   lie   so   that   I   may   have   time   to   think   about   where to get a needle
to sew my head
back on.

I keep trying to sink. But this wrist, this freakingly annoying wrist, keeps dragging me back up along the puppet string I so resent. *Stop it!* I scream at it, but wrists have no ears.

      wrists have no ears.

          wrists have no ears.

I whimper. *Let me sleep...*

A picnic table. I remember sitting here with friends, on some Saturday afternoons and watching children play in the baby pool. They would squeal with delight at the radiance of the sun dancing on their mini-waves and perk up, up, up! at their mom's and dad's voices.

I love my Mom and Dad.

"GET UP HERE." Someone demands, and I obey. I just want to sleep. "Now shut up about sleeping and fucking relax."

Relax...that sounds good...relax...

Cradling me in his palm he gives me a false sense of security. With closed eyes, I smile into him, thinking that surely this person is more sincere than the last, that somehow...despite his masculine smell...he's Sage...I'm safe here, and I am able to be quiet and secure...

Thrust. Eyes fly open, and I see him again. The crooked teeth, the 'dreamy eyes' so lusted after by all the girls. The muscles in his arms expand as he thrusts in and out, *again*, and I feel myself go rigid, detected, disgusted, diseased.

...you like this remember?...surely you do. why else would you let it happen? ah, because you want to prove that you are heterosexual? that this is love? *well, then. PERFORM. if he's enjoying it, something must be right. if only i could learn to feel how he feels. will he show me? show me, show me...*

> Twist.

> Ribbons.

> Change.

I morph. Victim to Bitch. I am angry. I cannot get him off me – I know this from experience. But I can fuck with his head, at least pretend to be in control, at least scream like I mean it.

"That's right, Steve...Fuck Me Harder." I hear myself slur. *He likes it when I say that.* Furious at life, I throw him down on the table, so that I am now in control. Sick triumph; he gleams. He only lets me do this because it's serving what he thinks he needs. Burying my head into his shoulder, I shield my eyes from his face. *Can't show, won't show weakness.* I pretend that it feels good. *I like the pain and the submission and the dirt. I do, don't I? I manipulate my expressions – extend the noises, as the cries of pain can sound like exclamations of pleasure.* "Ahhhhhhh! O...uch....." *Why does this hurt so much?*

Stop asking stupid questions. It ALWAYS fucking hurts.

* * *

Flashes. Time evaporates.

Sage?

Dark street lamps serenade us with light. Thin droplets of midnight dew extend magnum opuses along the ground. Muddy shoes slip on wet pavement. Ripped knees - ignored.

Cars. People. Now drumming rain upon opened umbrellas.

Confusion. Wailing. Desperation.

Writing.

Sage?

* * *

Our hands are shaking as we sit nestled in one another, two scared to move away but too to sacred look at one another. i have paper in my pocket and even a pen.

first, to process what just happened with steve. i look down at my calf and wipe a smear of blood and dirt off.

surely he's not all that bad? surely he's just a broken child...

hello

Steve,

11/10

10:35

I love you because you are my best friend cause your are my best friend. I

<3 best friend, I can see you I <3 you because you are my friend cause If you don't belief then I guess this is nothing. Nothing at all.

Deftones is apparently everything — but I wonder if you would hate me if i was stoned?

***

My lungs are screaming. I see rain, big fat droplets falling straight into my mouth as I look up and ask the clouds to drown me – just one time, the pain slips away as I cradle the only child I ever knew...it's her, in my face, in my eyes, in my lungs – I cough, an attempt to rid my body of her toxin, but she is not toxic – she is the air, the air I breathe each day, but it is illicit, not allowed,

merciless.

We are pulled apart – skin rips, and it desperately tries to heal itself in the same moment – our hands are bleeding, shredded – I reach out my hand and paradoxically love and hate her so intensely that I fear for my splitting personality – *please just reach out and grasp me, then we'll be together, and we can figure it out from there* – we are too volatile – straight jacket sleeves caress and suffocate our wrists – the whole jacket comes soon, and the padded walls... -

Invisible wooden doors stand in the middle of the street – they stand to separate us – their knots a mockery of my heart – the nurses push us through them, into padded cells and slam them upon us – they think they are being kind by containing us, but they are every person that has ever stifled true, raw emotion – suddenly a mime, i frantically seek a way out of the invisible door – the contraption containing us, between us, killing us –

No! God! Please! No! I need...her..

Nicole and Melantha inject an unwanted serum of Calmness into my desperate mind. Amy and Morgan, into hers.

* * *

Episodic memory plagues me; I can't remember what happened next.   All I
remember is finding these slips of paper in my pocket the next morning.

Holding her

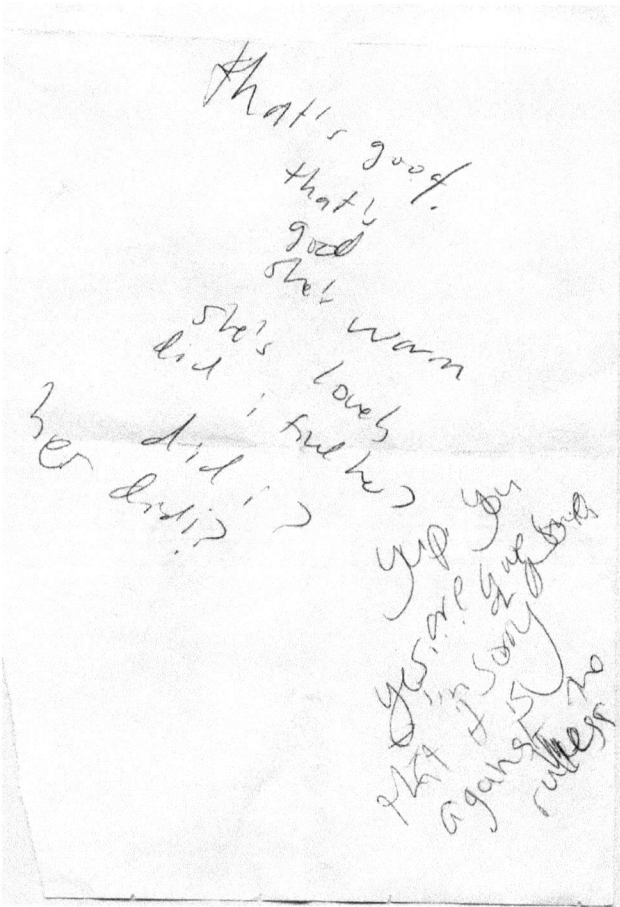

that's

good

she's warm

she's lovely

did i find her?

did i?

her   did   i?

yup   you   yes   are   awesome
im sorry that it is against the rules

          I

      i
      love
      you

          e
          r

          jasper who are you?

true love

          who are you love?

          who are you love?

          love jasper love who is

          love jasper love you

* * *

Steve, Melantha and I begin to walk downtown. I anxiously bid goodbye to the poison now weakening in my body, for I have neglected to add another layer to keep sobriety at bay.

394

Sobriety is the enemy – it is more physically kind but in my destabilized state of mind, it is the curse of integrity.

The poison slips off in malformed droplets, my toes struggle to reabsorb them, but they have no tongues   no tongues   no

The poison surrenders.

Sobriety overwhelms, almost unnoticed, drawing lies upon my spine, over my head – to suffocate

It begins plastering an artificial masterpiece; a disguise; a false sense of nature

The new skin is made up of unnaturally restrictive fibers – paper mâché soup

Strips of gummy glue and tatty newspapers with stories of the 1940s and 50s

I only want to clutch at my breast and rip the soggy bits of paper from my skin

        before they dry

    Too late.

I am a doll once more, mummified in traditions and encapsulated in cruel words

I explore my mouth, open, close, open, close

Sticky spider webs form between my lips – glue

My tongue is trapped – I make mere noises; articulation a lost skill.

                           no Voice

* * *

Sage is gone. I keel over at the thought and reach out to steady myself. As I do, miserable bile hurls itself throughout my mouth. Melantha catches me, holds onto my arm and pats my head murmuring, "You'll be ok, sweetie, just breathe. We'll get you some food, right Steve?" She turns to direct her voice at him. I vaguely see him nod.

She simply has no idea.

I wretch.

Life is always a polarity.

                    If   there   were   no
darkness
there   would   be   no   light.
             If   there   were   no   trouble   there
could   never   be   any   peace.

One day we will look back and say,

"We learned our best lessons not when
the sun was shining, but when the storm was
at its greatest, when the thunder roared, the
lightning flashed, the clouds obscured the
sun and all seemed dark and hopeless".

        - Silver Birch (Maurice Barbanell,
medium)

a raw hummingbird

website: www.JasperFaolan.com
facebook: Jasper Faolan
blog: http://jasperfaolan.wordpress.com

Jasper Faolan has been through a lot in her life due to her internal struggle about sexuality, rape, abuse and addiction.

She's now dedicated to being a significant and positive contributor to the queer youth movement & women's empowerment.

Contact

To connect with Jasper, email: JF@JasperFaolan.com. She'll reply as quickly as she can.

The Hummingbird Team

Occasionally, Jasper looks to employ Hummingbird team members. All jobs can be done remotely & from your own home. Email: Team@JasperFaolan.com if you'd like to work with her.

Street Team, Income &/or Fundraising

*Be a part of her street team/indie promotional team,
*Sell *a raw hummingbird* for personal commission, and/or
*Promote *a raw hummingbird* during one of your group/organization's fundraisers,

Email: IndiePromote@JasperFaolan.com.

Tour

To invite Jasper Faolan to your event during email: Tour@JasperFaolan.com.

Review

To review Jasper Faolan's work, please email: Review@JasperFaolan.com.

Ordering *a raw hummingbird*

Order *a raw hummingbird* & -

- Send it to the head of a women's resource group, rape crisis center, LGBTQ group, GSA, etc. at a high school, university or community college,

- Submit it to radio stations, newspapers or libraries,

- Gift it to a professor of women's studies, adolescent psychology and/or queer literature,

- Give it as a gift for a friend or family member.

Rock it out! Thank you.

Ordering Options:

Order online any time at www.JasperFaolan.com.

Send payment to arawhummingbird@gmail.com on PayPal.

Visit Amazon.com or BarnesandNobel.com.

> Note: For self published authors, much of the purchase price goes to Amazon.com and BarnesandNobel.com. So...if you don't mind, please go to www.JasperFaolan.com or use paypal! Thank you.

> (For sales outside the USA, do visit Amazon.com.)

OR use the personal Order Form on **page 403**.

Wholesalers, Professors & Reviewers see **page 402**.

Wholesale Orders

If you would like to carry *a raw hummingbird* in your stores, purchase a bulk amount for your class, book club, talk show, or event, your order might be eligible for a 20 – 40% discount.

Email Sales@JasperFaolan.com for details and terms.

Professors!

Lecture material is available for those who wish to incorporate *a raw hummingbird* into their course(s).

To include *a raw hummingbird* in your women's studies, queer literature or adolescent psychology course, please contact us with your interest & ideas at JF@JasperFaolan.com. Thank you!

Reviewers, Journalists, Bloggers & Magazine Editors

Jasper Faolan is an indie author & publisher. Her success depends utterly on her readers, her efforts, and you – our world's media.

If you have ethics *grins* and an interest in reviewing or interviewing Jasper Faolan about her work, *a raw hummingbird*, or how she is creatively promoting her mission & art as an independent entrepreneur, email: Press@JasperFaolan.com.

Looking forward to it.

Order Form for *a raw hummingbird*

Yes! Please send me ___ copies of *a raw hummingbird* for
$24 + $3 s/h per copy.

My credit card information,
money order or check is enclosed.

Please Mail me my copy/copies to:

Name: _____

Street: _____

Apartment/Unit: _____

City, State: _____

Postal code: _____

Country: _____

Phone: _____

Send order form to:

340 S LEMON AVE #5221
WALNUT, CA 91789
UNITED STATES

Credit Card details (optional):

Number: _____ - _____ - _____ - _____

Expiration date: __/__ CVS: _____

Signature: _____

Note: The 'CVS' number is the Card Verification System and
includes the last three numbers insider the signature box on
the back of your card. For American Express cards, this is
the four-digit number on the front of your card.

Please allow three weeks for delivery. **Thank You.**

NOTES:

405

www.ingramcontent.com/pod-product-compliance
Lightning Source LLC
Chambersburg PA
CBHW051747040426
42446CB00007B/247